Focus on GRAMMAR 2

FOURTH EDITION

Irene E. Schoenberg

W9-ANM-367

ALWAYS LEARNING

PEARSON

Focus on Grammar 2: An Integrated Skills Approach, Fourth Edition
Teacher's Resource Pack

Pearson Education, 10 Bank Street, White Plains, NY 10606

Staff credits: The people who made up the *Focus on Grammar Teacher's Resource Pack* team, representing editorial, production, design, and manufacturing, are, Iris Candelaria, Dave Dickey, Christine Edmonds, Nancy Flaggman, Ann France, Shelley Gazes, Lester Holmes, Stacey Hunter, Pamela Kohn, Theodore Lane, Christopher Leonowicz, Jennifer McAliney, Lise Minovitz, Jennifer Raspiller, Mary Perrotta Rich, Debbie Sistino, Ken Volcjak, Marian Wassner, and Adina Zoltan.

Contributing writers (Level 2): Carol Chapelle, Leslie Grant, Bethany Gray, Elizabeth Henly, Joan Jamieson, Xiangying Jiang, Hsin-Min Liu, Ruth Luman, Kathleen Smith, Raudy Lance Steele, Gabriele Steiner, Silvia Tiberio, BJ Wells, and Kevin Zimmerman.

Cover image: Shutterstock.com
Text composition: ElectraGraphics, Inc.
Text font: New Aster

ISBN 10: 0-13-216352-7
ISBN 13: 978-0-13-216352-1

Printed in the United States of America

1 2 3 4 5 6 7 8 9 10—V001—16 15 14 13 12 11

CONTENTS

ABOUT THE TEACHER'S RESOURCE PACK

This Teacher's Resource Pack offers a multitude of ideas for working with the material for the new edition of *Focus on Grammar 2: An Integrated Skills Approach*. The Teacher's Resource Pack includes:

- a **Teacher's Manual** (including General Teaching Notes, Unit Teaching Notes, Student Book Audioscript, and Student Book Answer Key)
- a **Teacher's Resource Disc** (including interactive PowerPoint® grammar presentations, placement test, reproducible Unit and Part assessments, and test-generating software)

THE TEACHER'S MANUAL

The Teacher's Manual includes the following sections:

- **General Teaching Notes** (pages 1–13) provide general suggestions for teaching and assessing the activities in the Student Book. A Strategies for Teaching Grammar section offers a quick reference for some of the most common and useful grammar teaching techniques. A Frequently Asked Questions section answers some of the most common issues that teachers encounter.

- **Unit Teaching Notes** (pages 15–158) provide step-by-step instructions on how to teach each unit and supplementary "Out of the Box Activities." They also include suggestions on when to use activities and tests from **www.myfocusongrammarlab.com**, assignments from the workbook, and materials from the Teacher's Resource Disc.

- The **Student Book Audioscript** (pages 159–169) includes scripts for the Listening and Pronunciation exercises in the Student Book.

- The **Student Book Answer Key** (pages 170–201) includes answers for the exercises in the Student Book.

THE TEACHER'S RESOURCE DISC

The Teacher's Resource Disc includes additional teaching resources and a complete assessment program:

Teaching Resources

- **PowerPoint® Presentations** of all Grammar Charts for each unit in the Student Book offer an alternative teaching tool for introducing the grammar presentation in the classroom. For select units, animated theme-based grammar presentations provide interactive follow-up practice activities for the contextualized instruction of grammar.

- **Internet Activities** for each unit in the Student Book provide opportunities for students to expand on the content and interact with each other creatively and fluently.

Assessments

- **Placement Test** in PDF format can be printed and used to place students into the appropriate level. Along with this 40-minute test is an audioscript and an answer key in PDF format, and audio as MP3 files.

- **Part and Unit Tests** in PDF format can be printed and used in class. These include Part Pre-Tests, Part Post-Tests, and Unit Achievement Tests. Also included are assessment audioscripts and answer keys in PDF format, and audio as MP3 files.

- **Test-Generating Software** provides thousands of questions from which teachers can customize class-appropriate tests.

GENERAL TEACHING NOTES

These notes are designed to guide you in teaching and assessing the recurring sections of the Student Book. Experimenting with the various options will enliven your classroom and appeal to students' different learning styles.

In the following section and in the Unit Teaching Notes, the icon (🕐) indicates an optional step you may wish to include if time permits.

PART OVERVIEW

The **Part Overview** previews the grammar and themes covered in each unit.

🕐 Part Pre-Tests

Before beginning each part, you may want to have students complete a diagnostic test. There are two options.

1. You can use the provided Part Pre-Tests to help you determine how well students know the material they are about to study in the next part of the Student Book. Since the material is usually new, students often score low on these tests. Each test takes about 50 minutes and includes about 60 items. The test begins with a listening exercise, includes several contextualized grammar exercises, and ends with an editing exercise. The tests are offered in two formats:
   • automatically graded tests at
     www.myfocusongrammarlab.com
   • reproducible tests on the Teacher's Resource Disc in this manual
2. You can use the **Test-Generating Software** on the Teacher's Resource Disc to create customized part diagnostic tests of any length. The test items focus on grammar.

UNIT OVERVIEW

The **Grammar Overview** portion of the Unit Overview (offered in this Teacher's Manual) highlights the most important grammar points of each unit. It also points out common grammar trouble spots for students. You may also find it helpful to review the Grammar Charts and Grammar Notes in the Student Book before teaching each unit. The **Unit Overview** previews the unit theme.

Step 1: Grammar in Context

Each unit opens with a reading selection designed to raise students' interest and expose them to the target grammar in a realistic, natural context. The selections include newspaper and magazine excerpts, websites, advertisements, reviews, brochures, biographies, blogs, emails, and other formats that students may encounter in their day-to-day lives. All of the texts are recorded and available on the audio program or at **www.myfocusongrammarlab.com**.

Before You Read (5 minutes)

This prereading activity creates interest, elicits students' knowledge about the topic, and encourages students to make predictions about the reading.

Suggested Procedure
1. Have the class look at the illustrations.
2. Ask students to respond to the questions. Ask these questions in a conversational way, instead of reading them from the book.
3. If you have time, you can ask additional questions to elicit students' personal experiences with or knowledge about the topic.

Option A
• Have the class read the questions in pairs or small groups and discuss their answers.
• Call on pairs to share their ideas with the class.

Option B
• Ask students to prepare questions they have about the topic in pairs.
• Call on pairs to share their questions and write them on the board.

Read (15–20 minutes)

Depending on the needs of your class, have students complete the reading in class or at home. Encourage students to read with a purpose, and to read the passage once or twice without stopping to look up new words.

Suggested Procedure
1. Write the comprehension questions from the Unit Teaching Notes on the board.
2. Play the audio and have students follow along in their books. Have them underline any new words.

3. Have students read the passage again silently, looking for answers to the questions.
4. 🕐 Have students discuss their answers with a partner or in small groups.
5. 🕐 Put students in pairs or small groups to discuss the reading. Invite them to respond to the reading in a way that is meaningful to them: What was most interesting? What did they learn? Refer to the discussion topics in the Unit Teaching Notes to help generate ideas for discussion.

Option A (At Home / In Class)
• Write a few personalized questions to consolidate the content of the reading.
• Have students copy the questions, or prepare them as a handout for students to take home.
• Have students read the passage and answer the questions at home.
• 🕐 Have students write a few additional questions about the reading.
• 🕐 In class, have students take turns asking and answering questions they prepared at home.

Option B (In Class)
• Have students work in pairs. Divide the reading in half, and have each student in the pair read one half.
• Have students summarize the information in their half of the reading for their partner.
• Follow steps 3–5 in the previous notes for Suggested Procedure for Read.

After You Read (10–20 minutes)
Depending on the needs of your class, have the students complete the exercises in class or at home. Following the Student Book practice, you may want your students to go to **www.myfocusongrammarlab.com** for automatically graded Vocabulary or Reading homework. The Vocabulary homework provides additional practice with the words in the Student Book; the Reading homework is on related topics.

A. Practice (10 minutes)
This practice helps students feel comfortable with the text of the reading and speaking the words aloud with a partner.

B. Vocabulary (5 minutes)
These questions help students develop vocabulary skills by focusing on the meaning of targeted words in the opening text. The words are recycled throughout the unit.

Suggested Procedure
1. Have students find and circle the target words in the opening text.
2. Elicit or explain the meanings of any new words.
3. Have students complete the exercise individually or in pairs.
4. Call on volunteers to read their answers aloud.
5. 🕐 Have students record new words in a notebook or on vocabulary cards. Have them write the word, part of speech, meaning, and a sample sentence.

C. Comprehension (5 minutes)
These post-reading questions help students focus on the meaning of the opening text. In some cases, they may also focus on the target grammar without explicitly presenting the grammar point.

Suggested Procedure
1. Have students answer the questions individually.
2. Have students compare answers in pairs.
3. Call on volunteers to read their answers aloud.

Step 2: Grammar Presentation

There are many ways to teach the material in the Grammar Presentation. As a general rule, the more varied and lively the classroom activities, the more engaged students will be—and the more learning will occur. Approaching grammar from different angles and trying out different classroom management options can help increase student motivation. The Strategies for Teaching Grammar on page 10 provide some guidelines to keep in mind when presenting a new grammar point. In addition to these strategies and the procedures outlined below, you can find specific suggestions for presenting the unit's grammar in the Unit Teaching Notes.

Grammar Charts (5–10 minutes)

The Grammar Charts provide a clear reference of all the forms of the target grammar. Students also become familiar with grammatical terminology. The charts also enable you to pre-teach some of the Grammar Notes that follow. You may want to use the charts in the PowerPoint® presentations on the Teacher's Resource Disc to help direct all of your students' attention to the same focus point. Select presentations also include colorful graphics, animations, and interactive practice activities that reinforce the grammar point.

Suggested Procedure

1. Using example sentences from the charts and/or the PowerPoint® presentations, draw students' attention to important features in the models by asking them questions or by pointing out the key features.
2. Confirm students' understanding by engaging them in some recognition activities. Try one or two activities from Strategies 3, 4, 5, or 6 (page 10).
3. Get students to manipulate the new structures through substitution or transformation drills. See Strategy 7 (page 10) for an example of a transformation drill.
4. Encourage students to make sentences that are personally meaningful using the new grammar.

Option A

- Have students study the Grammar Charts at home.
- In class, follow step 1 in the suggested procedure above.
- Move directly to the Grammar Notes section. Carry out steps 2, 3, and 4 in the suggested procedure above using the notes together with the charts.

Option B

- Assign pairs or groups of students responsibility for presenting one aspect of the target grammar to the class by combining the information in the charts and the relevant notes. You may want to give them large pieces of paper and markers to prepare posters.
- Ⓣ Meet with students individually. Allow them to practice their presentations and provide any coaching needed.
- Call on students to present their topics to the class. Encourage questions from the class.
- Choose appropriate practice activities from Strategies 4–8 (page 10) OR move directly to the Grammar Notes section.

Grammar Notes (20–30 minutes)

These notes provide helpful information about meaning, use, and form of the grammatical structures that students have encountered in the opening text and Grammar Charts. They include the following features to help students understand and use the forms:

- Where appropriate, timelines illustrate the meaning of verb forms and their relationship to one another.
- *Be Careful!* notes alert students to common errors among English-language learners.
- *Usage Notes* provide guidelines for using and understanding different levels of formality and correctness.
- References to related structures are provided below the notes.

Suggested Procedure

1. Have students read each note at home and/or in class.
2. For each note, write examples on the board and elicit or point out the key features of the form (see Strategy 1, page 10).
3. If possible, demonstrate the meaning of the grammatical form(s) by performing actions (see Strategy 6, page 10).
4. Model the examples and have students repeat after you so that they become comfortable with the appropriate stress, intonation, and rhythm.
5. Engage students with the grammar point by choosing appropriate activities, for example:
   - Elicit examples of the target structure.
   - Confirm students' understanding by having them categorize examples or perform actions that illustrate the structure (see Strategies 5 and 6, page 10).
   - Provide controlled practice with quick substitution or transformation drills (see Strategy 7, page 10).
   - Encourage students to make personally meaningful sentences using the new grammatical forms.
   - Use the Focused Practice exercises in the Student Book.
6. You may want to repeat steps 2–5 for each Grammar Note.

Option

- Photocopy one set of Grammar Notes for each group of three or four students in your class. Cut them up so that the notes and their corresponding examples are not attached.
- Divide the class into groups of three or four students, and give a set of cut-up notes to each group.

- Give students their task:
  1. Match the examples with the correct notes.
  2. Attach the notes and corresponding examples to a sheet of newsprint (a large piece of paper).
  3. Create and write more examples for each note.
- Circulate to insure that students are on the right track and provide help as needed.
- Have students post their results around the room, and invite groups to look at each other's work.
- Regroup as a class to answer questions.

Identify the Grammar (5–10 minutes)

This optional activity helps students identify the target grammatical structures embedded in the context of the opening text. This helps students learn the form, meaning, and usage of the target grammar point and helps you make a smooth transition from the Grammar Presentation to Discover the Grammar in Focused Practice.

Step 3: Focused Practice

The exercises in this section provide practice for the structures in the Grammar Presentation. You may want to have students complete the corresponding exercise immediately after you have presented the relevant Grammar Note. Another option is for students to complete one or more of the exercises at home.

If you decide to have students complete the exercises in class, you can keep them motivated by varying the order of the exercises and/or the way you conduct them. Following are various ways of conducting the exercises.

Following the Student Book practice, you may want students to go to **www.myfocusongrammarlab.com** for automatically graded grammar homework or to the workbook for traditional grammar exercises. You may want to assign these to be completed in class or as homework.

Discover the Grammar (5–10 minutes)

This opening activity gets students to identify the target grammar structures in a realistic context. It also sometimes checks their understanding of meaning. This recognition activity raises awareness of the structures as it builds confidence.

Suggested Procedure
1. Go over the example with the class.
2. Have students complete the exercise individually or in pairs.
3. Elicit the correct answers from the class.

Controlled Practice Exercises (5–10 minutes each)

Following the Discover the Grammar activity are exercises that provide practice in a controlled, but still contextualized, environment. The exercises proceed from simpler to more complex and include a variety of exercise types such as fill in the blanks, matching, and multiple-choice. Students are exposed to many different written formats, including letters, electronic bulletin boards and articles, newspaper and magazine excerpts, and conversations. Many exercises are art-based, providing a rich context for meaningful practice.

Options
- Have students complete the exercises in pairs.
- If the exercise is in the form of a conversation, have students practice the completed exercise in pairs and role-play it for the class.
- When going over answers with students, have them explain why each answer is correct.
- Whenever possible, relate exercises to students' lives. For example, if an exercise includes a timeline, elicit from students some important events that have happened in their own lives.

Editing (10 minutes)

All units have an editing exercise to build students' awareness of incorrect usage of the target grammar structures. Students identify and correct errors in sentences or in a contextualized passage such as a conversation, a journal entry, or an email. The direction line indicates the number of errors in the passage.

Suggested Procedure
1. Have students read the passage quickly to understand its context and meaning.
2. Have students read the passage line by line, circling incorrect structures and writing in the corrections.
3. Have students take turns reading the passage line by line, saying the structures correctly. Alternatively, read the passage aloud to the class and have students interrupt you with their corrections.
4. There are also usually examples of the correct usage of the structures in each editing exercise. After students have identified the errors, point out the correct usages and ask why they are not errors.

Step 4: Communication Practice

These in-class exercises give students the opportunity to use the target structure in communicative activities. These activities help develop listening and speaking fluency and critical-thinking skills, as well as provide opportunities for students to "own" the structures. As with the Focused Practice exercises, you may wish to vary the order of these activities to keep student motivation high.

Since there are many different exercise types in the Communication Practice section, specific ideas and guidelines are provided in the Unit Teaching Notes. Following are general suggestions for the three main types of exercises. (Note: See the FAQs on pages 11–13 for more information about setting up pair work and group work.)

Following the relevant Student Book practice, you may want your students to go to **www.myfocusongrammarlab.com** for automatically graded Listening, Pronunciation, Speaking, or Writing exercises and activities. The Pronunciation homework provides additional practice with the pronunciation feature from the Student Book; the Listening, Speaking, and Writing homework exercises and activities are on related topics.

Listening (10 minutes)

The first or second exercise in each Communication Practice section deals with listening comprehension. Students hear a variety of listening formats, including conversations, radio and television scripts, weather forecasts, and interviews. After listening, students complete a task that focuses on the form or meaning of the target grammar structure. The recordings for the listening exercises are on the audio program and at **www.myfocusongrammarlab.com**, so students can complete the exercises outside of class.

Suggested Procedure

Before Listening

1. Explain the situation or context of the listening passage. Provide any necessary cultural information and pre-teach any vocabulary students may need to know. Since some of these words and phrases may appear in the listening, not in the exercise itself, refer to the audioscript at the back of this manual as necessary.
2. Have students read the exercise questions first so that they know what to listen for.

First Listening Task

1. Play the audio. Have students listen with their pencils down.
2. Play the audio again. Have students listen and complete the task.
3. You may want to let students listen as many times as necessary to complete the task.

Second Listening Task

1. See steps 2–3 from the first listening task for general instructions.
2. Have student compare their answers in pairs or small groups.

After Listening

1. Elicit answers for the exercise items and write them on the board. Answer any questions the students may have.
2. ⏱ Students listen a final time and review the passage.

Option A

- Rather than play the audio, read the audioscript aloud.
- Speak with a lot of expression and at a natural pace. Change positions and tone of voice to indicate who the speaker is.
- Draw stick figures on the board and label them with the characters' names. Then point to the appropriate character as you change roles.

Option B

- Make photocopies of the audioscript and hand it out to students.
- Play the audio recording and have students read along with it in chorus. Explain that this exercise will help them to hear and practice the rhythms, stresses, and clusters of English sounds.

Option C

Have students listen and complete the exercise at home or in a language lab.

Pronunciation (10 minutes)

The first or second exercise in each Communication Practice section deals with pronunciation. The pronunciation exercise generally focuses on the grammar presented in the unit or a difficult sound that appears in the opening text. It also prepares students for the speaking activities that follow. The recordings for the pronunciation exercises are on the audio program and at **www.myfocusongrammarlab.com**, so students can practice the exercises outside of class.

Suggested Procedure

First Task
1. Go over the instructions and point out the Pronunciation Note.
2. Play the audio.

Second Task
1. Play the audio. Have students close their eyes and notice the pronunciation feature.
2. (🕐) Play the audio again. Have students listen again and follow along in their books.

Third Task
1. Play the audio again.
2. Have students repeat in pairs or small groups. Circulate and monitor their pronunciation.
3. (🕐) Call on volunteers to practice in front of the class.

Information Gaps (10–20 minutes)

Information Gaps are designed to encourage communication between students. In these activities, each student has a different set of information. Students have to talk to their partners to solve a puzzle, draw a picture (describe and draw), put things in the right order (describe and arrange), or find similarities and differences between pictures.

Advantages of Information Gaps
- Information Gaps are motivating and fun.
- There is a real need for communication in order to combine the information to solve a problem and complete the task.
- Information sharing allows students to extend and personalize what they have learned in the unit.

Suggested Procedure
1. Explain how the Student A and Student B pages relate to each other (how they are different or similar).
2. Refer students to the examples and to any language provided.
3. Divide the class into pairs (Student A and Student B). Have them position themselves so that they cannot see the contents of each other's books.
4. Tell the Students B what page to turn to. Circulate to check that they are looking at the correct page.
5. Have students read their separate instructions. Check comprehension of the task by asking each group, "What are you going to do?"
6. Remind students not to show each other the contents of their pages.

7. As students are working, circulate to answer individual questions and to help students with the activity.

Games (10–20 minutes)

Games are designed to encourage communication among students. In these activities, students compete in pairs or small groups to complete a task such as guessing something or winning points.

Advantages of Games
- They can create a fun and stress-free environment.
- They involve friendly competition and keep students engaged.
- They can improve students' ability to speak in a communicative way.

Suggested Procedure
1. Go over the instructions to make sure students understand the task.
2. Have students model the example or provide one of your own.
3. Have students carry out the instructions. Circulate and help as needed.
4. Go over answers as a class or ask who won.
5. (🕐) Write on the board any sentences you noticed using incorrect grammar. Have the students correct them as a class.

Role Plays / Interviews (10–20 minutes)

In these classroom speaking activities, students role-play a real-life encounter, such as a conversation between friends, a job interview, or a server and a customer at a restaurant.

Advantages of Role Plays / Interviews
- They are fun and motivating for most students.
- Role-playing characters often allows the more hesitant students to be more outgoing than if they are speaking as themselves.
- Interviews can help students build confidence in their ability to ask and answer extemporaneous questions.
- By broadening the world of the classroom to the world outside, role-playing allows students to use a wider range of language than less open-ended activities.

Suggested Procedure
1. When possible, bring in props or costumes to add drama and fun.
2. Review the task so students understand what is required.
3. Perform a sample role play with a volunteer in front of the class.

4. Divide the class into the suggested groupings and give them a fixed time limit for completing the task.
5. Have students write a script for the role play. Then have them write key words on cards and perform the role play using the cards as prompts OR have students plan the action without a script and present it extemporaneously.
6. While students are working, circulate among the pairs or groups to answer students' questions and help them with the activity.
7. Have various pairs or groups perform their role plays in front of the class. If possible, record the role plays for students' own listening or viewing.

Discussions (10–20 minutes)

In these classroom speaking activities, students express their ideas about a variety of topics. These activities include Likes, Last Weekend, Clothes and Customs, and Making Comparisons.

Advantages of Discussions
- They help students move from speaking accuracy to speaking fluency.
- They help students develop critical-thinking skills as they explore the pros and cons of a given topic.
- They help students build confidence in their ability to express opinions on a variety of topics.

Suggested Procedure
1. Go over the instructions so that students understand the task.
2. Elicit or present useful language and write it on the board.
3. Have two or three students model the example discussion.
4. Divide the class into the suggested groupings and give them a fixed time limit for completing the task.
5. Circulate while the students discuss the topic. Help with language or monitor their grammar as needed.
6. Ask volunteers from each group to summarize the discussion or conclusions.
7. ⏱ Write on the board any sentences you noticed using incorrect grammar. Have the students correct them as a class.

Writing (15–25 minutes)

These activities give students the opportunity to develop their writing skills and provide additional practice using the target grammatical structures. There is a variety of realistic formats, including short paragraphs, essays, emails, worksheets, fact sheets, and advertisements. The themes are related to material covered in the unit so that students already have some preparation for the writing task.

Suggested Procedure
Prewriting (in class)
1. Go over the instructions with the class.
2. Brainstorm ideas for the assignment with the class and write them on the board.
3. Encourage students to include grammar and vocabulary from the unit in their assignment.

Writing and Editing (at home)
1. Have students compose a draft of the writing assignment at home.
2. Have students use the Editing Checklist to correct their work.

Wrap-Up (in class)
1. Have students submit the draft to you or share it with a partner in class.
2. You can comment on the following features:
   - Content: Has the student responded appropriately to the task? Are the main points well supported?
   - Organization: Is the flow of ideas logical and effective?
   - Accuracy: Are there any major errors in the grammar points taught in the unit?
3. ⏱ Depending on your class's needs, you may want to have students complete a second draft at home. When you check these drafts, point out any further areas needing correction, concentrating especially on errors in the target grammar point or grammar points from a previous unit.

Option A
Have students share their final drafts in class. For example:
- Post students' work on the class bulletin board.
- Publish their work on a website or in a class magazine.
- Have students exchange papers with a partner.
- Have students read their papers aloud in small groups or to the class.

Option B

Have students put the final drafts of their written work in a folder, or portfolio, which you can review at the end of the course. This will allow your students and you to see the progress they have made.

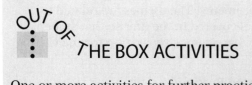

OUT OF THE BOX ACTIVITIES

One or more activities for further practice (in the Teacher's Manual only) can be found at the end of every unit in the Unit Teaching Notes. These exercises offer additional communicative practice with the target structure of the unit. Many can be done in class with no before-class preparation. The activities often involve a combination of skills, such as grammar and speaking or grammar and writing.

Unit Review

The last section of each unit of the Student Book is a review feature that can be used as a self-test. These exercises test the form and use of the grammar content presented and practiced in that unit. They give students a chance to check their knowledge and to review any problematic areas before moving on to the next part. An answer key is provided at the back of the Student Book.

Suggested Procedure
1. Have students complete the exercises at home and check their answers in the Answer Key.
2. During the next class, go over any remaining questions students may have.

Option
- Have students complete the exercises in class. Give them a time limit of 10 minutes, and circulate as they work.
- Have students use the Answer Key to check and correct their answers in pairs OR you can go over the answers as a class.

Unit Achievement Tests

After the Unit Review, you may want to have students complete an achievement test. There are two assessment options.

1. You can use the provided **Unit Achievement Tests** to help you assess students' knowledge of the specific grammatical topics presented in the unit. If students have mastered the material presented in the unit, they should answer most of the questions correctly. Each test takes about 30 minutes and includes about 30 items. The test begins with a listening exercise, includes two or three contextualized grammar exercises, and ends with an editing exercise. The tests are offered in two formats:
   - automatically graded tests at **www.myfocusongrammarlab.com**
   - reproducible tests on the Teacher's Resource Disc in this manual
2. You can use the **Test-Generating Software** on the Teacher's Resource Disc to create customized unit achievement tests of any length. The test items focus on grammar.

Part Post-Tests

At the end of each part, you may want to have students complete an achievement test. There are three assessment options.

1. You can have students go to **www.myfocusongrammarlab.com** for an automatically graded review. Students can complete the review on a computer in class, at home, or in a language lab. Each review takes about 25 minutes and includes about 30 items. The test focuses on grammar.
2. You can have students take the provided **Part Post-Tests** to help you determine how well students have mastered the material they have studied in that part of the Student Book. If students have mastered the material presented in the part, they should answer most of the questions correctly. Each test takes 50 minutes and includes about 60 items. The tests begin with a listening exercise, include several contextualized grammar exercises, and end with an editing exercise. The tests are offered in two formats:
   - automatically graded tests at **www.myfocusongrammarlab.com**
   - reproducible tests on the Teacher's Resource Disc in this manual
3. You can also use the **Test-Generating Software** on the Teacher's Resource Disc to create customized part achievement tests of any length. The test items focus on grammar.

From Grammar to Writing

The From Grammar to Writing section at the end of each Part of the Student Book integrates grammar presented in the units. It also goes beyond the grammar in the unit and gives additional information about writing in English. This information may include format and audience (e.g., emails, post cards, letters to the editor, invitations to a friend), cohesion (time connectors, subjects and verbs), or punctuation (e.g., capitalization, the apostrophe). Following these exercises, students practice prewriting strategies. These strategies may include the use of graphic organizers, such as charts, cluster diagrams, timelines, notes, and outlines. Finally, students apply the teaching point in a writing task. Text types include both formal and informal writing, such as notes, emails, and stories. The section concludes with peer review and editing.

Depending on your class's needs, you may want to have students go to an additional From Grammar to Writing exercise at **www.myfocusongrammarlab.com.**

Suggested Procedure

Prewriting

1. Have students complete the controlled practice exercises individually. Then have them exchange books and compare answers.
2. Go over the answers as a class and answer any questions.

3. Explain the prewriting task. Where appropriate, provide a model for students on the board or on an overhead.
4. Have students complete the prewriting task in pairs or small groups. Circulate and answer any questions.

Composing and Correcting

1. Go over the instructions to make sure students understand the task.
2. Have students complete the writing assignment at home.
3. In class, complete the peer review portion of the task. Circulate while students are working together to make sure they are on task and to provide appropriate feedback. (See Suggested Procedure for Writing on page 7 for examples.)
4. ⏱ Have students revise their writing and turn in the second draft to you. You may wish to correct these drafts and to include the drafts as part of the students' writing portfolios.

Option

- Have students complete the controlled practice exercise(s) at home.
- In class, have students compare answers in pairs.
- Follow the suggested procedure for steps 3 and 4 in the prewriting phase.

STRATEGIES FOR TEACHING GRAMMAR

1. Develop awareness
- Ask questions that help students become aware of the form of the structure. For example, for *can* to talk about ability (Student Book page 145), read the affirmative statements, "I can talk; He can talk," and ask: "How do you form affirmative statements with *can*?" (can + *base form of verb*) Ask students what *base form* means. *(the simple form without an ending)* Then ask: "Does *can* change when the pronoun changes?" (*no*) Point out that *can* is a modal and it is the same for all pronouns.
- Compare information in the Grammar Charts. For example, for the simple past (Student Book, pages 27–28) there are Grammar Charts for the past of *be*. Ask: "How many forms are there for the simple past of *be*?" (*two: was and were*) "How do you form the negative with *be* in the simple past?" (*wasn't, weren't*) Ask: "Do you use the base form for past *yes / no* questions with *be*?" (*no*) "Do you use the base form for *Wh-* questions with *be*?" (*no*)

2. Present meaning
Show the meaning of a grammatical form through a classroom demonstration. For example, to illustrate the use of the present perfect progressive, you could show a picture of a person pushing a grocery cart with bags full of food. *(He / She has been shopping.)*

3. Identify examples
Ask students to go back to the Grammar in Context section and label examples in the reading passage with the grammatical terms in the Grammar Charts.

4. Generate examples
Find examples from the reading or elsewhere that could fit into the Grammar Charts. An interesting way to do this is to photocopy and enlarge the Grammar Chart. White out the targeted structures and draw a blank line for each missing word. Make copies and distribute them to students in pairs or small groups. Have students fill in the blanks, using examples from the reading. Then generate more examples. Books can be open or closed, depending on the level of challenge desired.

5. Show understanding by categorizing
Check comprehension of a grammatical principle by asking students to label multiple examples appropriately. For example, students can label verbs "present" or "future," or they can label examples "correct" or "incorrect."

6. Show understanding by performing actions
Ask students to show their understanding of the meaning of a grammatical form by following instructions or devising a demonstration. Ask students, for example, to think of and perform a set of actions that they could describe using the present progressive.

7. Manipulate forms
Have students manipulate the examples in the Grammar Charts to practice the form. Drills such as substitution or transformation help students to build fluency. For example, in Unit 30 (Student Book page 350) you might put one form on the board (You should go.) and then elicit other forms by saying, "Negative" (*You shouldn't go.*), "Yes / no question" (*Should you go?*), "Short answer, affirmative" (*Yes, you should.*), "Wh- question, when" (*When should you go?*), and so on to get students to produce the other forms rapidly.

8. Personalize
Ask students to provide personal examples. For example, on page 188 of the Student Book, students see the examples, "Do you check Facebook® in the morning?" and "I own a smartphone." Ask students when they usually check email, if they own smartphones, etc. (*I check email in the evening. I don't own a smartphone.*)

9. Repeat, reinforce
Students need to be exposed to new grammar many times in order to internalize it completely. You can first present a new structure on the board, then point it out in the book, then have students use it in an informal oral exercise, then do a written exercise in pairs, and finally review the same structure in homework. Varying the content and focus of these activities will keep students interested, and the grammar will be reinforced almost automatically.

FREQUENTLY ASKED QUESTIONS (FAQs)

1. When should I have students work in pairs or groups rather than individually or as a class?

Varying your classroom organization to suit particular activity types will result in more effective and more interesting classes. Many students are not accustomed to working in pairs or groups, so it is important to use these groupings only when they are most beneficial.

- **Whole-class teaching** maximizes teacher control and is especially good for:
  — presenting information, giving explanations, and providing instructions
  — showing material in texts and pictures or on audio or video recordings
  — teacher-led drills (such as substitution or transformation) or dictations
  — reviewing answers or sharing ideas after students have completed an activity
  — enabling the whole class to benefit from teacher feedback to individuals
- **Students working individually** allows quiet, concentrated attention and is most effective for:
  — processing information or completing a task at students' own pace
  — performing writing tasks

For objective exercises such as fill-in-the-blank, matching, multiple-choice, and editing, vary your class organization to keep student motivation high. Students can sometimes complete these exercises individually, and sometimes they can work with a partner.

- **Students working in pairs** maximizes student speaking time, breaks up the routine and "teacher talk," and is ideal for:
  — information-gap activities
  — role plays
  — writing and/or reading dialogues
  — predicting the content of reading and listening texts
  — comparing notes on what students listen to or see
  — checking answers
  — peer assessment

Pair work can also be very effective for completing objective exercises such as fill in the blanks, matching, multiple choice, and editing.

- **Students working in groups** creates ideal conditions for students to learn from each other and works well for:
  — generating ideas
  — pooling knowledge
  — writing group stories
  — preparing presentations
  — discussing an issue and reaching a group decision

2. How should I set up pair work and group work?

Here are a few different techniques:

- **Streaming.** Grouping students according to ability or participation has certain advantages:
  — **ability:** Grouping weaker and stronger students together allows more proficient students to help their less fluent classmates.
  — **participation:** If you see that some students participate less than others, you could make a pair or group of weak participants. By the same token, you can also put especially talkative students together.
- **Chance.** Grouping students by chance has many benefits, especially if it results in students working with varied partners. You can group students by chance according to:
  — **where they sit:** Students sitting next to or near one another work in pairs or groups. This is the easiest option, but if students always sit in the same place, you will want to find other ways of grouping them.
  — **the "wheels" system:** Half the class stands in a circle facing outwards, and the other half stands in an outer circle facing inwards. The outer circle revolves in a clockwise direction, and the inner circle revolves in a counterclockwise direction. When you tell them to stop, students work with the person facing them. This is an effective way to have students engage in meaningful repetition, such as asking the same question of many different partners.
  — **assigned letters:** Assign each student a letter from A to E. Then ask all the As to form a group, all the Bs to form a group, and so on.

— **birthdays:** Students stand in a line in the order of their birthdays (with January at one end and December at the other). The first five students form one group, the second five students another group, and so on.

— **native language:** If possible, put students in groups or pairs with others who don't share a native language. This helps create an "English-only" classroom.

3. How can I make activities more successful?
Before the activity:

- **Motivate students and explain the purpose.** Make it clear that something enjoyable or interesting is going to happen. Explain the rationale for the activity. Making sure students understand the purpose of the activity helps them practice what they learned and encourages them to participate.

- **Provide clear directions.** Explain what students should do in every step of the activity. Have students paraphrase or demonstrate the task to be sure they understand it.

- **Demonstrate.** Show the class what is supposed to happen in an activity. This might involve asking a student to demonstrate the activity with you or having two students role-play at the front of the room.

- **Provide a time frame.** It is helpful for students to know how much time they have and exactly when they should stop. Approximate times are given for all the activities in this Teacher's Manual.

For open-ended activities, such as the Internet activity or writing exercises, you will also want to:

- **Stimulate thinking.** When there are choices for students to make, it is often helpful to set up small-group and/or whole-class brainstorming sessions to define the focus and/or content of their task.

- **Prepare language.** Review grammar and vocabulary that students may need to complete the task. This can be done as a follow up to a brainstorming activity where you elicit ideas and write key language on the board.

During the activity:

- **Observe students.** Walk around the room watching and listening to pairs or groups.

- **Provide assistance as needed.** (See FAQ 5 for suggestions on giving feedback and correcting errors.)

After the activity:

- **Elicit student responses.** For some activities, you may ask for volunteers or call on students to share some of their ideas with the class. For other types of activities, a few pairs or groups can be asked to role-play their discussions to demonstrate the language they have been using.

- **Provide feedback.** In many cases, this is most conveniently done in a whole-class setting. It may be preferable, however, for you to meet with individuals, pairs, or groups. While the principal focus in a grammar class is language use, it is also important to acknowledge the value of students' ideas. See FAQ 5 below for suggestions on feedback and error correction.

4. What can I do to encourage students to use more English in the classroom?
It is perfectly natural for students to feel the need to use their first language in an English class. There are a number of actions that teachers can take to promote the use of English.

- **Set clear guidelines.** Some teachers in monolingual classes find that activities such as providing vocabulary definitions, presenting a grammar point, checking comprehension, giving instructions, and discussing classroom methodology are best done in the students' native language.

- **Use persuasion.** Walking among the students during speaking activities and saying things such as "Please speak English!" or "Try to use English as much as possible" helps to insure that students will speak English most of the time.

5. What's the best approach to giving feedback and correcting errors?
Here are two considerations:

- **Be selective in offering correction.** Students can't focus on everything at once, so concentrate first on errors relating to the target grammar point and grammar points from units previously studied, as well as any errors that interfere with communication. Whether you respond to other errors depends on your judgment of students' readiness to take in the information. If you see a teachable moment, seize it! Rather than correct every error individual students make in the course of activities, it is generally preferable to note commonly occurring mistakes and give a short presentation to the class at the end of the activity.

- **Recasting.** If a student makes an error—for example, "I *didn't came* to class yesterday because I was sick."—you can recast it as, "You *didn't come* to class yesterday because you were sick?" The student ideally notices the difference and restates the original sentence: "Right. I didn't come to class yesterday because I was sick." This process can be effective because the student has the opportunity to self-correct an error that is still in short-term memory. As a variation, you can restate but stop, with rising intonation, right before the potential error: "You didn't . . . ?"

6. What can I do to accommodate different learning styles?

Focus on Grammar recognizes different styles of learning and provides a variety of activities to accommodate these different styles. Some learners prefer an analytical, or rule-learning (deductive), approach. Others, especially younger learners, respond best to an inductive approach, or exposure to the language in meaningful contexts. Indeed, the same students may adopt different styles as they learn, or they may use different styles at different times.

As teachers, we want to help the students in our classes who prefer to follow rules become more able to take risks and to plunge into communicative activities. We also want to encourage the risk-takers to focus on accuracy. *Focus on Grammar* provides the variety to ensure that students achieve their goal: to learn to use the language confidently and appropriately.

UNIT TEACHING NOTES

PART I OVERVIEW

Be: PRESENT AND PAST

UNIT	GRAMMAR FOCUS	THEME
1	Present of *Be*: Statements	Famous People
2	Present of *Be*: Yes / No Questions and *Wh-* Questions	First Day of School
3	Past of *Be*: Statements, Yes / No Questions, *Wh-* Questions	First Jobs

Go to **www.myfocusongrammarlab.com** for the Part and Unit Tests.

Note: PowerPoint® grammar presentations, test-generating software, and reproducible Part and Unit Tests are on the *Teacher's Resource Disc*.

UNIT 1 OVERVIEW

Grammar: PRESENT OF *Be*: STATEMENTS

Unit 1 focuses on the structure and use of *be* in simple present statements, including:

- Singular and plural forms of *be* in affirmative and negative statements
- Contractions
- Subject pronouns
- Placement of *be* in affirmative and negative statements

Theme: FAMOUS PEOPLE

Unit 1 focuses on famous people and language used to describe their occupations, home countries, and personal qualities.

Step 1: Grammar in Context (pages 2–3)

See the general suggestions for Grammar in Context on page 1.

Before You Read

- Have students look at the pictures. Ask: "Do you know any of these people?" "What are their names?" Try to elicit Carrie Underwood's name and why she's famous. (*She's a country singer.*)

- Form small groups. Have students complete the exercise in groups.
- Call on students to give answers.

Read

- Have a student read the title of the article. Elicit the meaning of *talented*.
- To encourage students to read with a purpose, write these questions on the board:
  1. Who is Carrie Underwood? (*She is an American country singer.*)
  2. What is her husband's name? (*Mike Fisher*)
  3. Where is their home? (*They live in Canada and the United States.*)
  4. Is Gisele Bündchen famous? (*Yes, she is.*)
  5. Where is she from? (*She's from Brazil.*)
  6. What sport does her husband play? (*football*)
- Have students read the text. (OR: Play the audio and have students follow along in their books.) Then call on students to share their answers to the questions on the board.

After You Read

A. Practice
- Have students complete the exercise in pairs.
- Then call on pairs to read the paragraphs aloud.

B. Vocabulary
- Have students complete the exercises individually.
- Have students compare answers in pairs. Then call on pairs to read the completed sentences.
- ⏱ Have students find and circle the vocabulary words in the reading text. Then call on students to read the sentences from the text.

C. Comprehension
- Have students complete the exercises individually.
- Have students compare answers in pairs. Then call on pairs to read the completed sentences.

Go to **www.myfocusongrammarlab.com** for an additional reading, and for reading and vocabulary practice.

Step 2: Grammar Presentation (pages 4–5)

See the general suggestions for Grammar Presentation on page 2.

Grammar Charts

- Have students silently read the examples of affirmative statements in the charts on page 4.
- On the board, write affirmative sentences:
  I am popular. You are popular.
  [Student's name] is popular.
  [Student's name] and [student's name] are popular.
- Have students read the sentences. Ask questions to draw students' attention to the forms in the sentences: "What is the subject here?" "Is it singular or plural?" "What is the verb?" "Is it singular or plural?"
- Write the following on the board to review the use of name and pronoun combinations:
  (name) + I = we, (name) + you = you,
  (name) + (name) = they
- ⏱ Conduct a matching drill. Say a noun or pronoun, singular or plural. Have the class respond with the appropriate form of be (am / is / are). Once the class is comfortable with the drill, have students try it in pairs.
- Write the following chart on the board. Have students combine elements to make their own affirmative statements.

I	am	hardworking
You	is	a student
He, She, It	are	cities
Tom		students
Anita and I		popular
We		hot
You		from London
They		
Seoul and Moscow		

- Explain contractions. Use mathematical formulas, such as you + are = you're. Do this for all forms. Have students repeat the forms after you.
- Have students use contractions to say the affirmative statements from the chart above. (Example: Tom's hardworking. They're students.)
- Give students time to read the negative statement charts on page 4. Highlight the two forms of the contractions.
- Repeat the previous steps with negative sentences. Add the word not to the chart above.
- Have students cover the charts in the book with their hands. Drill the two types of negative contractions, for example:
  T: We are not from London.
  S1: We aren't from London.
  S2: We're not from London.

Grammar Notes

Note 1
- Call on a student to read the note and the examples.
- To elicit the three forms of be, ask: "Who is from [Mexico]?" "What is your favorite sport?" "Where are [Lin] and [Mei Li] from?"
- Write students' responses on the board and underline the three forms of be.
- Call on students to use the three forms of be to give you more sentences about students in the class.
- Write students' responses on the board.

Note 2
- Call on a student to read the note and the examples.
- Ask: "In negative statements, where do we add the word not?" (after the form of the verb be)
- To review how to form negative sentences, have students come to the board and change the sentences to the negative by adding not in the correct places. (Example: I am not from Mexico.)

Note 3
- Call on a student to read the note and the examples.
- Ask: "When do we use contractions?" (in speaking and informal writing)
- To review, do a quick transformation drill. Say sentences with the full forms and call on students to change them to contractions. Elicit both forms of the negative contractions, for example:
  T: We are students.
  S1: We're students.
  T: They are not from Seoul.
  S1: They're not from Seoul.
  S2: They aren't from Seoul.
- To review all contractions in the affirmative and negative, write the following chart on the board (or make a handout):

Affirmative	Negative
1. (I) *I'm* _____	1. (I) _____
2. (you) _____	2. (you) _____
3. (he) _____	3. (he) _____
4. (she) _____	4. (she) *She's not, she isn't*
5. (it) _____	5. (it) _____
6. (we) _____	6. (we) _____
7. (you) _____	7. (you) _____
8. (they) _____	8. (they) _____

- Call on students to come to the front and fill in the chart.

Note 4

- Call on a student to read the note and the examples.
- Draw attention to the *Be Careful!* note.
- Write the following sentences on the board and have students tell you whether they are correct or incorrect. Ask them to correct the incorrect sentences and tell you the subject and verb in each sentence.
  I am a soccer fan. (*correct*)
  My favorite player is David Beckham. (*correct*)
  He from England. (*incorrect:* He is from England.)
  David and Victoria Beckham are famous. (*correct*)
  Victoria's nickname Posh Spice. (*incorrect:* Victoria's nickname is Posh Spice.)
  Not an athlete. (*incorrect:* She is not an athlete. / He is not an athlete. / I am not an athlete.)
  She a singer. (*incorrect:* She's a singer.)

Note 5

- To check comprehension, write a list of nouns and noun phrases on the board, including some noun / pronoun combinations, for example:
  my best friend and I
  Ali and Kenji
  English
  you and your sister
  footvolley
  my English teacher
- On the other side of the board, list the subject pronouns:
  I, you, he, she, it, we, they
- Ask pairs of students to write sentences using the subject nouns and noun phrases and then to rewrite them with the correct pronouns, for example:
  My best friend and I are soccer players.
  We are soccer players.
- Point out the *Be Careful!* note.

⏱ **Identify the Grammar:** Have students identify the grammar in the reading on page 2. For example:
  They're young. They're rich.
  The woman on the left **is** Carrie Underwood.
  Carrie **is** an American country singer.

Go to **www.myfocusongrammarlab.com** for grammar charts and notes.

Step 3: Focused Practice (pages 5–8)

See the general suggestions for Focused Practice on page 4.

Exercise 1: Discover the Grammar

A

- Ask: "What word do we add to make a statement negative?" *(not)* Elicit examples of negative statements, and prompt students to give you both forms of the negative contractions for *is* and *are*.
- Go over the example with the class. Then have students complete the exercise individually.
- Have students compare answers in pairs. Then call on pairs to give answers.

B

- Have students complete the exercise individually.
- Have students compare answers in pairs. Then call on pairs to give answers.

Exercise 2: Affirmative Statements

- Go over the example with the class. Ask: "What is the subject?" *(football and soccer)* "Why is *are* the correct answer?" *(because football and soccer are plural)*
- Have students complete the exercise in pairs.
- Call on pairs to give answers.

Exercise 3: Affirmative and Negative Statements

- Go over the example with the class. Remind students that they should write the full forms and not contractions for this exercise. Draw attention to number 7 and point out that negative forms are indicated with a *(not)*.
- Have students complete the exercise individually.
- Have students compare answers in pairs. Then call on students to read two or three consecutive sentences from the paragraph.

Exercise 4: Subject Pronouns and Contractions

- Go over the example with the class. Be sure students understand that they should use contractions in their answers.
- Have students complete the exercise individually.
- Have students compare answers in pairs. Call on students to read the original sentences first and then the new sentences.

Exercise 5: Affirmative and Negative Contractions

- Go over the example with the class. Make sure students understand that they should write true sentences. Sentences may be in either the affirmative or the negative, but they must contain a contraction.
- Have students complete the exercise individually.
- Have students compare answers in pairs. Then call on students to give answers.

Exercise 6: Editing

- Go over the example with the class. Point out that students should find eight more mistakes in the passage.
- Have students find and correct the mistakes in pairs.
- Combine pairs to form groups of four and have students compare answers. Then call on students to read the corrected passage. Have them explain why the incorrect structures are wrong.

Go to **www.myfocusongrammarlab.com** for additional grammar practice.

Step 4: Communication Practice (pages 8–11)

See the general suggestions for Communication Practice on page 5.

Exercise 7: Pronunciation

A

- Play the audio. Have students read along as they listen to the Pronunciation Note. Demonstrate the correct position of the mouth when you say *he's* (lips drawn back in a smile) and *she's* (lips relaxed, forward). Have students repeat.

B

- Play the audio. Have students listen.
- Play the audio again. Have students listen and complete the chart. If necessary, stop the recording after each statement to allow students time to confirm / correct their answers.

C

- Play the audio. Have students listen and repeat the statements.

Exercise 8: Listening

A

- Have students look at the pictures. Ask: "Do you know these talented people?" "What are their names?" "Where are they from?" "What do they do?"

- Have students complete the chart in pairs, using the information in the box. Tell them that it's OK if they do not know all of the answers. They will have a chance to check their guesses when they hear the audio.

B

- Play the audio. Have students listen and write the occupation and country.
- Go over the example with the class.
- Have students follow the example dialogue when they compare answers in pairs. Then call on pairs to give answers.

Exercise 9: Talking about Occupations

A

- Go over the pronunciation of the occupations. Ask students if they or any of their relatives or friends have the occupations listed. Have students check those occupations.
- Elicit sentences from the class. (Example: *I am a nurse. My sister is a writer.*)
- Have students brainstorm more occupations in pairs. Then call on students to give answers and write them on the board.

B

- Go over the adjectives in the box and ask the class to give you a few more adjectives to describe jobs. (Example: *fun, easy, well-paid*) Write students' ideas on the board.
- Call on a pair to read the example dialogue.
- Have students complete the exercise in pairs. Encourage them to use the adjectives and make both affirmative and negative statements. (Example: *My brother is a doctor. His job isn't easy, but it's interesting.*)

Exercise 10: Talking about Talented People

A

- Call on a student to read the list of qualities. Go over the meanings, if necessary.
- Have pairs add four more qualities to the list.
- Elicit ideas from pairs and write them on the board.

B

- Draw attention to the graphic organizer on page 11. Go over the meaning of *relationship*, if necessary. (who the person is: a friend, your sister, your uncle, etc.)
- Have students complete the circles individually.
- Read the example to the class. Then have pairs use the example as a guide to talk about their graphic organizers.

Exercise 11: Writing

A

- Go over the example with the class.
- Have students use the chart from Exercise 8 or their own information from the graphic organizer in Exercise 10 to write their sentences.

B

- Have students correct their work using the Editing Checklist.
- Have students exchange papers and check their partner's work.

OUT OF THE BOX ACTIVITIES

Writing and Speaking

- Bring in photos (or have students bring in photos) of various famous people, both local and international. (Example: *politicians, athletes, actors, musicians*) Post the photos around the classroom and have students talk in pairs about who the people are, where they are from, and their occupations.
- Have pairs choose three of the people and write a short description (four to five sentences) of each person. Tell them not to include the name of the person in their description.
- Have pairs read their description to another pair. The other pair should try to guess the person. (Example: *This person is a woman. She is from the United States. She is a famous singer.* [Beyoncé])

Reading and Speaking

- Bring in articles from the Internet or from entertainment magazines about famous people.
- Form small groups and give each group an article.
- Give students three or four minutes to skim through the article and circle the forms of *be*.
- Have groups tell the class three or four things learned about the famous person in the article. (Example: *Brad Pitt and Angelina Jolie are married. Their daughter's name is Shiloh.*)

Go to **www.myfocusongrammarlab.com** for additional listening, pronunciation, speaking, and writing practice.

Note:

- See the *Focus on Grammar Workbook* for additional in-class or homework grammar practice.

Unit 1 Review (page 12)

Have students complete the Review and check their answers on Student Book page UR-1. Review or assign additional material as needed.

Go to **www.myfocusongrammarlab.com** for the Unit Achievement Test.

> **UNIT 2 OVERVIEW**
>
> **Grammar:** PRESENT OF *Be*: YES / NO QUESTIONS AND *Wh-* QUESTIONS
>
> Unit 2 focuses on the structure and use of *be* in:
>
> - Singular and plural *yes / no* questions
> - Singular and plural *wh-* questions
> - Short and long answers to questions
>
> **Theme:** FIRST DAY OF SCHOOL
>
> Unit 2 focuses on the use of present *be* in *yes / no* and *wh-* questions to make small talk and get to know other people.

Step 1: Grammar in Context (pages 13–15)

See the general suggestions for Grammar in Context on page 1.

Before You Read

A

- Go over the example with the class. Demonstrate writing *yes* or *no* in the chart.
- Have students move around the classroom and choose four other students to talk with.
- Have students compare answers in pairs.

B

- Call on students to report their answers to the class.
- To review, elicit singular, plural, affirmative, and negative forms of *be*. (Example: *Carlos and Anita are always on time for dates. Hiro isn't always on time for school.*)
- Listen for students' use of the present forms of *be* and correct any errors as necessary.

Read

- Explain that students will read a conversation between some students on the first day of class.
- Ask: "What do you think the people might talk about?" "What questions might they ask each other?" Elicit several ideas, but do not correct students at this stage.
- Have students read the text (or play the audio and have students follow along in their books).

After You Read

A. Practice

- Have students read the conversation in pairs.
- Have pairs switch roles and read the conversation again.
- Call on several volunteer pairs to read the conversation.

B. Vocabulary

- Have students complete the exercise individually.
- Have students compare answers in pairs. Then call on students to read the complete sentences.

C. Comprehension

- Have students complete the exercise in pairs.
- Combine pairs to form groups of four and have students compare answers.
- Call on pairs to give answers. To reinforce the question-and-answer format, have one partner ask the question and the other give the answer.

Go to **www.myfocusongrammarlab.com** for an additional reading, and for reading and vocabulary practice.

Step 2: Grammar Presentation (pages 16–17)

See the general suggestions for Grammar Presentation on page 2.

Grammar Charts

- Write the following on the board. Don't write the final punctuation.
  I am late for class   Am I late for class
- Ask: "Which one is a question?" (*Am I late for class*) "How do you know?" (*subject-verb word order*)
- Write the following on the board, using names of students from the class:
  Is _____ here? / Yes, she is.
  Is _____ here? / No, he's not. (No, he isn't.)
- Call on students to read the singular and plural *yes / no* questions in the charts.

- Emphasize the rising intonation of the questions. Show the rising contour with your hand. Have students repeat.
- Do a quick drill. Include all the singular and plural forms.
  T: You are hungry.
  Ss: Are you hungry?
  T: He is hungry.
  Ss: Is he hungry?
- Drill the short answer using a question-and-answer format. Ask questions using all pronouns, singular and plural. Students should answer with true information. Begin with questions that take affirmative answers:
  T: Am I a teacher?
  S: Yes, you are.
  T: Is it Thursday today?
  S: Yes, it is.
- Repeat the previous step with questions that take a negative answer.
  T: Is today Thursday?
  S1: No, it's not.
  S2: No, it isn't.
  T: Are Diana and Kim absent?
- Go over the meanings of the *wh-* question words. Ask: "Which word asks about a person?" (*who*) "Which asks about a place?" (*where*) "Which asks about a reason?" (*why*)
- Call on several students to read the example questions and answers in the chart.

Grammar Notes

Note 1

- Call on a student to read the note and the examples.
- Use the conversation on page 14 to illustrate the difference between the two question types.
- Draw two columns on the board like this:

Yes / No questions	Wh- questions

- Have students find the examples of *yes / no* questions in the conversation. Write the answers on the board.
- Do the same with the *wh-* questions in the conversation, for example:

Yes / No questions	Wh- questions
No, we're right on time.	It's right here, next to the office.

- Ask the class to notice the types of information given in each set of answers. (*Answers to* yes / no *questions usually contain* yes *or* no. *Answers to* wh- *questions give various types of information, depending on the* wh- *question word.*)

Note 2
- Call on a student to read the note and the examples.
- Write a list of present *be* statements on the board, for example:
  I am here.
  She is here.
  We are sisters.
  They are happy.
  It is hot outside.
  Alina and Bao are late.
- Have students work individually to write the statements in question form. (*Am I here? Is she tired today?* etc.)
- Have students compare answers in pairs. Then call on students to write the questions on the board.

Note 3
- Call on a student to read the note and the examples.
- Ask the questions on the board from Note 2. Have students tell you both the long and short answers, for example:
  T: Am I here?
  S1: Yes, you are here.
  S2: Yes, you are.
- After each answer, write the incorrect contracted form on the board with an X through it, for example:

Yes, you're.

- Draw students' attention to the *Be Careful!* note.

Note 4
- Call on a student to read the note and the examples.
- Write the following on the board:
  October 10   My mother
  In Room 202   Because I like it
  It's interesting.   He is 18 years old.
- Explain that the phrases on the board are answers to questions.
- Have students tell you which *wh-* question word matches each type of information on the board. (Example: *October 10 = when*)

Note 5
- Call on a student to read the note and the examples.

- Using the phrases on the board from Note 4 above, have students work in pairs to come up with a possible question for each answer on the board. (Example: *When is / When's your birthday? October 10th.*)
- Call on pairs to give answers.

Note 6
- Point out that we often use contractions with *wh-* words in speaking and informal writing.
- Have students repeat the questions after you.
- Then call on students to answer the questions in the note. Remind them to use contracted forms. (*It's around the corner. The trip's on Monday.*)

Note 7
- Call on a student to read the note and the examples.
- Ask individual students questions and elicit both the short and the long answers, for example:
  T: Sun Yee, where's your book?
  S: On my desk. / It's on my desk.

Note 8
- Call on a student to read the note and the examples.
- Go around the class and ask questions to individual students. Encourage students to ask one another questions to find out the answers. Use a mix of *yes / no* and *wh-* questions, for example:
  T: Paru, is Elena from Mexico?
  PARU: I don't know.
  T: Please ask Elena the question.
  PARU: Elena, are you from Mexico?
  ELENA: Yes, I am.

  T: Yasmin, when is Juan's birthday?
  YASMIN: I don't know.
  T: Please ask Juan.
  YASMIN: Juan, when is your birthday?
  JUAN: November 23rd.

Identify the Grammar: Have students identify the grammar in the conversation on page 14. For example:
  Where's room 2?
  . . . are we late for class?
  Is the teacher here?

Go to **www.myfocusongrammarlab.com** for grammar charts and notes.

Step 3: Focused Practice (pages 18–21)
See the general suggestions for Focused Practice on page 4.

Exercise 1: Discover the Grammar
- Have students look at the picture and tell you what they see.
- Have students read the questions and answers. Make sure they understand key vocabulary such as *early, hungry, unhappy*.
- Have students complete the exercise individually. Then have them compare answers in pairs.

Exercise 2: *Yes / No* Questions
- Go over the example with the class. Ask: "What is the subject?" *(Today)* "What is the verb?" *(is)*
- Ask: "In *yes / no* questions with *be*, which comes first, the subject or the verb?" *(the verb)*
- Have students complete the exercise individually. Then call on students to read the questions.

Exercise 3: Word Order of *Yes / No* Questions
- Go over the example with the class. Remind students that they should use contractions when possible and that they should write true answers to the questions.
- Have students complete the exercise individually.
- Have students compare answers in pairs. Then call on pairs to read the questions and answers.

Exercise 4: *Wh-* Questions
- Go over the example with the class. Make sure students understand that they should read the answer first and then form the question.
- Have students complete the exercise individually.
- Have students read the questions and answers in pairs. Then call on pairs to give answers.

Exercise 5: *Yes / No* Questions and *Wh-* Questions
A
- Have students read the blog silently. Alternatively, call on a student to read it while the rest of the class reads along silently. Ask: "Who is Alejandra writing about?" "Why does she like him?" "What is the problem with him?"
- Go over the example with the class.
- Have students complete the exercise individually. Then have them compare answers in pairs.

B
- Have students read the blog response silently. Alternatively, call on a student to read it while the rest of the class reads along silently.

- Check that students know the meaning of *no big deal. (not important)* Then ask: "Why does SmartGirl think Oscar may be late?" *(he thinks he's important, he doesn't think it's a problem, or he's bad at planning his time)* "What advice does she give?" *(talk to him, try to help)* "What can we say when we don't know an answer to a question?" *("I don't know.")* "What can we say when we think something is true?" *("I think so.")* "What can we say when we think something is not true?" *("I don't think so.")*
- Go over the example with the class. Have students complete the exercise individually and then compare answers in pairs.

Exercise 6: Editing
- Go over the example with the class.
- Have students find and correct the mistakes individually.
- Have students compare answers in pairs. Then call on students to read the corrected passage. Have them explain why the incorrect structures are wrong.

Go to **www.myfocusongrammarlab.com** for additional grammar practice.

Step 4: Communication Practice (pages 22–23)
See the general suggestions for Communication Practice on page 5.

Exercise 7: Listening
A
- Tell students they will hear a conversation about a student's (Hugo's) English class.
- Play the audio. Have students listen and complete the exercise individually.
- Call on a student to give the answer.

B
- Call on students to read the questions.
- Play the audio. Have students listen and complete the exercise individually.
- Have students compare answers in pairs. Then call on pairs to read the questions and answers. Have them give the short answer after they give the long one.

Exercise 8: Pronunciation
A
- Play the audio. Have students read along as they listen to the Pronunciation Note. Say the example sentences and have students repeat them. Use your hand to show the rising or falling intonation contour as you say the end of each question.

B

• Play the audio. Have students listen.

C

• Play the audio. Have students listen and repeat the questions.
• To check that students understand the intonation, call on students to say the sentences with the correct intonation.

Exercise 9: Asking and Answering Questions

• Review the correct intonation of *yes / no* questions (rising) and *wh-* questions (falling).
• Have students look at Exercise 2 and complete the exercise in pairs. Remind them to focus on using the correct intonation.
• Have students form new pairs and practice asking and answering the questions again.

Exercise 10: Role Play: Meeting at a Party

• Have students make some notes about their new identity. Go around the class and help students with ideas as needed.
• Go over the example with the class.
• Have students complete the exercise in pairs. To make the situation more realistic, have students stand up and imagine that they are talking to someone at a party. Play some music, if desired.

Exercise 11: Writing

A

• Go over the example with the class.
• Have students complete the exercise in pairs. Remind students that the answers to the questions need to be found in the ad.
• Combine pairs to form groups of four. Have students read the ad once more and then close their books.
• Have pairs take turns asking and answering their questions. Remind them to use the correct intonation for each question type.

B

• Correct your work using the Editing Checklist.

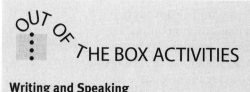

OUT OF THE BOX ACTIVITIES

Writing and Speaking

• Have students prepare ten biographical questions for an interview, including both *yes / no* and *wh-* questions.
• Have them interview a partner, taking notes on their partner's answers.

• Have students use their notes to write a one-page biography of their partner.
• Call on students to read their biographies to the class.

Speaking

• Form small groups. Have groups play the game 20 Questions.
• One student thinks of a person (or an animal / place / thing, etc.) but does not tell the group what it is.
• Other group members may ask up to 20 *yes / no* questions to guess the item.
• When a student has guessed the item, another student thinks of the next item.

Reading and Speaking

• Bring in a selection of short, level-appropriate readings. (Examples: news clips, articles, printed emails, blogs)
• Have students choose one of the readings and read it.
• Have students write five quiz questions about the reading.
• Have students find a partner who has a different reading and exchange quiz questions and reading papers.
• Have students use the reading to answer the quiz questions.
• Have students exchange papers and check one another's answers and give a quiz "score."

Go to **www.myfocusongrammarlab.com** for additional listening, pronunciation, speaking, and writing practice.

Note:
• See the *Focus on Grammar Workbook* for additional in-class or homework grammar practice.

Unit 2 Review (page 24)

Have students complete the Review and check their answers on Student Book page UR-1. Review or assign additional material as needed.

Go to **www.myfocusongrammarlab.com** for the Unit Achievement Test.

Grammar: PAST OF *Be*: STATEMENTS, *Yes /No* QUESTIONS, *Wh-* QUESTIONS

Unit 3 focuses on the structure and use of *be* in:

- Singular and plural past statements
- Negative statements in the past
- Questions in the past

Theme: FIRST JOBS

Unit 3 focuses on the use of past *be* statements and questions to talk about jobs people have held in the past and job changes.

Step 1: Grammar in Context (pages 25–26)

See the general suggestions for Grammar in Context on page 1.

Before You Read

- Read the two discussion questions and have students read along.
- Have students discuss the questions in pairs. Encourage them to explain the reasons for their opinions.
- Call on students to give answers. Write the responses on the board in past *be* sentences. (Example: *Franco was a cashier. Paulo and Andre were servers.*)

Read

- Have students look at the pictures and tell you what they see.
- Ask: "What do you think Hugo Rubio's first job was?" "What do you think he will say about it?" Go over any key vocabulary, such as *lifeguard, hero, slipped, mayor,* etc.
- Have students read the text. (OR: Play the audio and have students follow along in their books.)

After You Read

A. Practice

- Have students complete the exercise in pairs.
- Call on students to read portions of the story.

B. Vocabulary

- Have students complete the exercise individually.
- Have students compare answers in pairs. Then call on students to read the complete sentences.

C. Comprehension

- Have students complete the exercise in pairs.
- Combine pairs to form groups of four and have students compare answers.
- Call on students to give answers.

Go to **www.myfocusongrammarlab.com** for an additional reading, and for reading and vocabulary practice.

Step 2: Grammar Presentation (pages 27–28)

See the general suggestions for Grammar Presentation on page 2.

Grammar Charts

- Call on students to read the examples of affirmative statements in the charts.
- For each sentence, ask: "What is the subject?" "What is the verb?"
- Explain that time markers are words or phrases that tell when the action happened. Elicit the expressions in the examples that are past time markers.
- Do a quick drill. Provide a base sentence. Cue the class with different subjects and have students repeat the sentence with the proper verb, for example:
  T: I was in New York two weeks ago. You.
  Ss: You were in New York two weeks ago.
  T: He.
  Ss: He was in New York two weeks ago.
- Repeat the previous steps with non-contracted negative forms, for example:
  T: I was not at school last night. She.
  Ss: She was not at school last night.
- Repeat the previous steps, this time with contracted forms, for example:
  T: I wasn't at work last week. They.
  Ss: They weren't at work last week.
- Review the word order of *yes / no* questions with *be* (verb before subject).
- Call on students to read the example questions in the charts.
- Drill the question forms. Have students close their books. Write the following phrases on the board:
  . . . at the mall yesterday?
  . . . in class this morning?
  . . . home last night?
  . . . in the cafeteria at lunchtime?
  . . . at Javier's house last week?
  . . . on time to class today?
- Point to a student and say a subject, *he.* Then point to a phrase on the board and have the student make the question. (Example: *Was he at the mall yesterday?*) Be sure to include a variety of singular and plural subjects.

Grammar Notes

Notes 1–3
- Have students read Notes 1–3 silently.
- Write the following three columns on the board:

I you he, she, it we you they [Student's name] [Student's name and student's name]	at a party absent late at home at the library in class at the airport tired	this morning last night yesterday

- On a piece of paper, have students draw a large square and divide it into four smaller squares, like this:

was	were
wasn't	weren't

- Have students form pairs or small groups. Have students work together to write three true sentences for each verb form using the vocabulary on the board and the verb forms on their papers. Have groups share their sentences with other groups, or call on students to read selected sentences to the class.

Notes 4 and 5
- Have students read Notes 4 and 5 silently.
- Write the following prompts on the board:

Student 1's questions	Student 2's questions
in this country / last year	here / two months ago
in class / yesterday	with [student's name] last night
at home / last night	tired / yesterday
absent / the day before yesterday	sick / last week

- In pairs, have students use the prompts to interview each other using past *yes / no* questions. (Example: *Were you in this country last year? No, I was here two months ago.*) Remind students to use rising intonation at the end of questions.

🕐 **Identify the Grammar:** Have students identify the grammar in the reading on pages 25–26. For example:
  I **was** 16 years old.
  My days **were** long and boring.
  They **weren't** fun.

Go to **www.myfocusongrammarlab.com** for grammar charts and notes.

Step 3: Focused Practice (pages 29–31)

See the general suggestions for Focused Practice on page 4.

Exercise 1: Discover the Grammar
- Have students look at the pictures. Ask the class if they know the celebrities pictured (*actors Jennifer Aniston and Warren Beatty*).
- Explain that the cartoons show these celebrities' jobs before they became famous. Ask: "What do you think Jennifer Aniston's first job was?" "What was Warren Beatty's first job?" Elicit students' guesses, but do not correct them at this time.
- Have students read the text once quickly for meaning. Then have them read again and underline *was, were, wasn't,* and *weren't.*

Exercise 2: Questions and Answers
- Go over the example with the class. Ask: "How will you know whether to use the singular or plural form?" (*look at the subject*) "How will you know when to use a negative?" (*look for the word* not)
- Have students complete the conversation individually.
- Have students compare answers in pairs. Then call on a pair to read the complete conversation.

Exercise 3: Affirmative and Negative Statements
- Go over the example with the class. Remind students that if they see the word *not*, they should use the negative form.
- Have students complete the exercise individually.
- Have students compare answers in pairs. Then call on students to read the present and past sentences.

Exercise 4: Questions and Answers
- Go over the example with the class. Then review the formation of *wh-* questions. (wh-*word + verb + subject*)
- Have students complete the exercise individually. Then have them read the conversation in pairs.

- ⏱ Have students cover the completed conversation on the right. Then have them try to say the conversation just using the prompts on the left.

Exercise 5: Editing
- Go over the example with the class.
- Have students find and correct the mistakes individually.
- Have students compare answers in pairs. Then call on students to read the corrected sentences. Have students explain why the incorrect structures are wrong.

Go to **www.myfocusongrammarlab.com** for additional grammar practice.

Step 4: Communication Practice (pages 31–34)

See the general suggestions for Communication Practice on page 5.

Exercise 6: Listening

A
- Tell students they will hear five short telephone messages.
- Play the audio. Have students listen and check the appropriate columns in the chart to indicate whether the caller is a friend, a family member, or a business associate.
- Call on students to give answers.

B
- Go over the example with the class.
- Have students read the partial quotes quickly for meaning.
- Play the audio. Have students listen and complete the quotes. Then play the audio again and have students listen to confirm their answers.

Exercise 7: Pronunciation

A
- Play the audio. Have students read along as they listen to the Pronunciation Note.

B
- Play the audio. Have students listen and repeat the sentences.

C
- Play the audio again. Have students listen and check the past form of *be* that they hear.
- To extend the practice, play the audio again and have students repeat the sentences.

Exercise 8: Describing the Weather

A
- Have students think about their first day at their job or their first day at school. Ask: "What was the day like?" "How was the weather?" "How did you feel?"
- Have students study the words for weather.

B
- Go over the pronunciation of the international cities. Have students repeat them after you.
- Have students complete the exercise in pairs.
- Call on pairs to read the conversations they made.

Exercise 9: Talking about the First Day of School
- Go over the example with the class.
- Form small groups. Have students complete the exercise in groups.

Exercise 10: Writing

A
- Go over the example with the class. Then give students one minute to write down anything they can about last weekend: what the weather was like, what they did, where they went, who they spent time with, how they felt, and so on. If they don't know how to say something in English, they can draw a picture or write it in their own language, and they can look up the words later.
- Have students use their notes to write an email message to their friend about last weekend. Remind them that they can use both the present and past form of *be*, and they should use contractions where possible.

B
- Have students check their use of the forms of *be* and that they have used contractions where possible.
- Have them correct their work, using the Editing Checklist.
- If possible, set up student email accounts and have students type their emails on the computer and send them to another student in the class. Students can then highlight the forms of *be* and correct any errors in their partner's email.

OUT OF THE BOX ACTIVITIES

Reading and Writing

- Form small groups. Then have each group choose a celebrity that interests them.
- Have groups use the Internet or the library to research the past of their selected celebrity, including information about where the person was born, past jobs, movies or TV shows he or she appeared on, songs he or she sang, and so on.
- Have students make a true / false quiz about their celebrity. The quiz should be in the form of past *be* statements. (Example: *Brad Pitt's name was Brad Pittman. He was a clerk in a department store.*)
- Have groups give their quizzes to the class.

Speaking

- Have students play the game Two Truths and a Lie in pairs.
- Both students write three sentences about a past job they have had. Two sentences must be true and one must be a lie.
- When they finish, have students read their sentences to each other and try to guess which sentence is the lie.

Go to **www.myfocusongrammarlab.com** for additional listening, pronunciation, speaking, and writing practice.

Note:
- See the *Focus on Grammar Workbook* for additional in-class or homework grammar practice.

Unit 3 Review (page 35)

Have students complete the Review and check their answers on Student Book page UR-1. Review or assign additional material as needed.

Go to **www.myfocusongrammarlab.com** for the Unit Achievement Test.

From Grammar to Writing (pages 36–37)

See the general suggestions for From Grammar to Writing on page 9.

Go to **www.myfocusongrammarlab.com** for an additional From Grammar to Writing Assignment, Part Review, and Part Post-Test.

PART II OVERVIEW

NOUNS, ADJECTIVES, PREPOSITIONS

UNIT	GRAMMAR FOCUS	THEME
4	Count Nouns and Proper Nouns	Photographs and Photographers
5	Descriptive Adjectives	Cave Homes
6	Prepositions of Place	Locations

Go to **www.myfocusongrammarlab.com** for the Part and Unit Tests.

Note: PowerPoint® grammar presentations, test-generating software, and reproducible Part and Unit Tests are on the *Teacher's Resource Disc.*

UNIT 4 OVERVIEW

Grammar: COUNT NOUNS AND PROPER NOUNS

Unit 4 focuses on singular and plural count nouns and proper nouns, including:

- The formation of plural count nouns
- The use of article *a* and *an*
- Capitalization of proper nouns

Theme: PHOTOGRAPHS AND PHOTOGRAPHERS

Unit 4 focuses on the topic of photography and language used to discuss photographers and different types of photographs.

Step 1: Grammar in Context (pages 40–41)

See the general suggestions for Grammar in Context on page 1.

Before You Read

- If possible, before beginning this unit have students bring in a photograph to class. It may be a photo of a person / people or a place, or any photo that they like. If desired, bring in a photo album or show a slide show of some select photos of your own to introduce the topic.
- Go over the example with the class.
- Have students discuss the questions in pairs.

- Call on students to give answers and then ask them why they choose to keep their photos in those places.
- Have students stay in pairs and talk about a photo they have. If they do not have a photo, hand out photos cut out of magazines or printed from the Internet. Encourage students to use their imaginations to create information about the photo if they do not already know about it.

Read

- Have students look at the black-and-white photo and read the title of the article silently. Say: "You are going to read about Henri Cartier-Bresson, a famous French photographer. Look at his photo. What do you think made his photos special?"
- To encourage students to read with a purpose, write these questions on the board:
  1. Where did Cartier-Bresson take his photographs? *(on the "street" and all over the world)*
  2. What is "street photography?" *(photos of people in public places)*
  3. What do people say about his photos? *(They are striking and beautiful.)*
- Have students read the text. (OR: Play the audio and have students follow along in their books.) Then call on students to share their answers to the questions on the board.

After You Read

A. Practice

- Have students complete the exercise in pairs.
- Call on students to each read a paragraph to the class.

B. Vocabulary

- Have students complete the exercise individually. Have them refer to the reading to help them guess the meaning of the vocabulary.
- Have students compare answers in pairs. Then call on students to read the completed sentences and meanings.
- Highlight the importance of using the context (the words and sentences around a new vocabulary word) to guess the meanings of unknown words.

C. Comprehension

- Have students complete the exercise individually.
- Have students compare answers in pairs. Then call on students to say whether the sentences are true or false. Have them correct the false statements.

Go to **www.myfocusongrammarlab.com** for an additional reading, and for reading and vocabulary practice.

Step 2: Grammar Presentation (pages 42–43)

See the general suggestions for Grammar Presentation on page 2.

Grammar Charts

- Focus students' attention on the first two charts: Singular Nouns and Plural Nouns.
- Have students work in pairs to discuss the differences between the boldfaced nouns in both sets of sentences. Ask: "What do you notice about the ends of the plural nouns?" (*There is an* s.) "What do you see in front of the singular nouns?" (*a / an*) "When do we use *a* and when do we use *an* before a singular noun?" (*nouns beginning with a consonant =* a; *nouns beginning with a vowel =* an)
- Call on students to read the singular and plural forms of the irregular nouns. Go over the pronunciation of *women* and explain that the *o* is pronounced with the short *i* as in b*i*t.
- To reinforce these irregular forms, put students into pairs and have them write a sentence with each plural form. Call on pairs to share their sentences with the class.
- Focus students' attention on the Proper Nouns chart. Have students tell you what is important to remember about proper nouns. (*They must be capitalized.*)

Grammar Notes

Notes 1–3

- On the board, sketch a graphic organizer:

  singular

  a   an

- Demonstrate singular nouns with the article *a*. Hold up objects or photos, or point to objects in the room. Name the items using *a*. (Examples: *a book, a pencil, a phone*) Write the items under the article *a* on the board.
- Repeat with objects or photos that take the article *an*. (Examples: *an orange, an apple, an eye, an earring*) Again, write the examples on the board, this time under *an*.
- Ask the class for additional examples of singular nouns with *a / an*. Write them on the board.
- Call on two students to read the *Be Careful!* notes.

- Now write two columns on the board:

university	umbrella
uniform	undershirt
hand	honor
house	hour

- Point to each word and say it with *a* or *an*, as appropriate. Write a small *y* above the *u* in *university* and *uniform*. Put an *X* through the *h* in *hour* and *honor* so students understand that this sound is not pronounced. Have students repeat the phrases after you: "a university, an umbrella," and so on.

Note 4
- Sketch another organizer on the board:

  plural → regular
  plural → irregular
  plural → always plural

- Demonstrate examples of regular, irregular, and always plural nouns and write them on the board. Elicit further examples from the students.
- Drill the irregular plurals. Have students listen and repeat. (Example: *One man, two men. One woman, two women. One child, two children.*)
- Say a singular noun and have the class fill in the plural. Then do the reverse.
  T: One man, two . . .
  Ss: Men.
  T: One tooth, two . . .
  Ss: Teeth.
  T: Two feet, one . . .
  Ss: Foot.

Note 5
- On the board, write the title *Proper Nouns*. Write several names of places and people as examples.
- Have the class give further examples. Call students up to the board to write them.
- Point to the capital letters and underline them.

🕐 **Identify the Grammar:** Have students identify the grammar in the reading on page 40. For example:
  Henri Cartier-Bresson was **a photographer** . . .
  . . . he was almost 96 **years** old.
  His **photos** are from all over the **world**.

Go to **www.myfocusongrammarlab.com** for grammar charts and notes.

Step 3: Focused Practice (pages 43–46)

See the general suggestions for Focused Practice on page 4.

Exercise 1: Discover the Grammar

A
- Have students read the entire conversation once silently.
- Call on two students to read the conversation.

B
- Have students work in pairs to underline all the nouns in the conversation.
- Have students complete the exercise in pairs.
- Go over the answers as a class.

Exercise 2: *A* or *An*

A
- Go over the example with the class.
- Have students complete the exercise individually.
- Have students compare answers in pairs. Then call on students to read the correct phrases.

B
- Have students complete the exercise individually.
- Have students compare answers in pairs.
- 🕐 To extend the practice and review the plural forms, have students give you the plural form of each word on the list.

Exercise 3: *A* or *An*
- Have students complete the exercise in pairs.
- Combine pairs to form groups of four and have students compare answers. Then call on students to read the complete sentences.
- 🕐 Closed books. Ask the class questions about the information in the exercise:
  1. Who were Cartier-Bresson and Adams? (*They were photographers.*)
  2. What did Ansel Adams do before he became a photographer? (*He was a pianist.*)
  3. Where was Adams born? (*He was born in San Francisco.*)
  4. What should all good photographers be? (*They should be artists.*)

Exercise 4: Regular and Irregular Plural Nouns
- Go over the example with the class.
- Go over the spelling rules in Appendix 5 on page A-5 with the class. If students need extra practice, have them work in pairs to change the singular forms in the box to plurals before they begin the sentence completion task.
- Have students complete the exercise individually.

Exercise 5: Proper Nouns
- Review examples of types of proper nouns. *(names, cities, countries, etc.)*
- Go over the example with the class. Have students tell you whether any other words in the sentence need a capital letter. *(Lan)*
- Have students complete the exercise individually. Then have them compare answers in pairs.

Exercise 6: Editing
- Go over the example with the class. Make sure students know that they should look for errors in the use of *a* and *an*, spelling of plural nouns, and capitalization of proper nouns.
- Have students find and correct the mistakes in pairs.
- Combine pairs to form groups of four and have students compare answers. Then call on students to read the corrected passage. Have them explain why the incorrect structures are wrong.

Go to **www.myfocusongrammarlab.com** for additional grammar practice.

Step 4: Communication Practice (pages 47–49)
See the general suggestions for Communication Practice on page 5.

Exercise 7: Pronunciation
A
- Play the audio. Have students read along as they listen to the Pronunciation Note. Explain that there are three ways to pronounce *-s* / *-es* endings of plural nouns: /s/, /z/, and /ɪz/. Have students repeat the three sounds after you.

B
- Have students complete the sentences individually.
- Play the audio again for students to confirm their answers.

C
- Play the audio. Have students listen and check the correct ending in the boxes in Exercise B.

Exercise 8: Listening
A
- Have students read the question and answer choices silently.
- Play the audio. Have students listen and complete the exercise individually.
- Call on a student to say the answer.

B
- Have students read the questions and answer choices silently.
- Play the audio. Have students listen and complete the exercise individually.
- ⏱ Hand out the text for the audioscript and have students practice it in pairs.

Exercise 9: Game: Describing Things
- Say: "Go!" Have students complete the exercise in pairs. Remind them to correctly use *a* and *an* and capital letters where appropriate.
- After 5 minutes, have pairs exchange lists with another pair and check spelling, use of *a* and *an*, and capitalization.
- Have them return the lists, count the nouns, and tell you how many they found. The pair with the most nouns written correctly wins.

Exercise 10: Game: Naming People, Places, and Things
A
- Have a student read the list of items in the chart.
- Have students complete the exercise in pairs. Remind them to use *a* and *an* and to use capital letters where needed.

B
- Combine pairs to form groups of four and have students compare their answers from part A.
- Call on groups to give answers. Ask how many answers they had in common.
- To add an element of competition, points may be given for each different item (i.e., an item that no other pair in the class has listed).

Exercise 11: Writing
A
- Go over the example with the class.
- Have students use their own photos and give real information. Alternatively, hand out photos from magazines or printed from the Internet and have students use their imaginations to write a description.

B
- Have students correct their work, using the Editing Checklist.
- Have students exchange papers and check their partner's work.

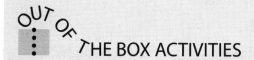

OUT OF THE BOX ACTIVITIES

Speaking and Listening

A.
- Show and tell. Form small groups. Have students bring in several photos of a recent trip or event to share with the class.
- Encourage the rest of the class to ask questions about the photos.

B.
- Play a chain game. Have students sit in a circle. Students will speak in turn. Take the first turn and say: "I'm going shopping. I need to buy a [ball]."
- The student on your right then says your sentence and adds an item of his or her own: "I'm going shopping. I need to buy a [ball] and an [elephant]." Each speaker repeats what has been said and adds one item until you make it all the way around the circle.

Reading and Speaking

- Post students' photos and writing from Exercise 11 around the room.
- Have the class stand and move around the room, reading the descriptions.
- Have them choose one they are particularly interested in, read the description carefully, and try to remember the details. Allow them to take notes, if desired.
- Call on students to tell the class (in their own words) about the photo they have chosen.

Go to **www.myfocusongrammarlab.com** for additional listening, pronunciation, speaking, and writing practice.

Note:
- See the *Focus on Grammar Workbook* for additional in-class or homework grammar practice.

Unit 4 Review (page 50)

Have students complete the Review and check their answers on Student Book page UR-1. Review or assign additional material as needed.

Go to **www.myfocusongrammarlab.com** for the Unit Achievement Test.

UNIT 5 OVERVIEW

Grammar: DESCRIPTIVE ADJECTIVES

Unit 5 focuses on the structure and use of descriptive adjectives including:
- Placement within sentences
- Use with articles *a* and *an*
- Various forms of descriptive adjectives

Theme: CAVE HOMES

Unit 5 focuses on the use of descriptive adjectives to talk about amazing, unusual, and interesting places.

Step 1: Grammar in Context (pages 51–52)

See the general suggestions for Grammar in Context on page 1.

Before You Read
- Have students look at the photographs and tell you what they see.
- Read the adjectives and have students repeat.
- Call on students to tell you two adjectives that they think describe the photos. More than one combination is possible, as students will have their own opinions.

Read
- Before students read, explain that the photos are of a place called Cappadocia, Turkey. If a world map is available, have students find Turkey on the map and tell you anything they know about it.
- Have students read the text. (OR: Play the audio and have students follow along in their books.)

After You Read

A. Practice
- Have pairs read the paragraphs aloud.
- (!) Have students find and circle the vocabulary words in the reading. Then call on students to read the sentences from the text.

B. Vocabulary

- Read the answer choices. Have students repeat. Then call on individual students to say them.
- Have students complete the exercise individually. Have them refer to the reading to help them guess the meaning of the vocabulary.
- Call on students to read the completed sentences.

C. Comprehension

- Have students complete the exercise individually.
- Call on students to give answers. Have students tell you the sentences in the reading in which they found the answers.
- (!) Lead a brief class discussion about the article. Ask: "Would you like to visit Cappadocia?" "Why or why not?" "Do you know of any other places that have unusual or interesting landscapes? Describe them."

Go to **www.myfocusongrammarlab.com** for an additional reading, and for reading and vocabulary practice.

Step 2: Grammar Presentation (page 53)

See the general suggestions for Grammar Presentation on page 2.

Grammar Charts

- Write the following sentences on the board:
  Cappadocia has a **long** history.
  They are full of **interesting** things to see.
  Awesome underground cities . . .
- Read the sentences. Point to the word *cities* and say: "Noun." Ask: "What kind of cities are they?" *(awesome)* Say: "Awesome is an adjective."
- Repeat with the other examples.
- Erase the sentences except for the nouns. Ask: "What kind of history?" *(a long history)* "What kind of things to see?" *(interesting things to see)* "What kind of cities?" *(awesome underground cities)*
- To reinforce the word order, write the following on the board:
  The [noun] is [adjective].
  It is a / an [adjective] [noun].
- Provide several sentences using the first pattern and have students transform them to the second pattern, for example:
  T: The day is warm.
  Ss: It is a warm day.

Grammar Notes

Note 1

- Call on one student to read the rule and another student to read the examples.
- Call on students to give you several new examples of sentences from the text that include descriptive adjectives.
- Write the sentences on the board. Underline the adjectives and draw arrows to the corresponding nouns.

Note 2

- Call on one student to read the rule and another student to read the examples.
- Have students give you several new examples of sentences from the text that include descriptive adjectives.
- Write the sentences on the board.
- Highlight the placement of the adjective in both types of sentences: after the verb *be* or before the noun it is describing.
- Explain that in some languages, adjectives may follow the noun (e.g., in Spanish, *la casa azul* = the blue house); however in English, adjectives come before the noun.

Note 3

- Call on one student to read the *Be Careful!* rule and another student to read the examples.
- Write a few incorrect examples on the board and cross out the *s* on the end of the adjectives. (Example: *These are interestings rocks. There are some beautifuls houses.*)

Note 4

- Write the examples from the chart on the board but replace the articles with blanks. Elicit the correct article from the class. Have them state the rule:
  "Use *a* if the adjective starts with a _____"
    (consonant sound)
  "Use *an* if the adjective starts with a _____"
    (vowel sound)
- Have students tell you the correct articles to fill in the blanks in the sentences on the board.
- Have students give you other adjectives to replace the two in the example sentences. (Example: *It's a boring / comfortable / safe place. It's an exciting / ordinary place.*)

Note 5

- Try to elicit more adjectives from the class by providing different contexts, for example, ask: "How do you feel when you have to wait for a long, long time?" *(bored)* "Is English grammar easy or confusing?" "What kind of city is this?" *(boring / exciting)* "Do you have a car? Is it new?" *(No, it's used.)*
- Examples of other adjectives include *angry, fascinating, sleepy, worried, early.*

⏱ **Identify the Grammar:** Have students identify the grammar in the reading on page 51. For example:
Cappadocia has a **long** history.
They are full of **interesting** things to see.
Awesome underground cities, . . .

Go to **www.myfocusongrammarlab.com** for grammar charts and notes.

Step 3: Focused Practice (pages 54–55)

See the general suggestions for Focused Practice on page 4.

Exercise 1: Discover the Grammar
- Have students look at the picture and tell you what they see. Try to elicit some of the descriptive adjectives from Steps 1 and 2. (Example: *It is an unusual place. It looks like a cave.*) Review the purpose of adjectives: to describe nouns.
- Have students read the message silently and underline the 11 adjectives.
- Go over the meaning of any new vocabulary. (Example: *modern, expensive, delicious*)

Exercise 2: Word Order
- Go over the example with the class.
- Have students complete the exercise individually. Then have students compare answers with a partner.
- ⏱ Have pairs try to continue each conversation for a few more lines, using their own ideas.

Exercise 3: Sentences with Adjectives
- Go over the example with the class. Elicit the singular and plural present forms of *be*. (is and are) Remind students to add *a* where needed.
- Have students complete the exercise individually.
- Have students compare answers in pairs. Then call on students to write their sentences on the board. Ask the rest of the class to help you correct any errors.

Exercise 4: Editing
- Go over the example with the class. Then have students find and correct the four remaining mistakes individually.
- Have students compare answers in pairs. Then call on students to read the corrected passage. Have them explain why the incorrect structures are wrong.
- ⏱ Have students practice the conversation in pairs, substituting their own adjectives for the ones in the conversation, for example:
  A: Is that an <u>old</u> carpet?
  B: Yes, it is. It's from Turkey.
  A: The colors are <u>interesting</u>.
  B: Thanks. I got it at a <u>big</u> market in Cappadocia.

Go to **www.myfocusongrammarlab.com** for additional grammar practice.

Step 4: Communication Practice (pages 56–58)

See the general suggestions for Communication Practice on page 5.

Exercise 5: Listening
A
- Tell students they will hear a telephone conversation.
- Have students read the question and answer choices silently.
- Play the audio. Have students listen and complete the exercise individually.

B
- Have students read the sentence stems and answer choices silently.
- Play the audio. Have students listen and complete the exercise individually.
- ⏱ Distribute copies of the audioscript and have students practice it in pairs.

Exercise 6: Pronunciation
A
- Play the audio. Have students read along as they listen to the Pronunciation Note.
- If students do not understand the concept of syllables, explain that a syllable is one "beat" of a word. Have students listen as you say the words in the chart one by one and clap the correct number of syllables.
- Say the word again and have students say them and clap with you. Then call on students to say the words and clap the syllables. Make sure students understand what a *stressed* syllable is: a syllable that is spoken a little more strongly than the others in a word.

B
- Play the audio. Have students listen and repeat.
- Play the audio again. Stop after each word and call on an individual student to repeat.

C
- Play the audio. Have students listen and mark stressed syllables.
- Have students compare answers in pairs. Then call on students to say the words with the correct stress pattern.

D
- Go over the example with the class.
- Have students complete the exercise in pairs. Then drill the class by saying the adjectives and having them reply with the opposites.
- 🕐 Have students create sentences with the words and read them in pairs.

Exercise 7: Guided Conversation
- Go over the example with the class.
- In pairs, have students brainstorm questions they could ask to find out information about a city or place. Encourage them to use as many adjectives from the unit as they can. For example:
  Is it a big city?
  Are there a lot of beautiful parks?
  Is the food delicious?
- Form small groups. Have students complete the exercise in groups.

Exercise 8: Writing

A
- Go over the example with the class.
- Have students write about the place they choose. Encourage them to include descriptive adjectives and *be* to discuss how the place looks, the weather, what the people are like, and so on.

B
- Have students check their work individually. Then have them exchange papers and check their partner's work.
- Have students correct their work, using the Editing Checklist.

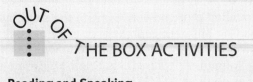
OUT OF THE BOX ACTIVITIES

Reading and Speaking
- Provide students with a selection of travel guides, travel brochures or magazines, and newspaper travel sections (or Internet travel sites).
- Have students scan the materials for sentences and phrases that contain descriptive adjectives.
- Have students choose one place and tell the class about it.

Reading, Writing, and Speaking
- Have students conduct independent research and give a report on a place they would like to travel to.
- Have them print photos from the Internet, get travel brochures or other informational material, and write a few paragraphs describing the place.
- Have them present their reports in groups or to the class.

Go to **www.myfocusongrammarlab.com** for additional listening, pronunciation, speaking, and writing practice.

Note:
- See the *Focus on Grammar Workbook* for additional in-class or homework grammar practice.

Unit 5 Review (page 59)
Have students complete the Review and check their answers on Student Book page UR-1. Review or assign additional material as needed.

Go to **www.myfocusongrammarlab.com** for the Unit Achievement Test.

Grammar: PREPOSITIONS OF PLACE

Unit 6 focuses on prepositions of place in:
- Descriptions of location of objects
- Locations inside buildings and around town
- Addresses
- Set phrases, such as *at school*, *in Canada*

Theme: LOCATIONS

Unit 6 focuses on the use of prepositions of place to give directions and talk about the locations of places around town.

Step 1: Grammar in Context (pages 60–62)

See the general suggestions for Grammar in Context on page 1.

Before You Read
- Assess students' knowledge of prepositions of place. Using locations around the classroom / school, try to elicit some prepositions. Ask questions and write any prepositions students give you on the board, for example:
  T: Where is Tomas sitting?
  S: Next to Andrea.
  T: Where is the cafeteria?
  S: Across from the office.
- Have students look at the map. Ask: "What is this place?" *(an art museum)* Lead a brief class discussion about any art museums students have visited and the types of art students like.
- Have students answer the questions in pairs. Then call on students to share their answers with the class.

Read
- Call on a student to read the instructions. Make sure students understand that they should read both the social network site posting and the conversation.
- To encourage students to read with a purpose, write these questions on the board:
  1. What advice does Marina ask her social network site friends for? *(a good eye doctor)*
  2. Where is the doctor that George recommends? *(7 East 89th Street, between Madison and Fifth Avenues, near the World Art Museum)*
  3. What is Marina going to do after she goes to the doctor? *(visit the art museum)*
  4. What two places does Marina ask the guard about? *(the African masks, the cafeteria)*

- Have students read the text. (OR: Play the audio and have students follow along in their books.) Then call on students to share their answers to the questions on the board.

After You Read
A. Practice
- Have students complete the exercise in pairs. Have them change roles and partners a few times.
- ⏱ For fluency practice, try a "backwards build-up" technique. Read the text at natural speed and have students try to repeat, each time a little faster, for example:
  T: . . . African masks?
  Ss: . . . African masks?
  T: . . . where are the African masks?
  Ss: . . . where are the African masks?
  T: Excuse me, where are the African masks?
  Ss: Excuse me, where are the African masks?

B. Vocabulary
- Say the words in the box and have students repeat.
- Have students complete the exercise individually.
- Have students compare answers in pairs. Then call on pairs to read the completed conversations.

C. Comprehension
- Have students complete the exercise in pairs.
- Combine pairs to form groups of four and have students compare answers.
- Call on students to give answers. Have them correct the false sentences.

Go to **www.myfocusongrammarlab.com** for an additional reading, and for reading and vocabulary practice.

Step 2: Grammar Presentation (pages 63–64)

See the general suggestions for Grammar Presentation on page 2.

Grammar Charts
- Write the following on the board: "It's **at** 7 East 89th Street, **between** Madison and Fifth Avenues." As you read the sentence aloud, underline the prepositions *(at, between)* and say: "These words are prepositions. Prepositions tell where something is."
- Write the following statements on the board. Then call a student up to the board to underline the other prepositions in the examples.
  So that's **near** the World Art Museum?
  They're **on** the second floor.

The elevator is **on your left, behind** the gift shop.
The African Masks are just **up the stairs**. They're **between** the sculpture and the Chinese garden.

- Have students look at the pictures in the Grammar Presentation. Say the sentences and have students repeat.
- Bring in a collection of common objects to demonstrate the prepositions. You can use a small box or bag and objects in the classroom (such as keys, pencils).
- Write the following prepositions on the board: next to, between, under, behind, near, in, in front of, in back of
- Use the objects to make sentences and write them on the board, for example:
The ball is in the box.
My keys are next to my glasses.
The pencil is on the floor. It's under the table.
- Ask a student to come up and read the sentences you wrote on the board. The student should position the objects according to the information in the sentences. Do this with several students.
- Next, position a pair of objects and have the whole class, then individual students, make sentences. Provide the preposition if students need help.
- Erase the sentences on the board, leaving only the prepositions, and call on students to come up, position the objects, and make sentences.
- Have students work in pairs to make sentences using the prepositions on the board with objects from their bags, pockets, or purses.

Grammar Notes

Note 1
- Read the note aloud. Call on students to read the examples.
- Use objects to demonstrate the difference between *near* and *next to*.
- Highlight that *behind* and *in back of* have the same meaning.

Note 2
- Before class, prepare a handout with a map of your neighborhood. Draw an *X* to show where your school is, and include several streets and other buildings. Write the address at the top. Alternatively, draw this map on the board.

- Model sentences, using the map, like the ones in the note. Say the sentences and have the class repeat. Also model sentences with the words *street* or *avenue* omitted as explained in the USAGE NOTE. (Example: *My house is on the corner of Center Street and Broad Avenue. It's on the corner of Center and Broad.*)
- Demonstrate different ways to say where you live, to emphasize the contrast among *in*, *on*, and *at*. (Example: *I live on Center Street. I live at 2110 Center Street. My apartment is on the second floor. I live in Detroit. I live in Michigan. I live in the United States.*)
- Call one student up to the board to write his or her address. Have the class make sentences like those above.
- Form small groups. Have students in each group sketch a quick map of their neighborhood and write their addresses at the top. Use this opportunity to make sure students know what their addresses are and how to write them. Then have them make sentences like those in the note.

Note 3
- Draw a horizontal line on the board representing your daily schedule. Underneath the line, fill in some times, for example:

7	8	9	10	11	12	1	2	3	4	5	6
Morning					*Afternoon*				*Evening*		

- Make sentences using the expressions in the note.
- Call one student to the board. Have him or her make sentences like yours about his or her own schedule.
- In pairs, have students repeat the above two steps.

🕐 **Identify the Grammar:** Have students identify the grammar in the reading on page 61. For example:
It's **at** 7 East 89th Street, **between** Madison and Fifth Avenues.
So that's **near** the World Art Museum?
The elevator is **on your left, behind** the gift shop.

Go to **www.myfocusongrammarlab.com** for grammar charts and notes.

Step 3: Focused Practice (pages 64–67)

See the general suggestions for Focused Practice on page 4.

Exercise 1: Discover the Grammar

- Have students scan the clues and circle the prepositions of location. Then have them compare answers in pairs.
- Have students complete the exercise in pairs. Combine pairs to form groups of four and have students check their answers to the puzzle.
- Elicit the answer from the class (*I love English*) and ask students if they agree.

Exercise 2: Prepositions of Place

- Go over the example with the class. Then have students look at the map and locate the places listed in the sentences.
- Have students complete the exercise in pairs.
- Ask questions to elicit the completed sentences. (Example: *Where is Fred's Flowers?*) Highlight the use of *on* and *at* in numbers 1 and 5 (*on* is used when just the street name is mentioned; *at* is used when the street number address is included).

Exercise 3: Prepositions of Place

- Go over the example with the class.
- Have students complete the exercise individually and compare answers in pairs.
- Call on students to read the completed sentences aloud.

Exercise 4: Prepositions of Place

- Go over the example with the class.
- Have students complete the exercise individually. Then call on students to read the completed sentences.
- ⏱ To extend the practice, write the following phrases on the board and have students make true sentences using the prepositions of place:
  I am . . . right now.
  At 9:00 P.M., I am usually . . .
  My house is . . .
  Our school is . . .
  I live . . .
  Our classroom is . . .

Exercise 5: Editing

- Go over the example with the class. Tell students that they need to find the remaining five mistakes.
- Have students find and correct the mistakes individually and then compare answers in pairs.
- Call on students to read the corrected conversations. Have students explain why the incorrect structures are wrong.

Go to **www.myfocusongrammarlab.com** for additional grammar practice.

Step 4: Communication Practice (pages 67–68)

See the general suggestions for Communication Practice on page 5.

Exercise 6: Pronunciation

A
- Play the audio. Have students read along as they listen to the Pronunciation Note. Explain that this type of stress is used to make a correction or to clarify information.

B
- Play the audio. Have students listen.
- Go over the example with the class.
- Play the audio again. Have students listen and mark a dot over the stressed words.

C
- Play the audio. Have students listen and repeat.
- ⏱ To extend the practice, give the class incorrect sentences and call on students to respond with a correct sentence, using the correct stress, for example:
  T: Our classroom is on the second floor.
  S: Our classroom is on the **first** floor. Not on the **second** floor.

Exercise 7: Listening

- Have students look at the map in Appendix 1, pages A-0–A-1. Tell them that they will hear a speaker describing the locations of four countries. Remind them to listen carefully for prepositions of location.
- Play the audio. Have students listen and take notes if necessary.
- Play the audio. Have students listen and write their answers.

Exercise 8: Guessing Countries

A
- Go over the example with the class.
- Form pairs and have them use the map in Appendix 1, pages A-0–A-1 to choose a country and write a description of the country's location.

B
- Combine pairs to form groups of four to play the game.
- Pairs take turns giving their clues. The other pair guesses.
- Call on groups to read their clues while the rest of the class guesses.

Exercise 9: Game: Describing Locations

- Go over the example with the class.
- Form small groups. Have students play the game in groups.

Exercise 10: Writing

A

- Go over the example with the class. To help students prepare for the task, have them make some notes about the date / day, time, and location for their party.
- Have students write their invitations.
- Have students check their work in pairs.

B

- Have students use the Editing Checklist to correct their work, especially their use of the prepositions of place.

OUT OF THE BOX ACTIVITIES

Speaking and Writing

A

- Have students work in groups to create a visitor's guide to their city or town.
- Have them list interesting or important places for visitors.
- Have them draw maps and write directions to make the visitor's guide useful.

B

- Have students interview a classmate or a family member about his or her daily schedule.
- Have students write a short "Day in the Life" essay describing where and how the person goes about his or her daily routine.

Speaking and Listening

- Create a map of a town with street names marked but buildings not labeled.
- Hand out a copy of the map to each student in the class.
- Have students listen as you describe the locations of the buildings on the map, using the target grammar from the unit.
- As they listen, students label the buildings according to your directions.
- Have students compare maps in pairs to confirm their answers.

Go to **www.myfocusongrammarlab.com** for additional listening, pronunciation, speaking, and writing practice.

Note:

- See the *Focus on Grammar Workbook* for additional in-class or homework grammar practice.

Unit 6 Review (page 69)

Have students complete the Review and check their answers on Student Book page UR-2. Review or assign additional material as needed.

Go to **www.myfocusongrammarlab.com** for the Unit Achievement Test.

From Grammar to Writing (page 70)

See the general suggestions for From Grammar to Writing on page 9.

Go to **www.myfocusongrammarlab.com** for an additional From Grammar to Writing Assignment, Part Review, and Part Post-Test.

PART III OVERVIEW

IMPERATIVES AND THE SIMPLE PRESENT

UNIT	GRAMMAR FOCUS	THEME
7	Imperatives; Suggestions with *Let's, Why don't we . . . ?*	Long Life
8	Simple Present: Affirmative and Negative Statements	Shopping
9	Simple Present: *Yes / No* Questions and Short Answers	Roommates
10	Simple Present: *Wh-* Questions	Dreams

Go to **www.myfocusongrammarlab.com** for the Part and Unit Tests.

Note: PowerPoint® grammar presentations, test-generating software, and reproducible Part and Unit Tests are on the *Teacher's Resource Disc.*

Grammar: IMPERATIVES; SUGGESTIONS WITH *Let's, Why don't we . . . ?*

Unit 7 focuses on the structure and use of affirmative and negative imperatives and *let's / why don't we . . . ?* to make suggestions.

Theme: LONG LIFE

Unit 7 focuses on language and expressions used to discuss how to live a long, healthy life.

Step 1: Grammar in Context (pages 72–73)

See the general suggestions for Grammar in Context on page 1.

Before You Read
• Have students discuss the questions in pairs.
• Call on students to give answers.

Read
• Have students look at the photo. Ask: "Where do you think this is?" "Why do you think people there live long lives?"
• To encourage students to read with a purpose, write these questions on the board:
  1. What advice does Buettner give? *(eat and drink healthy food, don't worry, take naps, walk, call friends, pray)*
  2. What does Joe think about the article? *(It sounds too healthy.)*
  3. What will Joe and Mary probably do? *(travel to Greece)*
• Have students read the text. (OR: Play the audio and have students follow along in their books.) Then call on students to share their answers to the questions on the board.
• ⏱ Focus students on the advice at the end of the article. Ask students which points they follow in their own lives.

After You Read
A. Practice
• Have students complete the exercise in pairs.
• Call on pairs to read the paragraphs aloud.

B. Vocabulary
• Have students complete the exercise individually. Alternatively, do the exercise with the class.
• Call on students to read the completed sentences and meanings.
• To highlight the importance of context, have students tell you the words or phrases in each sentence that helped them decide the answer.

C. Comprehension
• Have students complete the exercise individually. Have them try to complete the task without looking back at the text.
• Have students compare answers in pairs.
• Go over the answers with the class.

Go to **www.myfocusongrammarlab.com** for an additional reading, and for reading and vocabulary practice.

Step 2: Grammar Presentation (pages 74–75)

See the general suggestions for Grammar Presentation on page 2.

Grammar Charts
• Call on a student to read the examples in the first two charts.
• Explain that the imperative form is used to tell someone what to do (or what not to do).
• Have the class give more examples of both affirmative and negative imperative sentences following the examples in the chart. List students' ideas on the board, for example:
  Ride a bicycle.   Don't drive a car.
  Use the stairs.   Don't take the elevator.
• Call on a student to read the two examples using *let's*.
• Explain that *let's* is used to make suggestions.
• Highlight that the imperative indicates a stronger suggestion or an order, while *let's* is softer in tone. It is used to simply offer a possible suggestion.
• Have the class give more examples of suggestions with *let's* and write them on the board, for example:
  Let's join an exercise class. Let's not eat sweets.
• Call on a student to read the examples with *why don't we / you*.
• Elicit additional sentences from the class and write them on the board, for example:
  Why don't we go for walk? Why don't you eat more vegetables?
• Read the phrases in the last two charts and have students repeat.
• Use students' example suggestions on the board to drill the responses. Read one of the sentences from the board and call on a student to respond using one of the phrases in the chart, for example:
  T: Ride a bicycle.
  S1: No, I don't feel like it.
  T: Let's join an exercise class.
  S2: That's a good idea.

Grammar Notes

Notes 1–5

- Call on a student to read each note and the corresponding examples.
- Play a quick game of Simon Says to drill the base forms of the verbs. Have students stand up. When you say "Simon Says" followed by an imperative, students should follow your instructions. If you do not say "Simon Says" before the imperative, students should *not* follow the instruction. If they do, they are out of the game, for example:
  T: Simon Says, put your hands on your head.
  (Students put their hands on their heads.)
  T: Simon Says, sit down.
  (Students sit down.)
  T: Stand up.
  (Students stay sitting. Any students who stand up are out.)
- Call on students to come to the front and be "Simon."
- Ask: "How do we form the negative imperative?" (add *don't before the base form of the verb*)
- Have students use the negative imperative to tell you some examples of class / school rules, for example:
  Don't be late.
  Don't run in the halls.
  Don't write on the desks.
- Do a quick drill to highlight the use of *please* to make an imperative more polite.
  T: Hurry.
  S1: Please hurry.
  T: Don't run.
  S2: Please don't run.

Note 6

- Have students tell you some things they want to do and don't want to do over the coming weekend. Write their ideas on the board in two columns, for example:

want to	don't want to
sleep late	wake up early
go shopping	clean the house
watch a movie	do laundry
go out to eat	study for a test

- Call on students to turn the ideas on the board into suggestions using *let's* or *let's not*. (Example: *Let's sleep late. Let's not wake up early.*)
- 🕐 To extend the practice, call on students to give a response to each suggestion:
  S1: Let's sleep late.
  S2: That sounds good to me.

Note 7

- Highlight the difference between *Why don't we . . . ?* and *Why don't you . . . ?* Say: "When we use *why don't we . . . ?* we are making a suggestion that includes ourselves. When we use *why don't you . . . ?* we want to give another person advice."
- Have the class give some suggestions for things they want to do / study in class. (Example: *Why don't we take a class trip? Why don't we have a class party? Why don't we study the simple present?*)
- Tell the class you need advice for a problem you have. Think of a real problem or make one up. (Example: *you don't have enough time to exercise*) Have students make suggestions using *Why don't you . . . ?* (Example: *Why don't you get up earlier? Why don't you exercise during your lunch break? Why don't you ride your bike to work?*)

🕐 **Identify the Grammar:** Have students identify the grammar in the reading on page 72. For example:
  Eat a lot of green vegetables, . . .
  Don't worry.
  Let's move to Ikaria!

Go to **www.myfocusongrammarlab.com** for grammar charts and notes.

Step 3: Focused Practice (pages 75–77)

See the general suggestions for Focused Practice on page 4.

Exercise 1: Discover the Grammar

- Go over the example with the class. Then have students read the conversations quickly for meaning.
- Have students complete the exercise individually. Then have them compare answers in pairs.
- Call on students to read the examples of the imperatives. Then call on students to read the examples of suggestions.

Exercise 2: Imperative and Suggestions: Affirmative and Negative

- Go over the example with the class. Remind students to pay attention to the context of the sentences to help them.
- Have students complete the exercise individually.
- Have students compare answers in pairs. Then call on students to read the correct sentences.

Exercise 3: Imperative for Directions

A
- Have students look at the map.
- Highlight that for directions we usually use the imperative. We do not generally use *please, let's,* or *why don't we / you.* . . .
- Have students read the conversation and mark the location of the gym on their maps.

B
- Have students look at the map and complete the exercise individually.
- Call on a student to read the directions he / she wrote aloud.
- Ask students if those directions would work. If not, call on another student.

Exercise 4: Editing
- Go over the example with the class. Point out that they should find five more mistakes in the conversation.
- Have students find and correct the mistakes in pairs. Then combine pairs to form groups of four and have students compare answers.
- Call on a pair to read the corrected conversation. Then have them explain why the incorrect structures are wrong.

Go to **www.myfocusongrammarlab.com** for additional grammar practice.

Step 4: Communication Practice (pages 77–79)

See the general suggestions for Communication Practice on page 5.

Exercise 5: Listening

A
- Have students read the answer choices silently.
- Elicit some possible words and phrases students might hear for each choice. (Example: *in an ad for a spa, students might hear* relax, massage)
- Play the audio. Have students listen and complete the exercise individually.

B
- Read the answer choices and have students repeat.
- Play the audio. Have students listen and complete the exercise individually.
- ⏱ To extend the practice, ask the following questions. Play the audio again. Have students listen and answer the questions.
  When is the spa open?
  What does the spa serve for breakfast?
  What time can you get a massage?
  What do people do after they leave the spa?
  What do you get if you join now?

Exercise 6: Pronunciation

A
- Play the audio. Have students read along as they listen to the Pronunciation Note.

B
- Play the audio. Have students listen and notice the pronunciation of *don't you*.

C
- Play the audio again. Have students repeat the "why don't you" suggestions.

Exercise 7: Making Suggestions for Another Person
- Go over the example with the class. Then have the class brainstorm some possible suggestions for each of the problems listed.
- Have students complete the exercise in pairs. Remind them to use phrases for agreeing and disagreeing.
- Call on pairs to present their conversations to the class.

Exercise 8: Making Suggestions for You and Another Person
- Call on students to read the suggestions in the list. Have the class brainstorm more ideas for a healthy lifestyle and write them on the board.
- Go over the example with the class.
- Have students complete the exercise in pairs. Then call on several pairs to present their conversations to the class.

Exercise 9: Giving Advice
- Have students read the list of verbs and think about some possible additions of their own.
- Have students complete the exercise in pairs.
- Call on pairs to read their lists to the class.
- ⏱ Have pairs create a role-play conversation between a doctor and a patient (the patient visits the doctor with a variety of health problems and the doctor gives advice for being healthier).

Exercise 10: Give Directions

A
- Have students look at the map on page 76.
- Preteach expressions for asking directions: "Excuse me. Where is the . . . / Can you tell me how to get to . . . / How do I get to . . . ?"
- Have students complete the exercise in pairs. Pairs should play both roles.

B
- Have students complete the exercise in pairs. Pairs should play both roles.
- When they have each given directions to two or three places, call on students to give you directions to places on the map.

Exercise 11: Writing

A

- Go over the example with the class.
- To help them begin to write, have students make some notes about what to include in their ad. (Example: *the name of the hotel, words to describe the rooms, the food, the views, what people can do there*)
- Have students complete the exercise individually.

B

- Have students correct their work using the Editing Checklist. Then have them exchange papers and check their partner's work.

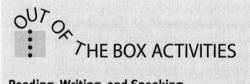

THE BOX ACTIVITIES

Reading, Writing, and Speaking

- Have students use cookbooks or cooking websites to research recipes for healthy dishes.
- Have them write the recipes and instructions for cooking the dish, using imperatives.
- Have students share their recipes in groups.
- Have groups choose one recipe to teach to the class.
- Have groups bring in the ingredients to demonstrate to the rest of the class how to make the dish.
- Compile all students' recipes to create a class cookbook.

Go to **www.myfocusongrammarlab.com** for additional listening, pronunciation, speaking, and writing practice.

Note:

- See the *Focus on Grammar Workbook* for additional in-class or homework grammar practice.

Unit 7 Review (page 80)

Have students complete the Review and check their answers on Student Book page UR-2. Review or assign additional material as needed.

Go to **www.myfocusongrammarlab.com** for the Unit Achievement Test.

UNIT 8 OVERVIEW

Grammar: SIMPLE PRESENT: AFFIRMATIVE AND NEGATIVE STATEMENTS

Unit 8 focuses on the structure and use of affirmative and negative statements in the simple present with both regular and irregular verbs.

Theme: SHOPPING

Unit 8 focuses on the use of simple present statements to talk about current youth fashion trends.

Step 1: Grammar in Context (pages 81–82)

See the general suggestions for Grammar in Context on page 1.

Before You Read

A

- Read the passage. Then elicit words and phrases in students' languages (and other terms they may know in English) to say that something is trendy or fashionable.

B

- Go over key vocabulary from the statements before students begin. (Example: *comfortable, trendy*)
- Have students complete the exercise individually.

Read

- Before students read, have them look at the photograph and tell you what they see. Ask: "Where do you think this girl is from?" "What do you think about the fashion?" "Is this style popular where you are from?"
- Have students read the article once quickly for meaning. Alternatively, read the article aloud while students follow along silently.
- To encourage students to read with a purpose, write these questions on the board:
  1. How old is Yumi? *(17)*
  2. Where does she live? *(Japan)*
  3. What does she wear? *(kawaii boots, jeans, and sunglasses)*
  4. What does *kawaii* mean? *(cute)*
  5. What is a trendsetter? *(the first to start a trend)*
  6. Who are the trendsetters now? *(high school girls)*
  7. Are trendsetters always girls? *(no)*
- Have students read the text. (OR: Play the audio and have students follow along in their books.) Then call on students to share their answers to the questions on the board.

After You Read

A. Practice
- Have students complete the exercise in pairs.
- Then call on pairs to read paragraphs.

B. Vocabulary
- Have students complete the exercise individually. Remind them to use the context to help them guess the meaning of the vocabulary.
- Call on students to read the completed sentences.
- ⏱ Have students work in pairs to write additional sentences using the vocabulary. Then have students share their sentences with the class.

C. Comprehension
- Have students complete the exercise individually.
- Have students compare answers in pairs. Then call on students to say whether the sentences are true or false. Have them correct the false statements.
- ⏱ Lead a brief class discussion about the article. Ask:
  Do you think the girl in the picture looks kawaii?
  Do you like the style of the girl's clothes and hair?
  What trends do you like in hair and clothes?
  Do you prefer to set trends or to follow them?

Go to **www.myfocusongrammarlab.com** for an additional reading, and for reading and vocabulary practice.

Step 2: Grammar Presentation (pages 83–84)

See the general suggestions for Grammar Presentation on page 2.

Grammar Charts
- Before the start of the lesson, prepare a large cutout of the letter *s* or draw a large *s* on a piece of paper that you can hold up for the class to see.
- Call on a student to read the example sentences from the chart.
- On the board, write the following examples of affirmative sentences from the reading:
  Yumi **wears** "kawaii" boots and jeans.
  She **carries** a "kawaii" phone.
  Businesses **look** at Yumi and her friends.
  They **study** their clothes.

- Point to each sentence and ask: "What is the verb in this sentence?" "Is it singular or plural?" "Is the ending of the verb always the same in affirmative sentences?" (*No. The third-person singular takes an -s ending.*)
- Model the affirmative forms with several verbs: *I work, you work, he works, I play, you play, she plays,* etc. When you get to the third person, hold up the cutout of the letter *s.*
- Drill the affirmative forms. Write several regular verbs on the board. (Example: *walk, eat, love, buy, meet*)
- Say the pronouns and have students respond with the correct form of each verb. Hold up the *s* cutout at the appropriate times. Mix up the order of the pronouns until students get the *s* every time. Then substitute other verbs, for example:
  T: (points to *walk* on the board) We.
  S1: We walk.
  T: (points to *eat* on the board)
  S2: We eat.
  T: (points to *love* on the board) She.
  S3: She loves.
- Call on a student to read the negative statements in the chart.
- Ask: "How do we make negative sentences?" (do / does + not + *verb*)
- Drill the affirmative and negative forms and all persons, for example:
  T: I like dogs. Maria.
  Ss: Maria likes dogs.
  T: Negative.
  Ss: Maria does not like dogs.
  T: We.
  Ss: We do not like dogs.
  T: Affirmative.
  Ss: We like dogs.
- If students make errors with third-person -*s,* simply hold up the *s* cutout (or write *s* on the board) as a reminder.

Grammar Notes

Note 1
- Call on one student to read the rule and another student to read the examples.
- Review frequency adverbs and time expressions. Write the following on the board: sometimes, often, always, never, every day, once a week, on Saturday, in the morning
- Use the time expressions to tell about your own life, for example:
  I always sleep late on Saturday morning.
  I read the newspaper every day.
- Elicit similar sentences from the class. Choose time expressions and have students make sentences by asking questions. (Example: *What do you do on Saturday morning, Yuki?*)

Note 2

- Call on one student to read the rule and another student to read the examples.
- Call on students to give you several examples of sentences from the reading that tell facts, for example:
  She's a senior in high school in Japan.
  *Businesses **look** at Yumi and her friends. They **study** their clothes.*
- Write four facts on the board. All but one should be true. Call on students to read the sentences aloud. Then point to each sentence and ask: "Is it true?" When students identify the false statement, have them correct it to make it true, for example:
  The sun is hot.
  Carlos isn't here today.
  Dogs love cats. (Dogs hate cats. / Dogs do not love cats.)
- Elicit several other facts from the class.

Note 3

- Write a mix of action and non-action verbs on the board. (Example: *eat, like, run, want, write, have, smile*)
- Mime each action verb and say "action verb." Stand still for each non-action verb and say "non-action verb."
- Have students stand up. Say a mix of action and non-action verbs. Students should mime the action verbs and stand still for the non-action ones.
- Read the note and examples with the class.

Note 4

- Hold up your cutout of the letter *s* and say a few third-person verbs. (Example: *eats, likes, watches, kisses*)
- Use the board or a handout like the one below to introduce the spelling rules. Read the lists aloud. Underline the last sound of each word and add *-s* or *-es*.

-s	-es
stop	kiss
kick	teach
eat	wash
need	box
learn	buzz
sing	
live	
laugh	
fall	
remember	
play	

- Write the following rules on the board and have students tell you the missing forms:
  If a word ends in *s, z, sh, ch,* or *x*, add
  _____. (*-es*)
  For other third-person singular verbs, add
  _____. (*-s*)
- ⏱ Optional game: Make up a list of verbs that take both *-s* and *-es* in the third person. Have students work in pairs. Give each pair a copy of the list and have them add *-s* or *-es* to each word as appropriate. The first pair to finish with no mistakes wins.

Note 5

- Do a quick review of the contracted forms. Say affirmative sentences and have students say the negative, for example:
  T: I eat eggs for breakfast.
  Ss: I don't eat eggs for breakfast.
- Write the contractions on the board. Draw an arrow. Then write the full forms. (Example: *don't → do not*)
- Highlight that we usually use the full form in writing and the contracted form in speaking.
- Read the *Be Careful!* note and write the following on the board:
  Right: He doesn't work or study on weekends.
  Wrong: He doesn't work or doesn't study on weekends.

Note 6

- Model the formation of *have, do,* and *go*. For *have*, take an object out of your pocket or bag and say: "I have a(n) _____." Call one or two students to the front of the class to do the same. Say to one student: "You have a(n) _____." Then turn to the class and say: "She / he has a(n) _____." Keep going in the same way but have students form the sentences.
- For *do*, make sentences about your routine: "Every day, I do the dishes. On Saturday I do the laundry. In the evening I do homework." Ask: "Do you do the dishes every day? When do you do the laundry?" Then ask: "Does [Jaime] do the dishes every day? When does [Jaime] do the laundry?"
- Repeat the procedure with *go*.
- Write the pronouns on the board: *I, you, he,* etc. Include the plural. Elicit the forms of each verb from the class. Write them on the board or have a student do it. Underline the irregular spelling of the third-person forms.

Note 7

- As a class, quickly recite the conjugation of the verb *be*.

- To reinforce the spelling of the third-person singular, give students a quick spelling quiz. Include the four irregular verbs and regular verbs with both -*s* and -*es* endings. Say a sentence with each verb, then repeat the verb. (Example: *Roberto goes to school every day. Goes.*)

⏱ **Identify the Grammar:** Have students identify the grammar in the reading on page 81. For example:

Yumi **wears** "kawaii" boots and jeans.
She **doesn't buy** "non-kawaii" things.
Businesses **look** at Yumi and her friends.

Go to **www.myfocusongrammarlab.com** for grammar charts and notes.

Step 3: Focused Practice (pages 84–87)

See the general suggestions for Focused Practice on page 4.

Exercise 1: Discover the Grammar
- Go over the example with the class.
- Have students complete the exercise individually.
- Have students compare answers in pairs. Then call on students to come to the board and write the verbs.

Exercise 2: Affirmative Sentences
- Go over the example with the class.
- Have students complete the exercise individually.
- Have students compare answers in pairs. Then call on pairs to read the sentences. Have students explain the reasons for their answer choices.

Exercise 3: Negative Statements
- Go over the example with the class. Then review the formation of negative statements. (Add *do not / don't* or *does not / doesn't* before the base form of the main verb.)
- Drill the negative forms using a variety of singular and plural subjects, for example:
  T: He likes pizza.
  Ss: He doesn't like pizza.
  T: I have a camera.
  Ss: I don't have a camera.
- Have students complete the exercise individually and then compare answers in pairs.

Exercise 4: Affirmative and Negative Statements
- Go over the example with the class.
- Have students complete the exercise in pairs.

- For each item, call on one student to read the answer for part a, and another student to read the answer for part b.

Exercise 5: Affirmative and Negative Statements

A
- Go over the example with the class. Then have students read the letter quickly for meaning.
- Have students complete the exercise in pairs. Then call on students to write their answers on the board.
- ⏱ To extend the practice, ask the following questions, which will elicit affirmative and negative responses:
  Who does the woman want advice about?
  What is the problem she describes?
  What does the woman think about spending a lot of money on clothes?
  What does the woman's son do with his spending money?
  What does the woman's husband think about a part-time job?

B
- Go over the example with the class. Then have students read the response quickly for meaning.
- Have students complete the exercise in pairs. Then call on a student to read the completed response.
- ⏱ Lead a brief class discussion about the letter and the response. Ask: "Do you agree with the response? Why or why not?" "What advice would you give the woman?" "Her son?"

Exercise 6: Editing
- Go over the example with the class.
- Have students find and correct the seven remaining mistakes individually and then compare answers in pairs.
- Call on students to read the corrected paragraph. Have students explain why the incorrect structures are wrong.

Go to **www.myfocusongrammarlab.com** for additional grammar practice.

Step 4: Communication Practice (pages 87–89)

See the general suggestions for Communication Practice on page 5.

Exercise 7: Pronunciation

A
- Play the audio. Have students read along as they listen to the Pronunciation Note.

- Point out the difference between voiceless /s/ and voiced /z/. (Note that many languages do not have a /z/, and many students will have difficulty making this sound.) Model by putting your hand on your throat and saying "sssss." Have students copy you. Ask: "Did you feel anything?" (*no*) Repeat with /z/. Students should feel their vocal cords vibrating. If a student is unable to do this, put the student's hand on your own throat and let him or her feel the vibration.

B
- Have students underline the verbs. Then play the audio and have students listen and check the appropriate columns.

Exercise 8: Listening

A
- Tell students they will hear a conversation between two friends.
- Play the audio. Have students listen and complete the exercise individually.

B
- Have students read the sentence stems quickly for meaning.
- Play the audio. Have students listen and complete the exercise individually.
- ⏱ Distribute copies of the audioscript and have students practice it in pairs.

Exercise 9: Conversation

A
- Have students read the statements quickly for meaning.
- Go over any unfamiliar vocabulary. (Example: *colorful, leather, designer, traditional*)
- Have students complete the exercise individually.

B
- Go over the example with the class.
- Model the task with a student, for example:
  T: Sanjit, do you wear colorful clothes?
  S: No, I don't wear colorful clothes. How about you?
  T: Yes, I wear colorful clothes.
- Have students complete the exercise in pairs.

Exercise 10: Discussion
- To stimulate more discussion, bring additional photos or Internet printouts of traditional clothing from around the world. You may also want to have students bring in examples of traditional clothing and / or jewelry from their countries. Alternatively, you can have students do Internet research to find out about traditional clothing around the world. Have students look at the pictures and tell you what they see. Try to elicit the countries where the clothing is worn.
- Go over the example with the class.
- Form small groups. Have students complete the exercise in groups.

Exercise 11: Writing

A
- Go over the example with the class.
- Have students think about and take notes on their own style and what kinds of clothes they like to wear. Then have them think of a relative (or a friend) who has a different style. Have them include descriptive adjectives to talk about the clothing and to add details about why they like it.
- Have students complete the exercise individually.

B
- Have students correct their work using the Editing Checklist.
- Have students exchange papers and check their partner's work.

OUT OF THE BOX ACTIVITIES

Speaking or Writing
- Have students compare shopping venues. (Example: *shopping at a store vs. shopping online, a big department store vs. a specialty store, a discount store vs. a boutique*) Students should write / discuss the advantages and disadvantages of each.

Reading and Speaking
- Bring in a variety of print advertisements for clothing stores.
- Have students read the ads and discuss the types of clothing each store offers, the prices, the location, what they like and dislike about each store, and so on.

Go to **www.myfocusongrammarlab.com** for additional listening, pronunciation, speaking, and writing practice.

Note:
• See the *Focus on Grammar Workbook* for additional in-class or homework grammar practice.

Unit 8 Review (page 90)

Have students complete the Review and check their answers on Student Book page UR-2. Review or assign additional material as needed.

Go to **www.myfocusongrammarlab.com** for the Unit Achievement Test.

UNIT 9 OVERVIEW

Grammar: SIMPLE PRESENT: *Yes / No* QUESTIONS AND SHORT ANSWERS

Unit 9 focuses on the structure and use of *yes / no* questions and short answers with *be* and other verbs.

Theme: ROOMMATES

Unit 9 focuses on the use of *yes / no* questions and short answers to find out about personality, hobbies, habits, likes and dislikes, and other issues in order to determine people's compatibility as roommates.

Step 1: Grammar in Context (pages 91–92)

See the general suggestions for Grammar in Context on page 1.

Before You Read
• Have the class tell you what a roommate is (*someone who shares a room or an apartment with you*). Ask for a show of hands from students who currently have a roommate.
• Ask: "Before you choose a roommate, what information should you find out about the person?"
• Form small groups. Then have students answer the questions in the book in these groups.

Read
• Have students read the questionnaire quickly for meaning. Then go over key vocabulary. (Example: *neat*, *bother*, *outgoing*, *private*, *easygoing*)

• Ask: "How are Dan and Jon the same? How are they different?" (Example: *They both dislike waking up early. Dan isn't quiet; Jon is quiet.*)
• Have students complete the exercise individually.

After You Read

A. Practice
• To review *yes / no* questions with *be*, ask: "Which questions use the verb *be*?" (*Are you . . . ?*)
• Have students complete the exercise in pairs.
• Call on students to read the questions to the class.

B. Vocabulary
• Read the words in the box and have students repeat.
• Have students complete the exercise individually.
• Have students compare answers in pairs. Then call on students to read the completed sentences.

C. Comprehension
• Have students complete the exercise individually. Have them try to complete the task without looking back at the text.
• Have students compare answers in pairs.
• Go over the answers as a class and have students correct the false statements using information from the questionnaire.

Go to **www.myfocusongrammarlab.com** for an additional reading, and for reading and vocabulary practice.

Step 2: Grammar Presentation (pages 92–93)

See the general suggestions for Grammar Presentation on page 2.

Grammar Charts
• Call on students to read the examples in the first chart using all of the pronouns.
• Ask questions to elicit the structure: "What's the main verb?" *(work)* "What verb do we add at the beginning of a question with *I*, *you*, *we*, or *they*?" *(do)* "What do we add for third-person questions?" *(does)*
• Drill. Write a verb on the board, such as *learn*. Say a pronoun. The class says the question, for example:
T: We.
Ss: Do we learn?
T: She.
Ss: Does she learn?

- Call on students to read the short answer forms in the second chart.
- Ask: "What are the four forms we use to give short answers?" (do, don't, does, doesn't) "Which ones are affirmative?" (do, does) "Which ones are negative?" (don't, doesn't)
- Model the short answers:
  T: Ask me if I work.
  Ss: Do you work?
  T: Yes, I do. Ask me if I stay up late.
  Ss: Do you stay up late?
  T: No, I don't.
- To model the third-person short answer, call two students to the front of the class:
  T: William, ask Bella if she likes rock music.
  WILLIAM: Do you like rock music?
  BELLA: Yes, I do. / No, I don't.
  T: Class, does Bella like rock music?
  Ss: Yes, she does. / No, she doesn't.

Grammar Notes

Notes 1–3
- Call on a student to read a note and another student to read the examples.
- Form pairs. Have students look at the opening questionnaire on page 91. Do a simple role play to practice the question forms.
- Have one student play the role of Dan and the other play the role of Jon.
- Have them ask the questions, for example:
  S1 (Dan): Do you wake up early?
  S2 (Jon): No, I don't. Do you wake up early?
  S1 (Dan): No, I don't.
- Ask the class questions about the questionnaire to elicit the third-person forms, for example:
  T: Does Dan wake up early?
  Ss: No, he doesn't.
- Contrast yes / no questions with be and those requiring the auxiliary do / does. Write the following examples on the board:
  <u>Are</u> you from New York? / <u>Do</u> you <u>live</u> in New York?
  <u>Is</u> Jon a good cook? / <u>Does</u> Jon <u>like</u> to cook?
- Go over the errors in Note 3. Write similar sentences with errors on the board and call on students to come up and correct them:
  Does he is your roommate? (Is he your roommate?)
  Do are you a student? (Are you a student?)
  Does Jon a teacher? (Is Jon a teacher?)

🕐 **Identify the Grammar:** Have students identify the grammar in the reading on page 91. For example:
  Do you **wake up** early?
  Do you **stay up** late?
  Are you neat?

Go to **www.myfocusongrammarlab.com** for grammar charts and notes.

Step 3: Focused Practice (pages 93–96)
See the general suggestions for Focused Practice on page 4.

Exercise 1: Discover the Grammar
- Have students read the passage and questions quickly for meaning. Then go over the example with the class.
- Have students complete the exercise individually. Remind them to check for matching subjects and verbs in the questions and answers.
- Have students compare answers in pairs. Then call on pairs to read the questions and answers.

Exercise 2: *Yes / No* Questions and Short Answers
- Go over the example with the class.
- Have students complete the conversations individually. Then have them compare answers in pairs.
- 🕐 Have pairs continue the conversation, adding one additional yes / no question and short answer, for example:
  S1: Do you listen to music?
  S2: Yes, I do.
  S1: Do you have an MP3 player?
  S2: No, I don't.

Exercise 3: *Yes / No* Questions and Short Answers
- Do a quick review of the formation of yes / no questions: Write the following on the board:
  Find out if your partner . . .
    takes the bus to school
    is hungry
    drinks coffee in the morning
    watches TV every day
    is from (city)
    has an iPad
    listens to rock music
    likes dancing
- Put students in pairs and have them ask each other yes / no questions to find out the information on the board.
- Have students complete the exercise in pairs. Remind them to check for subject-verb agreement.

Exercise 4: *Yes / No* Questions and Short Answers
- Go over the example with the class.
- Have students work in pairs to complete the conversation. Then combine pairs to form groups of four and have students compare answers.

- Ask the following questions and elicit answers from the class:
  Is Edward from England?
  Does he study music?
  Does he play the trumpet?
  Does his family live nearby?

Exercise 5: Editing
- Go over the example with the class.
- Have students find and correct the seven remaining mistakes individually and then compare answers in pairs.
- Call on students to read the corrected conversations. Have students explain why the incorrect structures are wrong.
- ⏱ Have pairs continue the conversation, adding one additional *yes / no* question and short answer.

Go to **www.myfocusongrammarlab.com** for additional grammar practice.

Step 4: Communication Practice (pages 96–100)

See the general suggestions for Communication Practice on page 5.

Exercise 6: Pronunciation
A
- Play the audio. Have students read along as they listen to the Pronunciation Note.

B
- Play the audio. Have students listen and repeat each question.

C
- Have students read the questionnaire quickly for meaning. Then go over the example with the class.
- Have students complete the exercise in pairs. Remind them to link *Does + he*.
- ⏱ To follow up, ask: "Would Serge be a good roommate for you? Why or why not?"

Exercise 7: Listening
A
- Call on a student to read the instructions aloud. Then have students read the chart quickly for meaning.
- Focus students' attention on the chart and ask questions about Leyla:
  Does Leyla like parties?
  Does she listen to hip-hop?
  Does she play basketball?
- Play the audio. Have students listen and complete the exercise individually.

B
- Have students complete the exercise in pairs.
- Take a class poll to find out how many students think Leyla and Andrea would make good roommates.

Exercise 8: Discussion: Comparing Habits and Personality
- Have students complete the questionnaire individually.
- Put students into pairs and have them compare answers. Remind them to not simply look at one another's answers; they should ask and answer the questions.
- To follow up, call on students to report on their answers to the class. (Example: *We both wake up early. Wan is neat, but I am not neat.*) Ask: "Do you think you would make good roommates?" Remind students to support their answers with reasons.

Exercise 9: Game: Find Someone Who . . .
- Call on students to read the questions in the chart. Then go over the example with the class.
- Have students stand and go around the class to ask their classmates questions. Remind them to write the names of students who answer *yes*.
- Call on students to report their findings to the class, following the example. Make notes about students' answers and then discuss who would be good roommates.

Exercise 10: Game: What's in Your Backpack?
- Have students read the list of items. Answer any questions about vocabulary. Then go over the example with the class.
- Form small groups. Then say: "Go!" and have groups check any items they have. Remind them to use the target structure: *yes / no* questions.
- The first group to check 10 items wins.

Exercise 11: Writing
A
- Have students read the example email quickly for meaning.
- To help them begin to write, have students make some notes about what to include in their email. (Example: *where they are from, their interests, hobbies, questions they have about their new roommate*)
- Have students complete the exercise individually.

B
- Have students correct their work using the Editing Checklist.

- Then have students exchange papers and check their partner's work.
- If possible, have students type and send their email to a classmate, who will respond in the role of the new roommate.

OUT OF THE BOX ACTIVITIES

Writing and Speaking
- Have students work in groups to create their own questionnaires to find out about their classmates' preferences in music, fashion, sports teams, food, free-time activities, or any other topic that interests them.
- Have groups distribute their questionnaires and collect them when they are completed.
- Have each group report on their findings.

Listening, Writing, and Speaking
- Find a short (one- to two-minute) video clip (on TV or online) of a question-and-answer type interview in English. It may be from a local news report, a celebrity news show, or another format.
- Play the video and have students write the questions the interviewer asks.
- Play the video again and have students write the interviewee's answers.
- Elicit the questions and answers from the class and write them on the board.
- Have students role-play the interview.

Go to **www.myfocusongrammarlab.com** for additional listening, pronunciation, speaking, and writing practice.

Note:
- See the *Focus on Grammar Workbook* for additional in-class or homework grammar practice.

Unit 9 Review (page 101)

Have students complete the Review and check their answers on Student Book page UR-2. Review or assign additional material as needed.

Go to **www.myfocusongrammarlab.com** for the Unit Achievement Test.

UNIT 10 OVERVIEW

Grammar: SIMPLE PRESENT: *Wh-* QUESTIONS

Unit 10 focuses on the structure and use of simple present *wh-* questions as well as on long and short answers to *wh-* questions.

Theme: DREAMS

Unit 10 focuses on the use of simple present *wh-* questions to talk about dreaming and to ask questions about people's dreams.

Step 1: Grammar in Context (pages 102–103)

See the general suggestions for Grammar in Context on page 1.

Before You Read
- Introduce the topic of dreams. Then call on a student to read the discussion questions aloud.
- Have students discuss the questions in pairs.
- Call on pairs to give answers. Have students share any types of dreams they may have frequently. (Example: *flying, falling*)

Read
- Have students look at the picture while you read the introduction to the text. Then have students read the text quickly for meaning.
- To encourage students to read with a purpose, write these questions on the board:
  1. Who is Helena Lee? (*the author of* Sleep and Dreams)
  2. Why do people dream? (*maybe to help us understand our feelings*)
  3. Does everyone dream? (*yes*)
  4. Do animals dream? (*yes*)
  5. What dreams do people remember? (*unusual ones*)
  6. What is the meaning of a dream you have again and again? (*It has special meaning. You have to think about it.*)
  7. When do people dream? (*during REM sleep*)
  8. Why is REM sleep important? (*without it we can't remember or think clearly*)
- Have students read the text. (OR: Play the audio and have students follow along in their books.) Then call on students to share their answers to the questions on the board.

After You Read

A. Practice
- Have students complete the exercise in pairs. Then call on pairs to read paragraphs aloud.

B. Vocabulary

- Read the words in the box and have students repeat.
- Have students complete the exercise individually. Remind them to use the context to help them guess the meaning of the vocabulary.
- ⓘ Have pairs try writing one or two more conversations using all of the words.

C. Comprehension

- Have students complete the exercise individually.
- Have students compare answers in pairs. Then call on students to give answers.
- Have students tell you the sentences from the text where they found the answers.

Go to **www.myfocusongrammarlab.com** for an additional reading, and for reading and vocabulary practice.

Step 2: Grammar Presentation (pages 104–105)

See the general suggestions for Grammar Presentation on page 2.

Grammar Charts

- Copy the following chart on the board. Use a contrasting color or underline the *wh-* words and the words in the long answer that answer the question, for example, for the first question, color *Who* and the answer, *Everyone dreams*.

Question	Long Answer	Short Answer
Who dreams?	Everyone dreams.	Everyone.
What dreams do they remember?	They remember unusual dreams.	Unusual ones.
When do people dream?	They dream during deep sleep.	During deep sleep.
Why do we need REM sleep?	We need it because without it, we can't remember or think clearly.	Without it, we can't remember or think clearly.

- Point to each *wh-* word, read the question, and ask: "Which words answer the question?" *(everyone; unusual dreams; during deep sleep; rapid eye movement; without it, we can't remember or think clearly)* "Which word repeats in every question?" *(do)*

- Add a row at the bottom of the chart:

What does REM mean?	It means rapid eye movement.	Rapid eye movement.

- Ask: "What's different about this question?" *(It uses does.)* "Why?" *(The subject is third person.)*
- On the board, write *When, Where, What, Why, Who(m)*. Name a topic such as a member of your family or your pet. Have students form questions with each *wh-* word + *do*. Answer each question with a long answer or have another student do the same, for example:
  T: My dog.
  S1: When does your dog sleep?
  T: He sleeps all afternoon and all night.
- Point to the question "Who dreams?" Point to the answer. Ask: "Which word answers the question?" *(Everyone.)* "Is it the subject or the object of the answer?" *(subject)* "Does the question use *do*?" *(no)*
- Practice a few subject-pattern questions and answers about the class, for example:
  T: Who comes from Turkey?
  Ss: Didem comes from Turkey.
  T: What happens every morning at 9 A.M.?
  Ss: Our class starts every morning at 9 A.M.

Grammar Notes

Note 1

- Call on a student to read the note and the examples.
- Pick a topic, such as students' daily habits or schedules, to use for drilling object-pattern questions.
- To drill, provide a core sentence. Then prompt students with *wh-* words. One student forms the question. Another student answers with the short answer, for example:
  T: Javier goes to sleep at 11 P.M. When.
  S1: When does Javier go to sleep?
  S2: At 11 P.M.
  T: Javier does his homework in the library. Where.
  S1: Where does Javier do his homework?
  S2: In the library.
- Have students ask and answer questions about each other's habits. First model the activity with a student. Then circulate as students talk in pairs.

Note 2

- To drill subject-pattern questions, ask some general-knowledge questions beginning with *who* or *what*. (Example: *What makes you sleepy? What causes nightmares? Who has a dog? Who remembers their dreams?*) Students should respond with long answers.
- Reverse the procedure. Provide answers. Have students ask the questions, for example:
  T: Creative people remember their dreams.
  Ss: Who remembers their dreams?
- Put students in pairs. Give students a context, such as household chores. Have students ask questions about who does what in their home. (Example: *Who washes the dishes? Who cooks dinner?*)
- Copy the wrong sentences from the *Be Careful!* note on the board. Have students correct the errors.

Note 3

- Model the way in which questions with *who* and *whom* are formed. On the board, write a subject-verb-object sentence. Both subject and object must be people. (Example: *John loves Mary.*)
- Cross out the subject, replace it with the word *who*, and add a question mark:
  ~~John~~ loves Mary.
  Who loves Mary?
- Write the sentence again. Cross out the object and replace it with *whom*. Draw an arrow to show that *whom* begins the question. Also point out that *loves* changes to *love*. Add *does*.
  John loves ~~Mary~~.
  John loves whom.

  Whom John loves?
       does
  Whom ↑ *John love?*

  Note: Point out to students that *John loves whom.* is not a correct sentence but is used here as part of the exercise since the change to *Whom does John love?* is grammatically correct.
- Write several sentences on the board and have students write the subject-pattern sentences, for example:

  Nati sings in the shower. (Who sings in the shower?)
- Write additional sentences and have students form object-pattern sentences. for example:

  Nati helps her aunt. (Whom does Nati help?)

⏱ **Identify the Grammar:** Have students identify the grammar in the opening text on page 102. For example:
  Why do we dream?
  Who dreams?
  How do we know?

Go to **www.myfocusongrammarlab.com** for grammar charts and notes.

Step 3: Focused Practice (pages 105–108)

See the general suggestions for Focused Practice on page 4.

Exercise 1: Discover the Grammar
- Have students look at the pictures while you read the introduction. Then ask: "Is Felix an early bird or a night owl?" *(a night owl)* "How about his mother?" *(an early bird)*
- Have students read the text quickly for meaning. Then go over the example with the class.
- Have students complete the exercise individually. Then go over the answers as a class.

Exercise 2: Word Order of *Wh-* Questions
- Go over the example with the class. Ask: "In each question, where will the *wh-* word go?" *(at the beginning)*
- Have students complete the exercise individually. Then have them compare answers in pairs.
- Highlight the third-person sentences with *does*.

Exercise 3: *Wh-* Questions about the Subject
- Go over the example with the class. Then review the formation of subject-pattern *wh-* questions. Ask: "What will be the ending of the verb?" *(-s)*
- Have students complete the exercise in pairs.
- Go over the answers as a class.

Exercise 4: *Wh-* Questions
- Go over the example with the class.
- Write the underlined portions from the sentences on the board. Then elicit the corresponding *wh-* word for each phrase. (Example: *Sabrina = who; during her math class = when*)
- Have students complete the exercise individually. Then call on pairs to read the questions and answers.

Exercise 5: *Wh-* Questions: Subject and Object

- Go over the example with the class. Elicit the subject *(my mother)* and the object *(me)*.
- Have students complete the exercise in pairs.
- Combine pairs to form groups of four and have students compare answers. Then call on pairs to read the conversations.

Exercise 6: Editing

- Go over the example with the class.
- Have students find and correct the nine remaining mistakes individually. Then have them compare answers in pairs.
- Call on pairs to give answers. Have them explain why the incorrect structures are wrong.

Go to **www.myfocusongrammarlab.com** for additional grammar practice.

Step 4: Communication Practice (pages 109–112)

See the general suggestions for Communication Practice on page 5.

Exercise 7: Listening

A

- Tell students they will hear a conversation between Mia and her doctor.
- Have students read the question silently.
- Play the audio. Students listen and complete the exercise individually.

B

- Go over the meaning of *symbolize* (mean; represent). Then have students predict the answers to the questions in pairs. Stress that prediction involves making guesses and that there are no right or wrong answers.
- Play the audio. Have students listen and complete the exercise individually.
- ⏱ To follow up, ask: "Have you ever had a dream like Mia's?" "Do you ever have dreams when you have stress?" "What kinds of things do you dream about?" "What do you think they symbolize?"

Exercise 8: Pronunciation

A

- Play the audio. Have students read along as they listen to the Pronunciation Note.

B

- Play the audio. Have students listen and repeat.
- Say the words on the list first with and then without the initial consonant. (Example: *rate . . . great . . . ream . . . dream*) Have students repeat.

C

- Have students complete the exercise in pairs. Encourage them to ask their partner to repeat if they do not understand.
- ⏱ Have pairs come up with a sentence using each of the words and have them share their sentences with the class.

D

- Play the audio. Have students read along.
- Have students listen and complete the exercise individually.
- ⏱ To follow up, ask: *wh-* questions to elicit the words with *r / l* consonant groups:
  What does Olivia buy in her dream? *(a black dress)*
  What does she do when she discovers a problem? *(She brings it back.)*
  What does the salesperson give her? *(a bright blue dress)*

Exercise 9: Interview

- Have students write their own answers to the questions in the You column.
- Have students complete the exercise in pairs. Make sure they know they should write their partner's answers in the Your Partner column.
- ⏱ To extend the practice, take notes as students give you the long answers. Then use your notes to ask *wh-* follow-up questions, for example:
  T: Who goes to bed after 11?
  Ss: Kim and Huang go to bed after 11.
  T: Who sleeps late on Wednesdays?
  Ss: Pablo sleeps late on Wednesdays.

Exercise 10: Group Interview

A

- Tell students they will interview their classmates to find out about their sleeping and dreaming habits. Go over the example with the class. Then have them read the questions quickly for meaning.
- Go over any unfamiliar vocabulary; for example, demonstrate *snore* and point out that *insomnia* means to have trouble sleeping.
- Form groups of five. Have students do the exercise in these groups. Remind them to take notes on their classmates' answers.

B

- Go over the example with the class.
- Call on students to give answers. Elicit both the long and short answer forms.

Exercise 11: Information Gap: Understanding Dreams

In pairs, have students choose A and B roles. Have Students B turn to page 112.

1.
- Have Students A read the questions quickly for meaning. Have Students B read the dream quickly for meaning.
- Have pairs ask and answer the questions.
- Call on students to tell you about the dream in their own words. Ask questions to help guide them.

2.
- Have Students B read the questions quickly for meaning. Have Students A read the dream quickly for meaning.
- Have pairs ask and answer the questions.
- Call on students to tell you about the dream in their own words. Ask questions to help guide them.

3.
- Have pairs discuss the meaning of each dream. Stress that this exercise asks for students' own opinions and ideas. Encourage them to make creative guesses.
- Elicit ideas from the class.
- ⏱ To follow up, ask: "Has anyone ever had a dream similar to these?" "What happened in the dream?" "What do you think it means?"

Exercise 12: Writing

A
- Have students read the questions quickly for meaning. Then go over the example with the class.
- To help them begin to write, have students make some notes about what to include in their description.
- ⏱ Have students illustrate a scene from their dream to go along with the piece of writing.

B
- Have students correct their work using the Editing Checklist.
- Then have students exchange papers and check their partner's work.
- ⏱ If desired, post the edited pieces of writing. Have students read their classmates' work and ask one another questions about the dreams.

OUT OF THE BOX ACTIVITIES

Writing and Speaking
- Play a game of Trivial Pursuit with the class.
- Prepare two lists of general-knowledge questions. Each list should have between six and eight questions. Alternatively, you may want to list topics on the board (Example: *history, math, art, music, TV, movies*), hand out small pieces of paper, and have students write the questions.
- Divide the class into two groups. Give each group one list of questions.
- First, students should try to answer the questions. Then have them write three or four new questions. Remind them to be sure they know the answers to the questions.
- Have the two groups quiz each other. Students should take turns asking and answering the questions. Teams get 1 point for each question they answer correctly.

Reading
- Do a reading scavenger hunt. Prepare two different news articles, or select two different websites or online articles.
- Assign each article / website to half the class.
- Have students work in pairs to write *wh-* questions about the article / website. They should try to come up with at least one question per *wh-* word (*who, what, when, where, why, how*).
- Have pairs join another pair that worked with the article.
- Have pairs exchange articles and questions and scan the article for the information.

Go to **www.myfocusongrammarlab.com** for additional listening, pronunciation, speaking, and writing practice.

Note:
- See the *Focus on Grammar Workbook* for additional in-class or homework grammar practice.

Unit 10 Review (page 113)

Have students complete the Review and check their answers on Student Book page UR-2. Review or assign additional material as needed.

Go to **www.myfocusongrammarlab.com** for the Unit Achievement Test.

From Grammar to Writing (page 114)

See the general suggestions for From Grammar to Writing on page 9.

Go to **www.myfocusongrammarlab.com** for an additional From Grammar to Writing Assignment, Part Review, and Part Post-Test.

PART IV OVERVIEW

There is / There are; POSSESSIVES; MODALS: ABILITY AND PERMISSION

UNIT	GRAMMAR FOCUS	THEME
11	*There is / There are*	Shopping Malls
12	Possessives: Nouns, Adjectives, Pronouns; Object Pronouns; Questions with *Whose*	Possessions
13	Ability: *Can* or *Could*	Abilities of Animals
14	Permission: *Can* or *May*	Health and Diet

Go to **www.myfocusongrammarlab.com** for the Part and Unit Tests.

Note: PowerPoint® grammar presentations, test-generating software, and reproducible Part and Unit Tests are on the *Teacher's Resource Disc.*

UNIT 11 OVERVIEW

Grammar: *There is / There are*

Unit 11 focuses on the structure and use of statements with *there is / there are* and questions with *is there . . . ? / are there . . . ?* to describe and ask about the existence of places and objects.

Theme: SHOPPING MALLS

Unit 11 focuses on language and expressions used to talk about shopping and shopping venues.

Step 1: Grammar in Context (pages 116–118)

See the general suggestions for Grammar in Context on page 1.

Before You Read
- Introduce the topic of shopping. Ask: "How often do you go shopping?" "Where do you like to go?" "What kinds of things do you shop for?"
- Have students discuss the questions in pairs. Then call on pairs to give answers.
- ⏱ Lead a brief discussion about the advantages / disadvantages of different types of shopping venues. (Example: *a mall vs. a boutique, a "big box" chain store vs. a local shop, shopping online vs. in a store*)

Read
- Have a student read the heading of the advertisement (ad). Ask: "What is this an advertisement for?" *(West Edmonton Mall)* Then elicit or explain the meanings of any unfamiliar vocabulary. (Example: *one-of-a-kind, young-at-heart, world-class*)
- To encourage students to read with a purpose, write these questions on the board:
  1. Have you been to a mall like West Edmonton Mall?
  2. Why do you think the ad calls it "a shopper's dream"?
  3. Which stores mentioned in the ad would you like to visit?
- Have students read the text. (OR: Play the audio and have students follow along in their books.) Then call on students to share their answers to the questions on the board.

After You Read

A. Practice
- Have students complete the exercise in pairs.
- Call on individual students to read the ad to the class.
- ⏱ To extend the intonation and fluency practice, try reading the ad line by line, in the style of a radio announcement. Have students try repeating after you in the same style.

B. Vocabulary
- Read the words in the box and have students repeat.
- Have students complete the exercise individually. Then have them compare answers in pairs.
- ⏱ Have pairs practice the conversations, changing roles and partners several times.

C. Comprehension
- Have students work in pairs to complete the exercise. Have them try to complete the task without looking back at the text.
- Call on pairs to give answers.

Go to **www.myfocusongrammarlab.com** for an additional reading, and for reading and vocabulary practice.

Step 2: Grammar Presentation (pages 119–120)
See the general suggestions for Grammar Presentation on page 2.

Grammar Charts
- Write several examples of the target grammar from the opening text on the board. Underline *There are*, *There's*, and *There isn't*. Say the phrases and have students repeat.
  There are more than 800 stores.
  There's a traditional Chinese market in Chinatown.
  There isn't a better time to get away.
- Ask questions to help students notice the structures:
  In the first sentence, what is the subject? *(stores)*
  Is it singular or plural? *(plural)*
  Do we use *there is* or *there are* with plural subjects? *(there are)*
  What does the contraction *there's* mean? *(there is)*
  What is the subject in the second sentence? *(a traditional Chinese market)*
  Is it singular or plural? *(singular)*
  Do we use *there is* or *there are*? *(there is)*
  How do we form the negative? *(there isn't)*
- To demonstrate the question form, give the students one minute to look around the room. Then have them close their eyes. Ask questions with *is there* and *are there*. (Example: *Is there a calendar in our room? Are there any windows in the back of the room? Are there any photographs on my desk?*)
- Call two volunteers up to the board. Have them write questions like the ones you just modeled about their school or campus using *is there* and *are there*.
- Have the students ask the class the questions and elicit the answers from the class.

Grammar Notes
Notes 1 and 2
- Call on students to read the notes and the examples.

- On the board, make a quick sketch of a room in your home. Draw the large pieces of furniture. Then say three or four sentences with *there is* and *there are*. As you speak, add these items to your sketch. (Example: *There's a painting above the fireplace. There are photos of my children on my desk. There's a lamp next to the couch.*)
- Draw attention to the *Be Careful!* note.
- Add more items to your sketch. Have students make sentences with *there is* and *there are*. Write students' sentences on the board to use for going over Note 3.

Note 3
- Call on students to read the notes and the examples.
- Have students use the sketch of your room and the sentences on the board from the previous step to make negative sentences comparing their own houses. (Example: *There isn't a fireplace in my house. There aren't any bedrooms on the first floor.*)
- Elicit sentences from several students. Highlight the use of *any* in plural negative statements.
- Draw attention to the *Be Careful!* note.
- To extend the practice, ask follow-up questions, for example:
  S: There isn't a TV in the bedroom at my house.
  T: Is there a TV in the living room?
  S: Yes, there is.

Note 4
- Do a short chain drill using *any* with *yes / no* questions. Ask about the students' homes, for example:
  T: Are there any plants in your house, Jasmine?
  S1: No, there aren't.
  T: Cats.
  S1: Are there any cats in your house, Enrique?
  S2: Yes, there are. / Yes, there's one.

Note 5
- Write the example sentences as a paragraph on the board. Replace *here*, *there*, and *their* with blanks. You may want to add two or three more sentences to the paragraph to further illustrate the teaching point.
- Call students up and have them fill in the blanks. Correct and discuss any errors.
- Draw attention to the *Be Careful!* note.

- Have students copy the paragraph but replace the information about Banff with information about another place, for example, a city nearby or one the students have visited in the past.
- Have students exchange and correct each other's papers.

Note 6
- On the board, write:
  There are
  There's
  There isn't
- Read the example sentences in Note 6, having students point to the words on the board as you say them.
- Make up similar sentences with *there is / are*. Have students follow up with an appropriate response containing *it's*, *he's*, or *they're*, for example:
  There's a book on the floor. *(It's Juan's.)*
  There's a sweater on the desk. *(It's red.)*
  There's a woman here to see you. *(She's waiting in the reception area.)*
  There are two cakes in the refrigerator. *(They're for the dinner party tonight.)*
  There are two new students in Ms. Jackson's class. *(They're from China.)*

🕐 **Identify the Grammar:** Have students identify the grammar in the reading on page 116. For example:
  There are more than 800 stores.
  There's a traditional Chinese market in Chinatown.
  There's Europa Boulevard . . .

Go to **www.myfocusongrammarlab.com** for grammar charts and notes.

Step 3: Focused Practice (pages 121–124)

See the general suggestions for Focused Practice on page 4.

Exercise 1: Discover the Grammar
- Have students study the mall directory for a minute or two. Then go over the example with the class.
- Ask questions to orient students to the shops on the directory and to review prepositions of location *(next to, between, to the left / right of)*, for example:
  Where is the shoe store? *(between the women's clothing store and the art supply store)*
  What is to the right of the gift shop? *(a bookstore)*

- Have students complete the exercise individually. Then have them compare answers in pairs. Have them rephrase the false sentences to make them true.

Exercise 2: Affirmative and Negative Statements
- Go over the example with the class. Stress that students will need to pay careful attention to the meaning of the sentences.
- Have students complete the exercise in pairs.
- Combine pairs to form groups of four and have students compare answers. Then call on students to read all of the correct sentences.

Exercise 3: Affirmative and Negative Statements
- Go over the example with the class.
- Have students complete the exercise individually. Then have them compare answers in pairs.
- 🕐 Have students brainstorm things they like and dislike about their city, school, or a local shop or restaurant. Then have them create sentences similar to those in the conversation, for example:
  There's a library at our school, but there aren't many computers in it.
  There are three classrooms on the second level, but there isn't an elevator.

Exercise 4: *There is / There are*, *There*, and *They are*
- Go over the example with the class.
- Have students complete the exercise in pairs. Make sure students are aware of the four expressions they may use to fill in the blanks.
- Have students practice the conversation in pairs, changing roles and partners a few times. Encourage students to try to make eye contact (rather than reading from the book) when they speak.

Exercise 5: Agreement with *There is / There are*
- Go over the example with the class. Then ask: "What is the subject of the first sentence?" *(café)* Elicit that the pronoun in the second sentence should agree with the subject of the first sentence.
- Have students complete the exercise individually.
- Call on students to read the completed sentences. Have the class listen and say whether the answer is correct and make any necessary corrections.

Exercise 6: *Yes / No* Questions with *Is there / Are there*

- Have students look at the calendar and read the text quickly for meaning. Then go over the example with the class. Ask: "Why does the example use *is there* and not *are there*?" *(because the subject, a dance performance, is singular)*
- Have students complete the exercise individually. Remind them to use the calendar to answer the questions.
- Call on pairs of students to read the questions and answers.

Exercise 7: Editing

- Go over the example with the class. Point out that students should find five more mistakes in the paragraph.
- Have students find and correct the mistakes in pairs.
- Combine pairs to form groups of four and have students compare answers. Then call on students to read the corrected passage. Have them explain why the incorrect structures are wrong.

Go to **www.myfocusongrammarlab.com** for additional grammar practice.

Step 4: Communication Practice (pages 125–128)

See the general suggestions for Communication Practice on page 5.

Exercise 8: Pronunciation

A

- On the board, write: *there, their, they're*. Read the words and have students repeat.
- Play the audio. Have students read along as they listen to the Pronunciation Note.

B

- Play the audio. Have students listen and complete the exercise individually.
- Have students compare answers in pairs. Then play the audio again for students to confirm answers.

Exercise 9: Listening

A

- Have students read the text quickly for meaning.
- Play the audio. Have students listen and write the question.
- Have students compare answers in pairs. Then call on a student to say the answer.

B

- Have students read the questions quickly for meaning.
- Play the audio. Have students listen and complete the exercise individually.
- Play the audio again for students to confirm answers. Then call on students to give answers.

Exercise 10: Comparing Pictures

- Go over the example with the class.
- Form pairs. Have students cover Picture B and give them one minute to study Picture A. After one minute, have students cover Picture A and look only at Picture B. Then have them write as many sentences as they can to describe the differences.
- Have students look at both pictures and report any differences they missed.

Exercise 11: Game: Tic Tac Toe

- Call on students to read the phrases in the boxes. Then have them quickly look at the tic tac toe board.
- Have students stand and move around the room to complete the game. You may want to tell students that they may ask only one question and then they should change partners.
- Call on students to tell you about their classmates' answers. (Example: *There is a skating rink near Yasmin's house.*)

Exercise 12: Writing

A

- Go over the example with the class.
- To help them begin to write, have students make some notes about what to include in their paragraph. (Example: *the shops and restaurants at the place, what they like and dislike about the place*)
- Have students complete the exercise individually.

B

- Have students correct their work using the Editing Checklist.
- Have students exchange papers and check their partner's work.

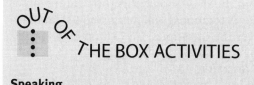

OUT OF THE BOX ACTIVITIES

Speaking

- Form small groups. Have students work together to design their dream shopping mall.
- Give them poster paper and markers and have them draw a floor plan of their mall, similar to the one on page 121.
- Then have them present their mall to the class.
- Encourage the rest of the class to find out more about their classmates' malls by asking questions using *Is there . . . ? / Are there . . . ?*

Reading and Speaking

- Have students use the Internet or the library to research interesting or famous shopping areas around the world. (Example: *the Champs-Élysées in Paris; Fifth Avenue in New York City; underground malls, such as PATH in Toronto; open-air night markets in Taipei*)
- Have students give a presentation to the class and talk about the features and attractions of their chosen shopping area.

Go to **www.myfocusongrammarlab.com** for additional listening, pronunciation, speaking, and writing practice.

Note:
- See the *Focus on Grammar Workbook* for additional in-class or homework grammar practice.

Unit 11 Review (page 129)

Have students complete the Review and check their answers on Student Book page UR-2. Review or assign additional material as needed.

Go to **www.myfocusongrammarlab.com** for the Unit Achievement Test.

UNIT 12 OVERVIEW

Grammar: POSSESSIVES: NOUNS, ADJECTIVES, PRONOUNS; OBJECT PRONOUNS; QUESTIONS WITH *Whose*

Unit 12 focuses on the structure and use of questions with *whose*, as well as object pronouns, singular and plural possessive nouns, adjectives, and pronouns.

Theme: POSSESSIONS

Unit 12 focuses on language and expressions used to ask about ownership and possessions and express relationships between people and belongings.

Step 1: Grammar in Context (pages 130–131)

See the general suggestions for Grammar in Context on page 1.

Before You Read
- Have students discuss their answers in pairs. Then elicit responses from the class.
- Ask two students to come to the board and write their names.
- Ask: "Whose name is longer?" "Whose name is shorter?" "Whose handwriting is smaller / larger / easier to read?"
- If students answer with the possessive *s* (Example: *Rick's*), write the sentences on the board. (Example: *Michelle's name is longer.*)
- Circle the examples of the apostrophe *s* in the sentences on the board.

Read
- Have students read the conversation quickly for meaning.
- To encourage students to read with a purpose, write these questions on the board:
  1. What is the teacher trying to do? *(find out who wrote the composition)*
  2. Why do you think Boris asks, "Is it a good paper?" *(because he wants to get a good grade)*
  3. In the end, does the teacher find out which paper Boris wrote? *(yes)*
  4. What does the teacher say about Boris's paper? *(It needs work.)*
- Have students read the text. (OR: Play the audio and have students follow along in their books.) Then call on students to share their answers to the questions on the board.

After You Read

A. Practice

- Have students in each group practice the conversation four times, changing roles each time. Encourage them to close their books and try the conversation without looking. Stress that they do not need to use the exact words from the book. They can use their own words.
- ⏱ Have groups stand and role-play the conversation.

B. Vocabulary

- Read the words in the box and have students repeat.
- Have students complete the exercise individually.
- Have students compare answers in pairs. Then call on pairs to read the completed sentences.

C. Comprehension

- Have students complete the exercise in pairs. Have them try to complete the task without looking back at the text.
- Call on pairs to give answers.

Go to **www.myfocusongrammarlab.com** for an additional reading, and for reading and vocabulary practice.

Step 2: Grammar Presentation (pages 132–133)

See the general suggestions for Grammar Presentation on page 2.

Grammar Charts

- Call on a student to read the examples in the chart.
- Ask: "How do we form possessives with singular nouns?" (*add 's*); "How do we usually form possessives with plural nouns?" (*add an apostrophe ['] at the end*) Highlight that with irregular plural nouns, such as *women, men, people*, or *children*, we add *'s*.
- Go around the room and hold up objects belonging to students. Drill the forms, for example:
  T: (holds up Oliver's jacket) Oliver.
  Ss: Oliver's jacket.
  T: (holds up Carla's book) Carla.
  Ss: Carla's book.
  T: (points to students' papers) The students.
  Ss: The students' papers.
- Call on a student to read the examples of questions and answers with *whose*. On the board, write *who's* and *whose* and elicit the difference.

- Repeat the drill above, this time calling on students to choose the items and ask and answer the questions, for example:
  S1: Whose shirt is red?
  S2: Tomas's is.
  S2: Whose hair is brown?
  S3: Kara's is.
- Read the examples of possessive adjectives and pronouns and have students repeat them.
- Ask the following questions:
  Which possessive pronouns are made by adding *s* to the possessive adjective? *(hers, yours, ours, theirs)*
  Which possessive adjective has no possessive pronoun? *(its)*
  Which has the same adjective and pronoun form? *(his)*
- Put students into pairs and have them practice by making new sentences using the examples in the chart. Explain that they should replace the nouns, for example:
  This is my <u>jacket</u>. This <u>jacket</u> is mine.
  Do you have your <u>cell phone</u>? Do you have <u>yours</u>?
- Call on pairs to tell you their sentences.
- Have students read the example sentences with object pronouns.
- Ask individual students questions to elicit the object pronouns, for example:
  T: Juan, do you know Yumi?
  Ss: Yes, I know her.
  T: Yumi, do you like Joao and Carlos?
  Yumi: Yes, I like them.
  T: Carlos, do you have your homework?
  Carlos: Yes, I have it.

Grammar Notes

Note 1

- Have students read the note and the examples.
- Demonstrate the possessive adjectives using objects belonging to different people in the class. (Example: hold up your purse and say: "This is my purse.") Have students repeat.
- Note that in many languages, possessive adjectives agree with the object (e.g., in languages with masculine and feminine gender nouns). However, in English they agree with the subject *(he-his, she-her, it-its)*. If any of your students' first languages have nouns with gender, you may want to spend some extra time practicing the adjectives.
- Drill. Hold up objects, point to people, and have students form phrases. (Example: *your book, his pencil, our desks*)
- To demonstrate relationships, draw a quick sketch of your family tree on the board using your family members' names.

- Explain your family tree. (Example: *Marla is my aunt. She is my mother's sister.*)
- Have students sketch their own family trees. Then have them form pairs and take turns explaining them.

Note 2
- Have students read the note and the examples.
- Dictate the following sentences to students and have them write them:
  Our teacher's car is blue.
  Where is John's mother's house?
  Good teachers listen to their students' ideas.
  The boys' restroom is on the second floor.
  Don't take other people's things.
  Here is the children's room.
- Have students exchange papers and correct them.
- Call on students to write the sentences on the board and have the class make any necessary corrections.

Notes 3 and 4
- Have students read the notes and the examples.
- Drill. Say phrases and have students transform them as follows:
  T: My mother's birthday.
  Ss: Her birthday.
  T: Jane's house.
  Ss: Her house.
  T: Kim and Jong's books.
  Ss: Their books.

Note 5
- Have students read the note and the examples.
- Drill. Say sentences and have students transform them, as follows:
  T: My eyes are blue.
  S1: Mine are blue.
  T: His car is red.
  S2: His is red.
- Draw attention to the *Be Careful!* notes.

Note 6
- Have students read the note and the examples.
- Draw attention to the *Be Careful!* note.
- To help students distinguish between *whose* and *who's*, do a drill similar to the one for *its / it's* below (see Note 8). Alternatively, do a dictation. Use the following sentences:
  Whose hat is this?
  Who's wearing jeans today?
  Do you know who's coming to the party?
  Whose car is in front of the school?
  Who's taller, you or your brother?
  Whose name is on that paper?

Note 7
- Have students read the *Be Careful!* note and the examples.
- To help students distinguish between possessive pronouns and object pronouns, write the following cloze activity on the board:
  It's mine. It belongs to _____.
  It's _____. It belongs to you.
  It's his. It belongs to _____.
  It's _____. It belongs to her.
  It's ours. It belongs to _____.
  It's _____. It belongs to them.
- Call on students to come to the board and fill in the blanks.
- Have the rest of the class correct errors as necessary.

Note 8
- Have students read the *Be Careful!* note and the examples.
- Write the following on the board:

  <u>1</u>   <u>2</u>
  it's   its

- Say the following sentences and have students tell you whether the word used is example number 1 or 2 from the board.
  We can't go outside because it's raining. *(1)*
  My cat loves its new toy. *(2)*
  Frank's car lost its tire. *(2)*
  Do you like my sweater? It's new. *(1)*
  The band finished making its new CD. *(2)*

Identify the Grammar: Have students identify the grammar in the conversation on page 130. For example:
  Whose composition is this?
  It's **my** composition.
  No, that's not **your** handwriting.

Go to **www.myfocusongrammarlab.com** for grammar charts and notes.

Step 3: Focused Practice (pages 134–138)
See the general suggestions for Focused Practice on page 4.

Exercise 1: Discover the Grammar
- Go over the example with the class. Explain that each question asks what the possessive adjective or pronoun refers to / talks about.
- Have students complete the exercise in pairs. Then combine pairs to form groups of four and have students compare answers.
- Call on pairs to read each conversation. Then elicit the answers from the class.

Exercise 2: Possessive Nouns

A
- Have students read the passage quickly for meaning. Then have them underline the possessive nouns in the reading.
- Have students work in pairs to identify each person in the picture. If necessary, review family vocabulary from the exercise. (Example: *niece, sister-in-law, cousin*)

B
- Go over the example with the class.
- Have students complete the exercise individually. Then have them compare answers in pairs.

Exercise 3: Possessive Adjectives
- Elicit the possessive adjectives *(my, your, his, her, its, our, their)* and write them on the board. Then go over the example with the class.
- Have students complete the exercise individually.
- Call on students to write their answers on the board. Then call on students to read the completed sentences.

Exercise 4: Possessive Pronouns
- Elicit the possessive pronouns *(mine, yours, his, hers, ours, theirs)* and write them on the board. Then go over the example with the class.
- Have students complete the exercise individually.
- Have students compare answers in pairs. Then call on pairs to read the conversations.

Exercise 5: Possessive Adjectives and Possessive Pronouns
- Have students read the conversations quickly for meaning. Then go over the example with the class.
- Have students complete the exercise in pairs. Then call on pairs to read the conversations.
- ⏱ Have students stand and move around the class, practicing each conversation with two more classmates.

Exercise 6: Subject and Object Pronouns, Possessives
- Go over the example with the class.
- Have students complete the exercise in pairs.
- Call on students to read the completed sentences. Have the class tell you whether the answer is correct or incorrect and correct any errors as necessary.

Exercise 7: Possessives: Questions and Verb Agreement
- Have students read the conversations quickly for meaning. Then go over the example with the class.

- Have students complete the exercise individually. Then have them compare answers in pairs.
- Call on pairs to read the completed conversations. Stop after each one and have the class tell you whether the answer is correct or incorrect and correct any errors as necessary.

Exercise 8: Pronouns and Possessive Adjectives
- Have students read the article quickly for meaning. Then go over the example with the class.
- Have students complete the article in pairs.
- ⏱ To extend the practice and prepare students for the writing activity at the end of the unit, have students make some notes about what they would include in a similar paragraph about themselves. Then have them share the information in pairs.

Exercise 9: Editing
- Go over the example with the class. Point out that students should find seven more mistakes in the conversations.
- Have students find and correct the mistakes in pairs.
- Combine pairs to form groups of four and have students compare answers. Then call on students to read the corrected passage. Have them explain why the incorrect structures are wrong.

Go to **www.myfocusongrammarlab.com** for additional grammar practice.

Step 4: Communication Practice (pages 139–141)

See the general suggestions for Communication Practice on page 5.

Exercise 10: Pronunciation

A
- Play the audio. Have students read along as they listen to the Pronunciation Note.

B
- Play the audio. Have students listen and circle their answers.
- Have students compare answers in pairs.
- Play the audio again, pausing after each item and calling on a student to tell you the answer.

Exercise 11: Listening

A
- Play the audio. Have students listen and mark their answer.
- Go over the answer as a class.

B

- Have students look at the pictures. In pairs, have them describe each bike and discuss the differences between them.
- Play the audio. Have students listen and write their answers.
- 🕐 To extend the listening practice, write the following questions on the board. Then play the audio again and elicit the answers.
  Where did Jasmine's family get their bikes? *(at a big sale)*
  What is Jasmine's brother's name? *(Johnny)*
  Who are Roger and Ted? *(Jasmine's uncles)*
  Why do they share a bike? *(because they don't ride much)*

Exercise 12: Talking about Family Photos

- Have students bring in a photo (or draw a picture) of a family member. To extend the activity, you can have them bring in / draw two or three photos / pictures.
- Collects students' photos. Check that students have marked their relationship to the person in the photo on the back. Then redistribute the photos randomly, making sure that no one gets their own photo.
- Have students walk around the room asking questions to try to find the owner of the photo, for example:
  Whose brother is this?
  Is this your brother?

Exercise 13: Game: Find Someone Whose / Who's . . .

A

- Have students read the sentences quickly for meaning. Elicit that the questions with *whose* will have a noun after the blank.
- Have students complete the exercise individually.

B

- Elicit possible questions students can ask to find out each piece of information. (Example: *Are you good in art? Does your name mean something?*)
- Have students ask their classmates questions to complete the questions in part A. Then have them report to the class.

Exercise 14: Writing

A

- Go over the example with the class.
- Have students look at Exercise 8 and make some notes about what to include in their own paragraph.
- Have students complete the exercise individually.

B

- Have students correct their work using the Editing Checklist.
- Then have students exchange papers and check their partner's work.
- 🕐 Collect the papers and have students bring in a photo of themselves. Compile the paragraphs and photos into a class newsletter and make a copy for each student in the class.

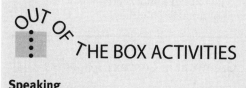

OUT OF THE BOX ACTIVITIES

Speaking

- Have students interview a classmate about his or her family. They can ask about family members' names, jobs, where they live, interests and hobbies, and so on.
- Have students give presentations about the classmate they interviewed, either for the class or in small groups.

Reading and Speaking

- Form small groups. Then hand back the paragraphs students wrote for Exercise 14. Have students in each group exchange paragraphs with a partner in their group.
- Have students read their partner's paragraph and continue exchanging until they have read all groups members' paragraphs.
- Have students ask their group members questions about the information in the paragraphs and try to find out more information about their classmates.

Go to **www.myfocusongrammarlab.com** for additional listening, pronunciation, speaking, and writing practice.

Note:

- See the *Focus on Grammar Workbook* for additional in-class or homework grammar practice.

Unit 12 Review (page 142)

Have students complete the Review and check their answers on Student Book page UR-3. Review or assign additional material as needed.

Go to **www.myfocusongrammarlab.com** for the Unit Achievement Test.

Grammar: ABILITY: *Can* or *Could*

Unit 13 focuses on the structure and use of the modals *can* and *could* to make affirmative and negative statements and ask questions about ability in the past and present.

Theme: ABILITIES OF ANIMALS

Unit 13 focuses on language and expressions used to talk about animals and pets with unusual or amazing abilities.

Step 1: Grammar in Context (pages 143–144)

See the general suggestions for Grammar in Context on page 1.

Before You Read

- Introduce the topic of animals and pets. Ask: "Who has a pet?" "What kind of pets do you have?" "What's interesting or unusual about your pet?"
- Have students discuss the questions in pairs.
- ⏱ Lead a brief class discussion about animals. Try to elicit any interesting or amazing stories students may have heard about animals in the news.

Read

- Preview the online article. Read the title of the article and have the class predict what the article may be about.
- To encourage students to read with a purpose, write these questions on the board:
  1. Who is N'kisi? *(an African gray parrot)*
  2. Where does he live? *(New York City)*
  3. What's interesting or special about him? *(He can say almost 1,000 words and use basic grammar.)*
  4. Why does the article compare him to apes or chimpanzees? *(because N'kisi thinks at high levels, just like apes and chimpanzees)*
- Have students read the text. (OR: Play the audio and have students follow along in their books.) Then call on students to share their answers to the questions on the board.

After You Read

A. Practice

- Have students complete the exercise in pairs.
- Call on individual students to read the online article to the class.
- ⏱ To extend the reading comprehension practice, have students close their books and explain the online article in their own words, recounting as many details as they can from the article.

B. Vocabulary

- Read the words in the box and have students repeat.
- Have students complete the exercise individually.
- Have students compare answers in pairs. Then call on pairs to read the completed sentences.

C. Comprehension

- Have students complete the exercise in pairs. Have them try to complete the task without looking back at the text.
- Call on students to read the sentences and tell you whether they are true, false, or unknown. Have them correct any false statements.

Go to **www.myfocusongrammarlab.com** for an additional reading, and for reading and vocabulary practice.

Step 2: Grammar Presentation (page 145)

See the general suggestions for Grammar Presentation on page 2.

Grammar Charts

- Call on students to read the examples in the charts.
- Ask the following questions to elicit information about the form of *can*, *can't*, *could*, and *couldn't*:
  Which forms express ability in the present? *(can and can't)*
  When do we use *could* and *couldn't*? *(to express ability in the past)*
  What form of the verb follows a modal? *(base form)*
  Where do modals go in statements? *(before the verb)*
  Where does the modal go in *yes / no* questions? *(before the subject)*
- Elicit the short answer forms for the questions:
  Yes, we can. / No, we can't.
  Yes, we could. / No, we couldn't.
- You may want to point out the following rules governing the pronunciation of these modals:
  Can and *could* are unstressed. The verb following them is stressed.
  Can't and *couldn't* are stressed, and so is the verb that follows them.

Grammar Notes

Note 1

- Say three or four sentences about things you can do very well. (Example: *I can speak French. I can sing. I can make chicken soup.*)

- Ask: "How about you?" Then go around the room in a chain, each student saying one thing he or she does well.

Note 2
- Repeat the procedure from Note 1 but have students form negative sentences.

Note 3
- Make a handout for each student with two lists of verbs such as the following:

Student 1	Student 2
swim	ski
whistle	play piano
touch your toes without bending your knees	speak Chinese

- Have students work in pairs, using the lists to interview one another. They should answer truthfully, for example:
  S1: Can you swim?
  S2: Yes, I can. Can you ski?
- As an optional follow-up, go around the room and have each student form a sentence about his or her partner, as follows: "Aki can swim, but he can't whistle."

Note 4
- Write the following chart on the board:

Now	Then
1. can	could
2. can't	couldn't
3. can't	could
4. can	couldn't

- Form small groups. Have students in each group use the cues in the chart to form sentences. (Example: their first sentence should be about something they can do now and could do in the past: *I can ride my bike to the river. I could ride my bike to the river when I was 16.*)
- Follow up as in the last step of Note 3.

Note 5
- Use the handout from Note 3 but instruct students to use *could*. Give them a past time to talk about. (Example: *when you were 12, before you moved to the United States, before you learned English*)
- Have students work with different partners.
- Follow up as in previous notes, if desired.

Note 6
- Have a student read the question and answer example in the note aloud.
- Have students work in pairs to take turns asking each other questions using *can* and *could*. Students can ask "crazy" questions to make it more fun. (Can you fly? Could you understand what that dog said?) Remind them to use short answers.
- Circulate as students work to help with the short answers.

🕐 **Identify the Grammar:** Have students identify the grammar in the reading on page 143. For example:
  Everyone knows parrots **can talk.**
  By "talk" we mean they **can repeat** words.
  Most parrots **can't** really **express** ideas.

Go to **www.myfocusongrammarlab.com** for grammar charts and notes.

Step 3: Focused Practice (pages 146–148)
See the general suggestions for Focused Practice on page 4.

Exercise 1: Discover the Grammar
A
- Have students read the sentences quickly for meaning. Then go over the example with the class.
- Have students complete the exercise in pairs.
- Call on students to write the target phrases including the modals and base forms on the board. Have the class tell you which ones are the negative statements. Circle them.

B
- Have students complete the exercise individually.
- Have students compare answers in pairs. Then call on students to read each statement followed by the reason.

Exercise 2: *Can* and *Can't*
- Go over the example with the class. Stress that students will need to pay careful attention to the meaning of the sentences. Ask: "What forms of the verbs are shown in parentheses?" *(base form)* "Will those change in the sentences?" *(no)*
- Have students complete the exercise in pairs. Then call on students to read the correct sentences.
- 🕐 Have the class think about the abilities of their own pets. Elicit sentences with *can / can't / could / couldn't* about students' pets and write them on the board.

Exercise 3: Can / Can't: Yes / No Questions and Answers

- Have students read the conversation quickly for meaning. Then go over the example with the class.
- Have students complete the exercise individually. Then have them compare answers in pairs.
- ⏱ Have pairs write another conversation between Aimee and N'kisi, using *can / can't / could / couldn't*. Then have them read their conversations for the class.

Exercise 4: Past Abilities: Could / Couldn't

- Ask: "What forms of the verbs are shown in parentheses?" *(base form)* "Will those change in the sentences?" *(no)* Then do the first item with the whole class.
- Have students complete the exercise individually.
- Call on students to read the completed sentences. Have the class listen and say whether the answer is correct and then make any necessary corrections.

Exercise 5: Editing

- Go over the example with the class. Point out that they should find six more mistakes in the conversation.
- Have students find and correct the mistakes in pairs.
- Combine pairs to form groups of four and have students compare answers. Then call on students to read the corrected passage. Have them explain why the incorrect structures are wrong.

Go to **www.myfocusongrammarlab.com** for additional grammar practice.

Step 4: Communication Practice (pages 149–151)

See the general suggestions for Communication Practice on page 5.

Exercise 6: Pronunciation

A
- Play the audio. Have students read along as they listen to the Pronunciation Note.

B
- Play the audio. Have students listen and complete the sentences.
- Have students compare answers in pairs.
- ⏱ Have students write three more sentences about animals' abilities using *can* and *can't* and share them with the class.

C
- Say the reduced pronunciations of *can* (/kæn/ and /kən/) several times and have students repeat.
- On the board, write: We can dance. We can't dance. Say the affirmative sentence with the reduced pronunciation of *can*. Then say the negative sentence, stressing the modal and the verb. Have students repeat both sentences chorally and then individually until the difference is clear.
- Play the audio. Have students listen and repeat.

Exercise 7: Listening

A
- Preview the listening. Tell students they will hear a conversation about dolphins. Say: "Dolphins are very intelligent animals. What are some things dolphins can do?" Elicit several ideas from the class.
- Call on a student to read the list of words and phrases.
- Play the audio. Have students listen and circle their answers.

B
- Have students read the questions and answer choices quickly for meaning.
- Play the audio. Have students listen and mark their answers.
- Have students tell you the answers in complete sentences. (Example: *The dolphins can exchange paper for fish.*)

Exercise 8: Game: Find Someone Who

A
- Call on two students to read the model conversation. Then call on students to read the phrases in the chart.
- Have a student stand up and model the task with you. Make sure students understand that they should write the person's name only if they answer "yes."
- Have students ask their classmates questions. Tell them that they should change partners after they ask each question in the present and the past.

B
- Go over the example with the class.
- Call on students to report their findings to the class.

Exercise 9: Game: What Can Your Group Do?
• Call on students to read the questions.
• Form small groups. Have groups choose one member to write down their answers. Remind students that this is a race. When they complete a task they should raise their hands quickly.
• When a group finishes, have one member call out answers. If all answers are correct, the group wins the round. If any answers are incorrect, play continues until another group finishes with all answers correct.

Exercise 10: Writing

A
• Go over the guiding questions and the example with the class.
• To help them begin to write, have students make some notes about what to include in their paragraph.
• You may want to give students time to research amazing animal stories on the Internet or at the library, especially those without pets of their own. Then have them complete the exercise individually.

B
• Have students correct their work using the Editing Checklist.
• Have students exchange papers and check their partner's work.

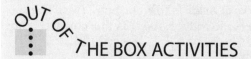

OUT OF THE BOX ACTIVITIES

Speaking and Writing
• Have students complete a survey to find out about their classmates' special or unusual abilities, skills, or talents.
• Elicit questions from the class to create one questionnaire. Alternatively, have students work individually to create their own questionnaires.
• Have each student interview five other classmates and write a few sentences to describe each student's talents.
• Have students report on their classmates' talents in small groups.
• To follow up, hold a class talent show and have students perform or teach a skill to the class.

Go to **www.myfocusongrammarlab.com** for additional listening, pronunciation, speaking, and writing practice.

Note:
• See the *Focus on Grammar Workbook* for additional in-class or homework grammar practice.

Unit 13 Review (page 152)

Have students complete the Review and check their answers on Student Book page UR-3. Review or assign additional material as needed.

Go to **www.myfocusongrammarlab.com** for the Unit Achievement Test.

UNIT 14 OVERVIEW

Grammar: PERMISSION: *Can* OR *May*

Unit 14 focuses on the structure and use of modals *can* and *may* to ask for, give, and deny permission to do things.

Theme: HEALTH AND DIET

Unit 14 focuses on language and expressions used to talk about healthy and unhealthy foods and recommendations for a healthy diet.

Step 1: Grammar in Context (pages 153–154)

See the general suggestions for Grammar in Context on page 1.

Before You Read
• Call on a student to read the introductory text. Help with pronunciation if needed. Then call on students to read the words in the box.
• Have students complete the categories in pairs.
• ⏱ Elicit more examples of foods for each category, for example:
  Protein: eggs, cheese, nuts, ham
  Carbohydrates: cereal, crackers
  Fat: cream, potato chips

Read
• Ask students if they have ever heard of Weight Watchers or the Atkins Diet. Elicit anything they may know about either one. Go over any key vocabulary from the article. (Example: *overweight, nutritionist, calorie*)
• To encourage students to read with a purpose, write these questions on the board:
  1. How much weight did Marita gain in college? (*She gained 5 pounds.*)
  2. How did she try to lose weight at first? (*She tried on her own.*)

3. How do people lose weight on Weight Watchers? *(They use a point system. They can't eat more than a certain number of points in a day.)*
4. On Weight Watchers, where can dieters meet other dieters? *(in a weekly class)*
5. How much weight did Marita lose? *(5 pounds)*
6. Why is Bill overweight? *(He works long hours and eats many meals out.)*
7. What diet is he following? *(Atkins)*
8. What can Bill eat on his diet? *(foods high in protein and fat)*
9. How much weight did Bill lose? *(10 pounds)*
- Have students read the text. (OR: Play the audio and have students follow along in their books.) Then call on students to share their answers to the questions on the board.

After You Read

A. Practice
- Have students complete the exercise in pairs.
- Then call on pairs to read paragraphs aloud.
- ⏱ To extend the reading comprehension practice, have students close their books and explain the article in their own words, recounting as many details as they can.

B. Vocabulary
- Read the words in the box and have students repeat.
- Have students complete the exercise individually.
- Have students compare answers in pairs. Then call on pairs to read the completed sentences.

C. Comprehension
- Have students complete the exercise in pairs. Have them try to complete the task without looking back at the text.
- Call on students to read the sentences and tell you whether they are true, false, or it doesn't say. Have them correct any false statements.
- ⏱ Lead a brief class discussion comparing the two types of diets. Ask: "Which diet do you think would be easier for you? Why?"

Go to **www.myfocusongrammarlab.com** for an additional reading, and for reading and vocabulary practice.

Step 2: Grammar Presentation (page 155)
See the general suggestions for Grammar Presentation on page 2.

Grammar Charts
- Call on students to read the examples in the chart.
- Ask: "Which words do we use to give permission?" (can / may + *verb*) "Which words do we use to deny permission?" (can't / may not + *verb*)
- Call on pairs to read the *yes / no* questions and answers. Ask: "What is the subject in each example?" *(I)* Explain that when we ask for permission, the subject is usually *I* or *we*.
- Call on students to read the questions in the last chart. Elicit possible answers to the questions. *(tomorrow / this evening; behind the building / on the other side of the street)*

Grammar Notes

Note 1
- Have students read the note and the examples.
- Elicit examples of things students can (may) and can't (may not) do in your classroom. Have them write these rules on the board. (Example: *Students can drink coffee. They can't sit on the desks.*) Call on different students to read the sentences and correct any errors.
- Change *can't* to *may not* in the sentence on the board. Ask: "Is this correct?" *(yes)* Then change it to *mayn't*. Ask: "Is this correct?" *(no)*

Note 2
- Call on students to read the note and the examples.
- Point out that we often ask for permission when we want to borrow something. Do a chain drill in which students ask to borrow items from each other, for example:
T: May I please borrow your dictionary?
S1: Sure. [To S2] Can I borrow your pencil?
S2: I'm sorry. I'm using it. [To S3] Can I borrow your car?
- To contrast the difference in the level of formality of *can* and *may*, give students situations and have them tell you sentences with *can* or *may* that would be used. Examples:
T: You need to leave work early. Ask your boss.
S: May I leave early?
T: You want to see your friend's new computer.
S: Can I see your new computer?

Note 3
- Have a student read the note. Have two students role-play the examples.
- Ask students where people might ask, "May I help you?" *(any place where people do services for clients, such as restaurants, stores, or a dry cleaner)*
- Make sure students understand the phrase *I'm just looking.*

🕐 **Identify the Grammar:** Have students identify the grammar in the reading on page 153. For example:

> You **can eat** any food, but you **may not eat** more than a certain number of points each day.
> Dieters **can follow** . . .
> . . . you **may eat** foods . . .

Go to **www.myfocusongrammarlab.com** for grammar charts and notes.

Step 3: Focused Practice (pages 156–158)

See the general suggestions for Focused Practice on page 4.

Exercise 1: Discover the Grammar

A
- Call on two students to read the conversation.
- Have students work individually to underline the target grammar.
- Have students compare answers in pairs.

B
- Call on a student to read the instructions.
- Have students complete the exercise in pairs.
- Go over the answers as a class.

Exercise 2: *Can / May:* Affirmative, Negative, *Yes / No* Questions
- Have students read the conversations and words in the box quickly for meaning. Then go over the example with the class. Ask: "Do you need to change the form of these verbs for the sentence?" *(no)* "Why not?" *(because the base form follows modals)* Point out that the modal is indicated above each conversation. Remind students to use the context of the conversation to select the correct verbs.
- Have students complete the exercise individually.
- 🕐 Have pairs write two more conversations using at least three of the verbs from the box in each conversation. Then have them read their conversations to the class.

Exercise 3: Permission: *May / Can*
- Call on students to read the conversation, including the sentences in parentheses.
- Have students complete the exercise individually. Then call on a pair to read the conversation.
- 🕐 Have the class brainstorm other permission questions a patient might ask a doctor, as well as the doctor's possible answers. Then have pairs role-play the questions and responses.

Exercise 4: Editing
- Go over the example with the class. Point out that they should find five more mistakes in the conversations.
- Have students find and correct the mistakes in pairs.
- Combine pairs to form groups of four and have students compare answers. Then call on students to read the corrected passage. Have them explain why the incorrect structures are wrong.

Go to **www.myfocusongrammarlab.com** for additional grammar practice.

Step 4: Communication Practice (pages 159–161)

See the general suggestions for Communication Practice on page 5.

Exercise 5: Listening

A
- Explain that a woman is calling a doctor to get the x-ray results of her ankle. Based on that information, have students make some predictions about what permission the doctor might give or deny.
- Have students read the questions quickly for meaning. Then play the audio.

B
- Play the audio again. Then have students complete the exercise individually.

Exercise 6: Pronunciation

A
- Play the audio. Have students read along as they listen to the Pronunciation Note.

B
- Play the audio. Have students listen and repeat the words with the /eɪ/ sound.
- Call on students to say the words they circled.

C
- Play the audio. Have students listen and repeat the words with the /ɛ/ sound.

D
- Go over the example with the class.
- Have students work in pairs, taking turns reading the sentences. Have them check the sound in the chart in pencil.
- Play the audio. Have students listen and complete the exercise in pairs.

Exercise 7: Information Gap
- Have students work in pairs and choose A and B roles. Then have the Students B turn to page 161.
- Have students read their information.
- Have students ask and answer the questions, role-playing a patient and a receptionist.

Exercise 8: Writing
A
- Call on a student to read the information in the chart and the example.
- Have students write the text by hand and then, if possible, type it in email format and send it to a classmate.

B
- Have students read and correct their partner's work.
- Have students correct their work using the Editing Checklist before handing in (or emailing) their work to you.

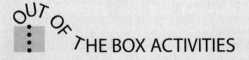

OUT OF THE BOX ACTIVITIES

Writing and Speaking
- Form small groups. Have students in each group come up with their own diet ideas. Encourage them to be creative, for example:
  - the round foods diet
  - the chocolate diet
  - the international diet
  - the crunchy foods diet
- Students should write what people on the diet can and can't eat / do.
- Have each group join another group to present their diet ideas. Encourage students to ask questions about their classmates' diets.

Go to **www.myfocusongrammarlab.com** for additional listening, pronunciation, speaking, and writing practice.

Note:
- See the *Focus on Grammar Workbook* for additional in-class or homework grammar practice.

Unit 14 Review (page 162)
Have students complete the Review and check their answers on Student Book page UR-3. Review or assign additional material as needed.

Go to **www.myfocusongrammarlab.com** for the Unit Achievement Test.

From Grammar to Writing (pages 163–164)
See the general suggestions for From Grammar to Writing on page 9.

Go to **www.myfocusongrammarlab.com** for an additional From Grammar to Writing Assignment, Part Review, and Part Post-Test.

PART V OVERVIEW

PRESENT PROGRESSIVE

UNIT	GRAMMAR FOCUS	THEME
15	Present Progressive: Affirmative and Negative Statements	High School
16	Present Progressive: *Yes / No* and *Wh-* Questions	Movies
17	Simple Present and Present Progressive; Non-Action Verbs	Smartphones

Go to **www.myfocusongrammarlab.com** for the Part and Unit Tests.

Note: PowerPoint® grammar presentations, test-generating software, and reproducible Part and Unit Tests are on the *Teacher's Resource Disc.*

Grammar: PRESENT PROGRESSIVE: AFFIRMATIVE AND NEGATIVE STATEMENTS

Unit 15 focuses on the structure and use of the present progressive in affirmative and negative statements.

Theme: HIGH SCHOOL

Unit 15 focuses on language and expressions used to compare schedules and norms at high schools in different countries.

Step 1: Grammar in Context (pages 166–167)

See the general suggestions for Grammar in Context on page 1.

Before You Read

- Have students discuss the questions in pairs. Encourage them to explain the reasons for their opinions.
- Ask the questions to the whole class and elicit responses from several students.
- Have the class debate the last question, giving reasons and examples to support their opinions.

Read

- Have students look at the photos. Say: "These two high school girls are cousins. Where do you think they live? How do you think their lives are similar? How do you think they are different?" Elicit responses from the class.
- To encourage students to read with a purpose, write these questions on the board:
  1. What time does Mi Young start school? *(8:00 A.M.)* How about Julie? *(9:00 A.M.)*
  2. What does Mi Young do after school? *(goes to a private study school)*
  3. What does Julie do after school? *(swims on the swimming team and then does homework)*
  4. Why are the girls working and studying so hard? *(they want to attend top colleges)*
- Have students read the text. (OR: Play the audio and have students follow along in their books.) Then call on students to share their answers to the questions on the board.

After You Read

A. Practice
- Have students complete the exercise in pairs.
- Call on individual students to read portions of the online article to the class.

B. Vocabulary
- Read the words on the left side of the chart and have students repeat.
- Have students complete the exercise individually. Then have them compare answers in pairs.
- Call on students to suggest a sentence for each word. Write the correct sentences on the board.

C. Comprehension
- Have students complete the exercise individually.
- Have students compare answers in pairs.
- Call on students to give answers in complete sentences. (Example: *Mi Young is in school.*)

Go to **www.myfocusongrammarlab.com** for an additional reading, and for reading and vocabulary practice.

Step 2: Grammar Presentation (pages 167–168)

See the general suggestions for Grammar Presentation on page 2.

Grammar Charts
- Call on students to read the examples in the chart.
- Write the following on the board: present progressive = present form of _____ + _____ form of the verb + _____
- Ask: "How do we form the present progressive?" and have students fill in the blanks on the board: (present form of *be* + base form of the verb + *-ing*)
- Ask: "How do we form negative statements in the present progressive?" *(by adding* not *after the present form of* be)
- Drill the conjugations. In the affirmative, say a verb and a pronoun. Students say the complete verb. Encourage them to use contractions, for example:
  T: Study. I.
  Ss: I am studying.
  T: You.
  Ss: You are studying.
- Provide an affirmative verb. Students transform it to the negative. Encourage students to use contractions, for example:
  T: She is reading.
  Ss: She is not reading.
  Ss: She isn't reading.

Grammar Notes

Note 1

- Walk around the room. As you walk, use the present progressive (also called present continuous) to narrate what you see students doing. (Example: *Akira is drinking coffee. Sofia is looking for something in her bag.*)
- Ask: "When are these things happening?" *(now)* On the board, write *now, right now, at this moment.* Repeat some of the sentences with each of these phrases. (Example: *Akira is drinking coffee now. At this moment, Sofia is looking for something.*)
- Elicit similar sentences from students.
- Draw attention to the *Be Careful!* note. Elicit the rule about non-action verbs by asking questions: "I'm thirsty. I want to drink something. Can I say *I am wanting*?" *(no)*
- Walk around again. This time make sentences with non-action verbs, for example:
  I'm thirsty. I want some water.
  I don't see Lana. Where is she?
  How much does this dictionary cost?
- Call on a student to read the *Be Careful!* note and the examples. Have students form a few more sentences with non-action verbs such as *need, like, hear, cost,* and *have.*

Note 2

- Call on a student to read the note and the examples.
- Drill the affirmative and negative contracted forms, for example:
  T: I am teaching.
  Ss: I'm teaching.
  T: Negative.
  Ss: I'm not teaching.
  T: John and I are eating.
  Ss: We're eating.
  T: Negative.
  Ss: We aren't eating.

Note 3

- Call on a student to read the note and the example.
- Have individual students transform statements into the present progressive (using contractions), for example:
  T: She eats and drinks.
  Ss: She's eating and drinking.
  T: We study and listen to music.
  Ss: We're studying and listening to music.

Note 4

- Call on a student to read the note and the examples.

- Dictate the following sentences and have students write them down, paying attention to the spelling rule.
  I'm writing a book.
  He's closing the door.
  We're sharing a room.
  They're moving to a new house.
  She's leaving now.
- Call on students to write their sentences on the board. Ask the rest of the class to correct any errors if necessary.

Note 5

- Draw a simple timeline on the board:

- Tell a simple story that illustrates the extended meaning of *now*, for example, *this moment, this week, this month, this year.* Use contractions, for example:
  My cousin is a computer designer. He normally lives in Italy, but this year he's living in the United States. He's studying at Harvard University in Boston. He's on vacation this week, so he's visiting me. Right now he's at the Fine Arts Museum.
- Form small groups. Students in each group make four sentences, saying what they are doing right now, this week, this month, and this year. Encourage them to use contractions.

⏱ **Identify the Grammar:** Have students identify the grammar in the reading on page 166. For example:
  She**'s working** on some tough math problems.
  She's tired, but she**'s not giving up.**
  . . . they**'re hoping to** go to a top college.

Go to **www.myfocusongrammarlab.com** for grammar charts and notes.

Step 3: Focused Practice (pages 168–171)

See the general suggestions for Focused Practice on page 4.

Exercise 1: Discover the Grammar

A

- Have students read the statements quickly for meaning. Then go over the example with the class.
- Ask: "What three letters will tell you whether the verbs are in the present progressive?" *(-ing)* "What else will you find and underline, besides the *-ing* form?" *(the present form of the verb)*

- Have students complete the exercise individually. Then have them compare answers in pairs.

B
- Go over the example with the class.
- Have students complete the exercise individually.
- Call on students to come to the board and write the base forms. Highlight the verbs that end in silent *e* (*take, have, ride*) and elicit the spelling rule.

Exercise 2: Present Progressive Statements
- Go over the example with the class. Remind students to pay attention to subject-verb agreement with the forms of the verb *be*, as well as to the spelling of any verbs with silent *e* endings.
- Have students complete the exercise in pairs. Then combine pairs to form groups of four and have students compare answers.
- To follow up, ask some questions about the schedule:
  Why isn't Julie eating breakfast? *(because she's late)*
  How is she getting to her class? *(She's taking the bus.)*
  It's 4:00. What is Julie doing? *(She's studying physics.)*
  What are Julie and her friends doing at 8:00? *(They're relaxing and having fun.)*

Exercise 3: Present Progressive Statements
- Go over the example with the class. Point out the negative items in the box and ask: "Where does the *not* go in the present progressive?" *(after the present form of* be*)*
- Have students complete the exercise individually.
- Have students compare answers in pairs. Then call on students to read the completed sentences.

Exercise 4: Present Progressive Statements
- Have students read the paragraphs quickly for meaning. Then go over the example with the class.
- Have students complete the exercise individually.
- Have students exchange books and check each other's work.

Exercise 5: Editing
- Go over the example with the class. Point out that students should find seven more mistakes in the journal.
- Have students find and correct the mistakes in pairs.

- Combine pairs to form groups of four and have students compare answers. Then call on students to read the corrected passage. Have them explain why the incorrect structures are wrong.

Go to **www.myfocusongrammarlab.com** for additional grammar practice.

Step 4: Communication Practice (pages 171–172)
See the general suggestions for Communication Practice on page 5.

Exercise 6: Listening
A
- Play the audio. Have students listen and write their answer.

B
- Have students read the questions quickly for meaning.
- Play the audio. Have students listen and answer the questions.
- Call on students to read the questions and answers.

Exercise 7: Pronunciation
A
- Play the audio. Have students read along as they listen to the Pronunciation Note. Read the examples and have students repeat, stressing the base form of the word but not the *-ing* ending.

B
- Play the audio. Have students listen and read along.
- Play the audio again. Have students listen and repeat.

Exercise 8: Game: Describing a Photo
A
- Form small groups. Give groups ten minutes to write as many statements as they can about the photo. Remind them to use both affirmative and negative statements.
- Call on students to read their statements to the class.
- Groups get 1 point for any correct sentence not used by another group. The group with the most points wins.

B
- Lead a class discussion about the differences and similarities between your class and the class in the photo.

Exercise 9: Writing

A
- Go over the example with the class.
- Assign the task for homework or give students time to leave class in order to complete their observations.

B
- Have students correct their work using the Editing Checklist. Then have them exchange papers and check their partner's work.
- Have students make any necessary corrections before handing in their papers.

OUT OF THE BOX ACTIVITIES

Speaking
- Have students play charades to practice forming the present progressive.
- Prepare sets of cards with present progressive verbs on them, for example:
  brushing your teeth   taking a shower
  eating a hamburger   baking a cake
  riding a horse
- Form small groups. Then hand out one set of cards to each group, placed face down on the table / desk.
- Students take turns choosing a card and miming the action for the group.
- Group members make guesses. (Example: *You're brushing your teeth.* [or use the question form: *Are you brushing your teeth?*])
- The first group to finish guessing all of the actions on their cards wins.

Speaking and Writing
- Play several scenes from a movie that show an actor doing a variety of actions.
- As students watch, they should use present progressive sentences to describe what's happening (either saying what's happening or writing it down). (Example: *A police officer is driving his car. He's stopping at a house. He's getting out of the car. He's walking to the house. He's knocking on the door. A woman is opening the door. She's talking to the police officer.*)

Writing
- Have students keep a journal in English.
- A few times a week, students should write in their journals, describing where they are and what's happening around them.

Go to **www.myfocusongrammarlab.com** for additional listening, pronunciation, speaking, and writing practice.

Note:
- See the *Focus on Grammar Workbook* for additional in-class or homework grammar practice.

Unit 15 Review (page 173)

Have students complete the Review and check their answers on Student Book page UR-3. Review or assign additional material as needed.

Go to **www.myfocusongrammarlab.com** for the Unit Achievement Test.

UNIT 16 OVERVIEW

Grammar: PRESENT PROGRESSIVE: *Yes / No* AND *Wh-* QUESTIONS

Unit 16 focuses on the structure and use of *yes / no* questions in the present progressive.

Theme: MOVIES

Unit 16 focuses on language and expressions used to describe the actions and themes in different movie genres.

Step 1: Grammar in Context (pages 174–176)

See the general suggestions for Grammar in Context on page 1.

Before You Read

A
- Introduce the topic of movies. Ask. "Where do you usually watch movies?" "What's a movie you'd like to see?" "Who are the actors in it?" "What kind of movie is it?"
- Have students check their favorite place to watch movies.
- Elicit responses from the class. Have students give reasons for their answers.

B
- Have students look at the three stamps. Call on a student to read the caption under each one.
- Elicit additional movie titles for each genre (Example: *Fantasy:* The Lord of the Rings, Twilight; *Romance:* Titanic; *Action:* The Bourne Identity, The Terminator)

- Have students check their preferred movie type and then compare answers in pairs. Encourage them to give reasons for their selections.

C
- Read the list of movie genres and have students repeat. Explain or elicit any unfamiliar vocabulary. Try to elicit movie titles to provide examples.
- Have students check the movie genres they like.
- Elicit students' movie preferences. Then have students tell the class about some of their favorite movies.

Read
- Have students look at the picture. Ask: "What movie is this scene from?" *(The Wizard of Oz)* Have students raise their hands if they have seen the movie. Elicit some information students know about the movie, for example, some of the characters' names and a basic summary of the plot.
- To encourage students to read with a purpose, write these questions on the board:
  1. Where is Abby? *(at home)*
  2. What is she doing? *(watching a DVD)*
  3. What's happening in the movie scene? *(Dorothy is meeting the Tin Man)*
  4. Where is Greg? *(at work)*
  5. How is Greg feeling? *(he thinks he's catching a cold)*
- Have students read the text. (OR: Play the audio and have students follow along in their books.) Then call on students to share their answers to the questions on the board.

After You Read

A. Practice
- Have students practice the conversation in pairs. Encourage them to close their books and try the conversation without looking. Stress that they do not need to use the exact words from the book. They can use their own words.
- Call on pairs to read the conversation for the class.

B. Vocabulary
- Read the words in the box and have students repeat.
- Have students complete the exercise individually.
- Have students compare answers in pairs. Then call on pairs to read the completed sentences.

C. Comprehension
- Have students complete the exercise in pairs. Make sure they understand that all of the sentences are false and they must change them to make them correct.
- Have them try to complete the task without looking back at the text.
- Call on pairs to give answers.

Go to **www.myfocusongrammarlab.com** for an additional reading, and for reading and vocabulary practice.

Step 2: Grammar Presentation (pages 177–178)

See the general suggestions for Grammar Presentation on page 2.

Grammar Charts
- Call on pairs to read the example sentences and answers in the charts.
- Write a *yes / no* question in large letters on a piece of paper. (Example: *Are we studying English right now?*) Cut the sentences into individual words and mix them up.
- Have a student arrange the words in the correct order. Repeat with two to three more questions.
- Drill the form of *yes / no* questions. Have students change statements into questions, for example:
  T: I'm teaching.
  Ss: Am I teaching?
  T: You're reading.
  Ss: Are you reading?
- Call on pairs to read the examples of *wh-* questions and answers.
- Repeat the procedure above using cut-up *wh-* questions.
- Drill the form of object-pattern *wh-* questions. Begin with a *yes / no* question. Then cue students with a *wh-* word. Have them form the new question, for example:
  T: Are you reading? What.
  Ss: What are you reading?
  T: Are you going? When.
  Ss: When are you going?
- Call on pairs to read the subject-pattern questions and answers.
- Ask: "Which *wh-* words can be used as subjects?" *(who and what)*
- Repeat the procedure from above using subject-pattern questions. To make it a little more challenging, cut up two questions and have a student sort them out.

- Drill as above. Provide a statement and have students transform it into a question, for example:
  T: Sarah is writing a composition. Who.
  Ss: Who is writing a composition?
  T: Something is burning. What.
  Ss: What is burning?

Grammar Notes

Note 1
- Have students read the note and examples.
- Have students work in pairs to write three or four new questions.
- Call on pairs to write their questions on the board.

Note 2
- Call on students to read the note and the examples.
- Have students think of a family member.
- Put students into small groups and explain that they will ask and answer questions about their classmates' family members.
- Write the following on the board:
  Who is . . .
  Why is . . .
  What is . . .
  Where is . . .
  When is . . .
- Model the activity with a student. Ask: "Who's your family member?" Then ask *wh-* questions about the person using the cues on the board. (Examples: *Where is your brother living now? Who is he living with? What is he studying? Where is he working?*)

Note 3
- To practice subject-pattern *wh-* questions, ask about students' relatives and friends.
- Have students think about people they know. Ask questions like the following:
  Who is sleeping now?
  Who is working?
  Who is studying?
- Elicit answers from the class.

- ⏱ **Identify the Grammar:** Have students identify the grammar in the conversation on page 175. For example:
  Are you resting?
  What are you watching?
  What's happening?

Go to **www.myfocusongrammarlab.com** for grammar charts and notes.

Step 3: Focused Practice (pages 178–180)
See the general suggestions for Focused Practice on page 4.

Exercise 1: Discover the Grammar

A
- Go over the example with the class.
- Have students turn back to the opening conversation and find three other *yes / no* questions.
- Have students compare answers in pairs. Then go over the answers as a class.

B
- "What two words could go in the first column?" (*who* or *what*)
- Have students complete the exercise individually.
- Draw the same chart on the board and call on students to come up and write in the answers.

Exercise 2: Present Progressive: *Yes / No* and *Wh-* Questions
- Go over the example with the class.
- Have students complete the exercise individually. Then have them compare answers in pairs.
- ⏱ Have pairs practice the entire conversation several times, changing roles. Then have them choose a movie that both students have seen and repeat the conversation substituting the movie title, actors' names, and scene description to fit that movie.

Exercise 3: Present Progressive: *Yes / No* and *Wh-* Questions
- Go over the example with the class. Then have students read the partial conversation and the question prompts quickly for meaning.
- Have students complete the exercise in pairs.
- ⏱ Have students practice the conversation in pairs, substituting Meryl Streep with any actor of their choice. Then call on pairs of students to role-play the conversation for the class without looking at the book.

Exercise 4: Common Two-Word Verbs
- Read the list of two-word verbs and have students repeat. Then go over the example with the class. Highlight that the questions are formed in the same way as for regular verbs. However, the preposition (particle) must be included after the *-ing* form.
- Review the importance of using the context to figure out which verb best fits the conversation.
- Have students complete the exercise individually. Then have them compare answers in pairs.

Exercise 5: Editing

- Go over the example with the class. Point out that they should find five more mistakes in the conversations.
- Have students find and correct the mistakes in pairs.
- Combine pairs to form groups of four and have students compare answers. Then call on students to read the corrected conversations. Have them explain why the incorrect structures are wrong.

Go to **www.myfocusongrammarlab.com** for additional grammar practice.

Step 4: Communication Practice (pages 181–183)

See the general suggestions for Communication Practice on page 5.

Exercise 6: Listening

A
- Make sure students understand that they should listen for which item Dan is shopping.
- Play the audio. Have students listen and circle their answer.

B
- Call on students to read the questions.
- Play the audio. Have students listen and write their answers. Then have students compare answers in pairs.
- (🕐) To extend the listening practice, write the following questions on the board. Then play the audio again and have students listen and say the answers.
  Why is Dan buying his father a DVD player? *(because his dad takes the train and loves movies)*
  Why does Dan's friend suggest a Blu-ray? *(because they don't cost much more than a DVD player)*
  Why is Dan "in luck"? *(because the store is having a sale this week)*

Exercise 7: Pronunciation

A
- Play the audio. Have students read along as they listen to the Pronunciation Note.

B
- Play the audio. Have students listen and repeat.
- Point out that *"a Master's Degree"* changes to *"an MA"* because "M" begins with a vowel sound.

C
- Play the audio. Have students listen and complete the exercise individually.
- Have students take turns reading the sentences in pairs.

D
- Play the audio. Have students listen and check their pronunciation.
- Play the audio again. Have students listen and repeat.

Exercise 8: Role Play

- You may want to go back to the opening conversation and tell students that they can use it as a model.
- To help with ideas, brainstorm with the class a list of popular movies they have seen. Encourage students to think about their favorite scene or a scene that was especially surprising, funny, suspenseful, or scary. Have each student choose a movie and scene so that they can take turns playing roles A and B.
- Have students complete the exercise in pairs.

Exercise 9: Describing Pictures

A
- Have students look at the picture. Ask: "What movie is this scene from?" *(The Wizard of Oz)*
- Have students work in pairs to use the present progressive to write questions about the picture.
- Combine pairs to form groups of four and have students ask and answer their questions.

B
- Have students complete the exercise individually.

C
- Go over the example with the class.
- Have students take turns describing their own sketches to their partners. Partners listen and try to draw what they hear being described. Stress that they may ask questions, for example:
  Is she holding the basket in her right hand or her left hand?
  What is the man wearing?

Exercise 10: Writing

A
- Have students read the questions quickly for meaning.
- Have students complete the exercise in pairs.

B
- Go over the example with the class.
- Have students complete the exercise individually.

C
- Have students correct their work using the Editing Checklist.
- Then have students exchange papers and check their partner's work.

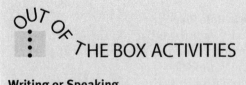

OUT OF THE BOX ACTIVITIES

Writing or Speaking
- Tell students to watch a movie they have never seen and do a movie review.
- Have the class decide on an icon to use as a rating system. (Example: *stars, popcorn kernels, thumbs up / down*)
- Have students write a brief review of the movie, describing the characters and their favorite (or least favorite) scenes.
- Reviews can be posted on a class blog or in a class newsletter.
- To do this as a speaking activity, have students role-play movie critics on a TV or Internet-based show.

Go to **www.myfocusongrammarlab.com** for additional listening, pronunciation, speaking, and writing practice.

Note:
- See the *Focus on Grammar Workbook* for additional in-class or homework grammar practice.

Unit 16 Review (page 184)

Have students complete the Review and check their answers on Student Book page UR-3. Review or assign additional material as needed.

Go to **www.myfocusongrammarlab.com** for the Unit Achievement Test.

UNIT 17 OVERVIEW

Grammar: SIMPLE PRESENT AND PRESENT PROGRESSIVE; NON-ACTION VERBS

Unit 17 compares and contrasts the meanings and contextual uses of the simple present and the present progressive, as well as the use of non-action (stative) verbs.

Theme: SMARTPHONES

Unit 17 focuses on language and expressions used to talk about features of modern electronic devices, such as smartphones, and popular Internet technologies such as social networking sites.

Step 1: Grammar in Context (pages 185–186)

See the general suggestions for Grammar in Context on page 1.

Before You Read
- Have students look at the pictures and tell you what they see. Have them describe the various ways people in the pictures are using their cell phones.
- As a class, brainstorm ways / situations in which cell phones can be used. Write students' ideas on the board. (Example: *to find a friend in a crowd, to make a call in an emergency situation, as an alarm clock, as a calendar, as a clock / watch / stopwatch, to check the weather, to check sports scores, to listen to music, to watch movies or TV*)
- Use the two discussion questions and students' ideas on the board to lead a class discussion. Ask some or all of the following questions:
  What do you use your cell phone for most often?
  Have you ever used it in an emergency?
  Tell about a time when you were very glad you had your cell phone.
  Tell about a time when you needed your cell phone but didn't have it.
  Would you be able to give up your cell phone?

Read
- Tell students they will read an online article about today's cell phones. Then preview the glossed vocabulary at the bottom of the article.
- Have students read the text. (OR: Play the audio and have students follow along in their books.)

- Ask some questions to generate discussion about the article:
  What features do you wish your cell phone had?
  Do you think Emily, Michael, and Robert's wishes might come true in the future?
  What interesting features do you think future cell phones might have?

After You Read

A. Practice
- Have students complete the exercise in pairs.
- Then call on pairs to read paragraphs aloud.

B. Vocabulary
- Have students read the sentences and answer choices quickly for meaning.
- Have students complete the exercise individually.
- Have students compare answers in pairs. Then go over the answers as a class and have students explain how they decided on the answers.

C. Comprehension
- Have students read the questions and answer choices quickly for meaning.
- Have students complete the exercise individually. Encourage them to do so without looking back at the text.
- Have students compare answers in pairs. Then call on students to give answers.

Go to **www.myfocusongrammarlab.com** for an additional reading, and for reading and vocabulary practice.

Step 2: Grammar Presentation (pages 187–188)

See the general suggestions for Grammar Presentation on page 2.

Grammar Charts
- On the board, write an example present progressive sentence from the opening article. (Example: *He's texting a friend.*)
- Call on a student to read the example on the board. Ask: "What is the verb?" *(is texting)* "When is it happening?" *(right now)*
- Call on students to read the simple present sentences in the chart. Ask: "How often does the person eat at 8:00?" Elicit time expressions like *every day, usually, always.* Contrast the simple present and the present progressive. Elicit that the simple present is used to talk about habits and actions that happen regularly. Elicit similar statements with action verbs. (Example: *I take the bus to work. She reads the newspaper in the morning. Franklin gets up early.*)

- Call on students to read the present progressive sentences in the chart. Elicit the verb and the time *(right now)* for each one.
- Have students look around the class and give you several examples of present progressive sentences. (Example: *The students are listening to the teacher. Mugdha is looking out the window. Paolo is writing in his notebook.*)
- Elicit an example of a simple present sentence from the opening article. (Example: *He needs a ride to a party that evening.*) Elicit the verb *(needs)* and the time *(now)*.
- Say: "The action is happening right now. Can we use the present progressive?" *(no)* Explain that non-action verbs do not use the present progressive.
- Have students look at the opening article and give you examples of action verbs (Examples: *text, take, check*) and non-action verbs (Examples: *be, have, want*).
- Have students read the list of non-action verbs in the chart.

Grammar Notes

Notes 1 and 2
- Call on students to read the notes and examples.
- Ask: "Which tense do we use to talk about activities that are usual, habitual, or normal?" *(simple present)* "Which tense do we use to talk about something that is happening right now?" *(present progressive)*
- Elicit five or six action verbs and write them on the board.
- Have students work in pairs to write a simple present sentence and a present progressive sentence for each verb. Then have them join another pair to share their sentences.

Note 3
- Have students read the note and the examples.
- Elicit other examples of non-action verbs.

Notes 4 and 5
- Before students read Note 4, ask: "What is the difference between an action verb and a non-action verb?" *(Action verbs describe actions; non-action verbs describe feelings, thoughts, possession, etc.)*
- Do a quick drill to help students differentiate between the two types of verbs. Provide verbs and subjects and have students give you either the simple present form (for non-action verbs) or the present progressive form (for action verbs). Example:
  T: Want. She.
  Ss: She wants.
  T: Play. I.
  Ss: I am playing.

⏱ **Identify the Grammar:** Have students identify the grammar in the reading on page 185. For example:

People under 30 **don't know** a world without them.

They **come** in all colors and shapes

The man **is taking** a photo with his phone.

Go to **www.myfocusongrammarlab.com** for grammar charts and notes.

Step 3: Focused Practice (pages 189–190)

See the general suggestions for Focused Practice on page 4.

Exercise 1: Discover the Grammar

- Go over the example with the class. Ask: "Why is *has* underlined twice?" *(because it is a non-action verb)*
- To help students focus on the verb forms first, suggest that they first go through and underline the simple present and circle the present progressive forms and *then* go back and add a second underline to the non-action verbs.
- Have students complete the exercise in pairs. Then call on pairs to give answers.

Exercise 2: Simple Present; Non-Action Verbs; Present Progressive

- Have students read the conversation quickly for meaning. Call on students to say whether each verb in parentheses is an action or a non-action verb.
- Have students complete the exercise individually. Remind students to use contractions when possible.
- Call on pairs to read the completed conversation.

Exercise 3: Simple Present; Non-Action Verbs; Present Progressive

- Have students read the conversation quickly for meaning.
- Have students complete the exercise individually and go over answers as a class.
- Call on two students to read the conversation to the class.

Exercise 4: Simple Present; Non-Action Verbs; Present Progressive

- Read the list of verbs in the box. Have students repeat and then tell you whether each one is an action or a non-action verb.
- Go over the example with the class.
- Have students complete the exercise in pairs. Then call on students to read the completed paragraph aloud.

Exercise 5: Editing

- Go over the example with the class. Point out that they should find five more mistakes in the paragraph.
- Have students find and correct the mistakes in pairs.
- Combine pairs to form groups of four and have students compare answers. Then call on students to read the corrected passage. Have them explain why the incorrect structures are wrong.

Go to **www.myfocusongrammarlab.com** for additional grammar practice.

Step 4: Communication Practice (pages 191–193)

See the general suggestions for Communication Practice on page 5.

Exercise 6: Listening

A
- Play the audio. Have students listen and write their answers in the chart.
- Call on students to give answers, explaining how they got their answers.

B
- Play the audio. Have students listen and complete the messages.
- Have students compare answers in pairs. Then go over the answers as a class.

Exercise 7: Pronunciation

A
- Play the audio. Have students read along as they listen to the Pronunciation Note. Explain that intonation is the *tone* we use to say something, that is, the emotion or feeling we express with our voice. To demonstrate, write the following on the board:
  A: How are you?
  B: Fine.
- Have several students ask you: "How are you?" Each time answer using a different tone, for example:
  S1: How are you?
  T: Fine! (cheerful)
  S2: How are you?
  T: Fine . . . (sighing, sad)
  S3: How are you?
  T: Fine! (irritated / angry)

B
- Play the audio. Have students listen and complete the exercise individually.
- Play the audio again. Have students listen and confirm their answer.

C
- Play the audio. Have students listen and complete the exercise individually.
- Play the audio again. Have students listen and confirm their answer.

D
- Have students complete the exercise in pairs.

Exercise 8: Conversation
- Go over the example with the class. Then have students read the other scenarios quickly for meaning.
- Brainstorm as a class some words and phrases for students to use in their discussions. (Example: *I think . . . What do you think . . . ? probably . . .*)
- Have students complete the exercise in pairs. Stress that there are no right or wrong answers for this activity. Students should feel free to make guesses.

Exercise 9: Survey
A
- Call on students to read the phrases. Explain any unfamiliar vocabulary.
- Form small groups. Have students in each group complete the matching exercise.
- ⏱ Take a class poll about the activities shown in pictures. Ask: "How many of you use social networking sites / read e-books / have a landline?" Have students raise their hands.

B
- Go over the example with the class.
- Have students complete the survey individually. Remind them to write both their preferences and their reasons.

C
- Go over the example with the class.
- Form small groups. Have students in each group complete the exercise.

Exercise 10: Writing
A
- Go over the example with the class.
- Have students write several sentences about each picture.
- Have students compare answers in pairs.

B
- Elicit situations when or reasons why students need to do many things at once. (Example: *when you are very busy, when you are at work, when you are riding the bus or train*) Then tell students about a time when you do several things at once. (Example: *At home in the evening, I often listen to music, drink tea, and correct English papers.*) Write the sentence on the board and ask: "What tense did I use?" *(simple present)* "Why?" *(because the action is regular / not happening right now)*
- Have students use the simple present to write about times they do many things at once.

C
- Have students correct their work using the Editing Checklist.
- Then have students exchange papers and check their partner's work.
- ⏱ Collect the papers and have students bring in a photo of themselves. Compile the paragraphs and photos into a class newsletter and make a copy for each student in the class.

OUT OF THE BOX ACTIVITIES

Writing
- Give students a field observation assignment.
- Have them go to a public place such as the cafeteria, a mall, a park, or a train station and observe people.
- As they observe, they should take notes on what people are doing. They should also guess why the people are doing those actions. (Example: *A man is running. He doesn't want to miss the train. A woman is walking into a clothing shop. She needs a new coat. A little boy is crying. He feels sad because he dropped his ice cream.*)

Go to **www.myfocusongrammarlab.com** for additional listening, pronunciation, speaking, and writing practice.

Note:
- See the *Focus on Grammar Workbook* for additional in-class or homework grammar practice.

Unit 17 Review (page 194)

Have students complete the Review and check their answers on Student Book page UR-4. Review or assign additional material as needed.

Go to **www.myfocusongrammarlab.com** for the Unit Achievement Test.

From Grammar to Writing (page 195)

See the general suggestions for From Grammar to Writing on page 9.

Go to **www.myfocusongrammarlab.com** for an additional From Grammar to Writing Assignment, Part Review, and Part Post-Test.

PART VI OVERVIEW

SIMPLE PAST

UNIT	GRAMMAR FOCUS	THEME
18	Simple Past: Affirmative and Negative Statements with Regular Verbs	Travel
19	Simple Past: Affirmative and Negative Statements with Irregular Verbs	You Never Know
20	Simple Past: *Yes / No* and *Wh-* Questions	Interviews

Go to **www.myfocusongrammarlab.com** for the Part and Unit Tests.

Note: PowerPoint® grammar presentations, test-generating software, and reproducible Part and Unit Tests are on the *Teacher's Resource Disc*.

UNIT 18 OVERVIEW

Grammar: SIMPLE PAST: AFFIRMATIVE AND NEGATIVE STATEMENTS WITH REGULAR VERBS

Unit 18 focuses on the structure and use of the simple past in affirmative and negative statements with regular verbs, as well as past time markers *(yesterday, last week, a month ago)*.

Theme: TRAVEL

Unit 18 focuses on language and expressions used to narrate past travel experiences.

Step 1: Grammar in Context (pages 198–199)

See the general suggestions for Grammar in Context on page 1.

Before You Read

- Have students look at the pictures of the tourist attractions. Call on a student to name the places. Assist with pronunciation as necessary.
- Have students discuss the question in pairs.
- ⏱ Lead a brief class discussion about which countries students want to visit and why.

Read

- Have students read the messages quickly for meaning.
- To encourage students to read with a purpose, write these questions on the board:
  1. Where are Karen and Julian? How do you know? *(Rio de Janeiro; because they mention Ipanema Beach and Sugarloaf)*
  2. What kind of game did they see? *(foot-volley)*
  3. What is Sugarloaf? *(a mountain)*
  4. What is a *churrascuria*? *(a barbecued meat restaurant)*
  5. How was their flight? *(bad, bumpy)*
  6. How is their room? *(beautiful)*
  7. What is the relationship between Karen and Dahlia? *(coworkers)*
- Have students read the text. (OR: Play the audio and have students follow along in their books.) Then call on students to share their answers to the questions on the board.

After You Read

A. Practice
- Have students complete the exercise in pairs.
- Call on pairs to read the messages.

B. Vocabulary
- Have students read the words in the box for meaning.
- Have students complete the exercise individually. Then have them compare answers in pairs.
- Go over the answers as a class and have students explain how they decided on the answers.

C. Comprehension
- Go over the example with the class. Then have students read the statements quickly for meaning. Make sure they understand that all of the statements contain false information.
- Have students complete the exercise individually. Encourage them to do so without looking back at the text.

- Have students compare answers in pairs. Then call on students to write the corrected statements on the board.

Go to **www.myfocusongrammarlab.com** for an additional reading, and for reading and vocabulary practice.

Step 2: Grammar Presentation (pages 200–201)

See the general suggestions for Grammar Presentation on page 2.

Grammar Charts

- Call on students to read the example sentences in the first two charts.
- Ask: "How do we form the regular past tense?" (*by adding -ed to the base form*) "How do we form the negative?" (did not / didn't + *base form*)
- Recite the complete conjugation with the verb walk (*I walked, you walked, he walked,* etc.) in both the affirmative and the negative. Then ask: "Does the form of the past tense change from singular to plural?" *(no)* "Is it the same for all persons?" *(yes)*
- On the board, write:
  yesterday   ago   last
- Model several sentences with these time expressions. Use a common verb such as *talk.* (Example: *I talked to my mother yesterday morning. I also talked to her two days ago. I didn't talk to her last week because she was out of town.*)
- Have the class brainstorm a list of additional past time expressions. Write students' ideas on the board.
- Call on several students to form similar sentences with different verbs and time expressions. You may want to provide verbs for them to use. (Example: *call, check email, exercise, visit*)
- Do a transformation drill, from affirmative to negative and vice-versa, as follows:
  T: I talked to my mother.
  Ss: I didn't talk to my mother.
  T: Alice called a friend.
  Ss: Alice didn't call a friend.
  T: We didn't watch a movie.
  Ss: We watched a movie.
  T: They didn't walk to work.
  Ss: They walked to work.

Grammar Notes

Note 1

- Prepare a handout of regular verbs for students to use in this unit. Alternatively, write the list on the board or dictate it and have students write it in their notebooks. Here are some useful verbs:

answer	help	study
arrive	hurry	travel
brush	learn	type
call	like	use
change	listen	visit
check (email)	live	walk
decide	open	wash
enjoy	play	watch
exercise	rain	work
finish	relax	worry
happen	start	

- Call on a student to read the note and the examples.
- Draw the following timeline on the board.

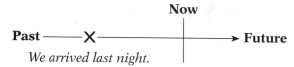

We arrived last night.

- Ask: "When did we arrive?" *(last night)* "Are we arriving now?" *(no)* Say: "No, the action is finished."
- Put students into pairs and have them use their list of verbs to think of two more true examples of actions they finished yesterday or last night. Have them make simple past sentences using time expressions, for example:
  Sanjit exercised last night.
  We both worked yesterday.
- Elicit several examples from the class and write them on the board.

Note 2

- Call on a student to read the note and the examples.
- Have students work in pairs to deduce the spelling rules from the examples. Elicit students' ideas and write them on the board. Ask guiding questions to elicit the correct rules:
  Which ending do we use for regular verbs ending in a consonant? *(-ed)*
  Which ending do we use for regular verbs ending in *y* when the *y* is pronounced /iy/? *(-ied)*
  What do we do before we add the *-ied*? (drop the *-y*)
  Which ending do we use for regular verbs ending in *e*? *(d)*

- Have students use the list of verbs provided in Note 1 to write the past forms.
- Elicit the answers from the class.
- Dictate the following sentences and have students write them:
  We hurried to class.
  My friends surprised me.
  The teacher ended class on time.
  John and Jim played chess yesterday.
  She watched TV last night.
  Kim cooked breakfast this morning.
- Have students exchange papers and correct any errors.
- Call on students to write the correct verb forms on the board.

Notes 3 and 4

- Call on a student to read the notes and the examples.
- To review the negative forms, have students play a game of Two Truths and One Lie. (This will prepare students for the similar activity in Step 4: Communication Practice.)
- Model the task on the board. Write three negative simple past sentences about yourself. Two statements must be true and one must be false, for example:
  I didn't visit Spain a year ago
  I didn't watch TV last night.
  I didn't eat breakfast this morning.
- Have the class guess which sentences are true and false.
- Have students write three negative simple past statements about themselves; two should be true and one should be false.
- In pairs, have students exchange papers and try to guess which sentences are true and which are false.
- To follow up, call on students to share information about their partners. (Example: *Sheri didn't ride her bicycle to school today.*)

Note 5

- Call on students to read the note and the examples.
- Reinforce the position of time markers by asking students to form a few sentences about what they did yesterday. Call on a student to say a sentence. Then transform it, for example:
  T: What did we study yesterday morning?
  S1: We studied the past tense yesterday morning.
  T: What's another way of saying it?
  S2: Yesterday morning we learned the past tense.

- Have the class brainstorm a list of ten to twelve past time expressions. Write them on one side of the board. Then elicit a list of regular verbs and write the base forms on the other side of the board.
- Call on students to make sentences by selecting a time expression and a verb from the board. If the sentence is correct, cross off the time expression and the verb. Then call on the next student. Make this a game by dividing the class into two teams. Give teams 1 point for each correct sentence.

🕐 **Identify the Grammar:** Have students identify the grammar in the reading on page 198. For example:
  Yesterday morning Julian and I **watched** foot-volley on Ipanema Beach.
  Then in the afternoon we **visited** Sugarloaf.
  . . . we **didn't land** until 11:30 at night.

Go to **www.myfocusongrammarlab.com** for grammar charts and notes.

Step 3: Focused Practice (pages 201–205)

See the general suggestions for Focused Practice on page 4.

Exercise 1: Discover the Grammar

A
- Go over the example with the class.
- Have students complete the exercise individually.
- Elicit first the affirmative forms and then the negative forms and write them on the board.

B
- Have students complete the exercise in pairs. To add an element of competition, have pairs race to find all five past time expressions. They should raise their hands when they have done so.
- Elicit the time expressions and write them on the board.
- 🕐 Have students use the time expressions and verbs listed on the board (from Parts A and B) to create new sentences.

Exercise 2: Affirmative Statements
- Call on students to read the verbs in the box. Then go over the example with the class.
- Have students complete the exercise individually.
- Call on students to read the completed sentences. Have the rest of the class listen and make corrections as necessary.

Exercise 3: Negative Statements

- Have students complete the exercise in pairs. Then call on students to read the completed sentences.
- ⏱ To extend the practice, write the following on the board:
  During my last vacation:
  travel
  stay home
  visit another country
  exercise
  watch TV
  study
  learn a language
  call home
  work
- Form small groups. Have students in each group take turns using the verbs on the board to make affirmative and negative statements about their last vacation, for example:
  S1: During my last vacation, I traveled.
  S2: I didn't travel, I stayed home.
  S3: I didn't stay home. I visited another country—Canada!

Exercise 4: Affirmative and Negative Statements

- Have students read the paragraph quickly for meaning. Then go over the example with the class.
- Have students complete the exercise in pairs.
- ⏱ Have students read the completed passage again silently. Then have them close their books and tell you about Camila's trip, for example:
  S1: Camila traveled to San Francisco.
  S2: It rained.
  S3: She shopped at Fisherman's Wharf.

Exercise 5: Past Time Markers

- Go over the example with the class.
- Have students complete the exercise in pairs. Then call on pairs to read portions of the conversation.
- ⏱ Have students practice the conversation in pairs, changing roles and partners several times.

Exercise 6: Simple Past and Simple Present Statements

- Go over the example with the class. Ask: "How will you know when to use the simple past?" *(look for past time markers)*
- Have students complete the exercise in pairs.
- Call on pairs to read the conversation. Have the rest of the class listen and make any necessary corrections.

Exercise 7: Editing

- Go over the example with the class. Point out that they should find five more mistakes in the postcard.
- Have students find and correct the mistakes in pairs.
- Combine pairs to form groups of four and have students compare answers. Then call on students to read the corrected passage. Have them explain why the incorrect structures are wrong.

Go to **www.myfocusongrammarlab.com** for additional grammar practice.

Step 4: Communication Practice (pages 205–207)

See the general suggestions for Communication Practice on page 5.

Exercise 8: Listening

A
- Have students look at the picture. Say: "You're going to hear about Marta's trip. This is a picture of where she stayed. What country do you think she visited?" Elicit answers from students, but do not correct any incorrect guesses at this point.
- Go over the example with the class. Then have students read the statements quickly for meaning.
- Play the audio. Have students listen and complete the exercise individually.

B
- Play the audio. Have students listen and complete the exercise individually.
- Have students compare answers in pairs. Then elicit the answers from the class.

Exercise 9: Pronunciation

A
- Play the audio. Have students read along as they listen to the Pronunciation Note.

B
- Draw a three-column chart on the board. Add the headings as follows:

/d/	/t/	/ɪd/

- Say several verbs with different ending sounds. (Example: *played /d/; landed /ɪd/; tried /d/; watched /t/; wanted /ɪd/*) Have students listen for the ending of the verbs and tell you which sound they hear. Write the verbs in the appropriate columns on the board. Have the class brainstorm additional verbs for each category on the board.
- Demonstrate the difference between the three ending sounds. Say: */d/, /t/, /ɪd/* and have students repeat.
- Play the audio. Have students listen and complete the exercise individually.
- Have students compare answers in pairs. Then play the audio again and have students confirm their answers.

C
- Have students complete the exercise in pairs.
- Call on students to tell the class about their partner's weekend.

Exercise 10: Game: Truths and Lies

A
- Go over the example with the class.
- Have students complete the exercise individually.

B
- Go over the example with the class.
- Have students take turns reading their sentences in small groups. Group members guess which sentence is false.

Exercise 11: Writing

A
- Go over the example with the class. Have students identify examples of the simple past as well as past time markers.
- To help them begin to write, have students make some notes about what to include in their postcard. (Example: *where they went during their vacation, what they did, who they went with*)
- Have students complete the exercise individually.

B
- Have students correct their work using the Editing Checklist.
- Then have students exchange papers and check their partner's work.
- ⏱ Have students design the front of their postcard to show a sight they saw during their trip. Pass the postcards around so students can see and read about one another's vacations.

OUT OF THE BOX ACTIVITIES

Reading and Speaking
- Have students find travel blogs or travel review websites. Alternatively, bring in travel magazines or travel sections of newspapers.
- Have students read the information, noting any examples of simple past statements and time expressions.
- Have students imagine they went on a trip to the place and write down what they saw, did, ate, and so on.
- Have students talk about their imaginary trips in pairs.

Go to **www.myfocusongrammarlab.com** for additional listening, pronunciation, speaking, and writing practice.

Note:
- See the *Focus on Grammar Workbook* for additional in-class or homework grammar practice.

Unit 18 Review (page 208)

Have students complete the Review and check their answers on Student Book page UR-4. Review or assign additional material as needed.

Go to **www.myfocusongrammarlab.com** for the Unit Achievement Test.

UNIT 19 OVERVIEW

Grammar: SIMPLE PAST: AFFIRMATIVE AND NEGATIVE STATEMENTS WITH IRREGULAR VERBS

Unit 19 focuses on the structure and use of the simple past in affirmative and negative statements with irregular verbs and *be*.

Theme: YOU NEVER KNOW

Unit 19 focuses on language and expressions used to narrate and discuss folktales and other stories with unexpected or surprising endings.

Step 1: Grammar in Context (pages 209–210)

See the general suggestions for Grammar in Context on page 1.

Before You Read
- Call on a student to read the quotation and the question.
- Have students discuss their ideas in pairs. Then elicit the answer from the class.
- Lead a brief class discussion about any folktales, stories, books, or movies students know of that have surprise endings.

Read
- Have student read the title of the folktale. Ask students what they think the story is about.
- To encourage students to read with a purpose, write these questions on the board:
  1. Where did this folktale happen? *(China)*
  2. What did the farmer say when the horse appeared? *(You never know what will happen.)*
  3. What happened two days later? *(The horse ran away.)*
  4. How did the farmer feel? *(He didn't get excited.)*
  5. What happened a week later? *(The horse returned with three other horses.)*
  6. What happened to the peasant's son? *(A horse ran into him, and he hurt his leg.)*
  7. What happened a month later? *(Soldiers took all the young, healthy men to fight.)*
  8. What happened to the young men? *(They were all killed.)*
  9. What happened to the peasant's son? *(Nothing. He lived a long and happy life.)*
- Have students read the text. (OR: Play the audio and have students follow along in their books.) Then call on students to share their answers to the questions on the board.

After You Read

A. Practice
- Have pairs take turns reading the paragraphs of the folktale.
- Call on students to read the folktale to the class.

B. Vocabulary
- Read the words in the box and have students repeat. Then have students read the sentences quickly for meaning.
- Have students complete the exercise individually.
- Have students compare answers in pairs. Then call on students to read the completed sentences

C. Comprehension
- Go over the example with the class. Then have students read the sentences quickly for meaning.

- Have students complete the exercise in pairs. Encourage them to do so without looking back at the text.
- Combine pairs to form groups of four and have students compare answers. Have groups go back to the text and discuss any that are in question.

Go to **www.myfocusongrammarlab.com** for an additional reading, and for reading and vocabulary practice.

Step 2: Grammar Presentation (page 211)

See the general suggestions for Grammar Presentation on page 2.

Grammar Charts
- Write several examples of simple past statements from the reading on the board. Include both regular and irregular verbs and at least one negative example. Call a student to the board.
- Ask other students to read each sentence and identify the verb. The student at the board should underline the verbs.
- For each affirmative verb, ask: "Is it regular or irregular?" Elicit the base forms of the regular verbs. Then try to elicit the base forms of any irregular verbs students may recognize.
- For the negative example, ask: "Is there any difference in form between regular and irregular verbs?" *(no)*
- Call on students to read the examples in the charts.
- Ask: "What are the affirmative past forms of *be*?" *(was, were)* "What are the negative forms?" *(wasn't, weren't)*

Grammar Notes

Note 1
- Because English has so many irregular verbs, you will need to help students learn them in manageable chunks. One way to do this is to choose several verbs a day for students to memorize and practice. You can choose the verbs from an alphabetical list, or you can present groups of verbs with the same morphology. (Example: *the* -aught *verbs such as* teach / taught *and* catch / caught)
- To begin, make a handout of the verbs in this chapter. (Students may also refer to the list of irregular verbs in Appendix 11 on page A-11.)

be	find	see
become	give	sell
begin	go	sit
bring	have	speak
buy	know	stand
come	lose	take
do	make	teach
eat	meet	tear
fall	(re)build	understand
feel	ride	write
fight	run	

- Call on students to read Note 1 and the examples.
- Say the base form and the past form of the verbs on the handout. Have students repeat.
- Say only the base form of each verb. Have students say the past form. Then reverse the order.
- Have students work in pairs. Have them drill each other. One student says the base form, and the other says the past form.

Note 2

- Have students read the note and the examples. Remind students that regular and irregular verbs are the same in the negative.
- Draw attention to the *Be Careful!* note. Remind students to use the base form after *didn't*.
- Drill. Say the base form of a verb from the handout in Note 1. One student says the affirmative, and another student says the negative, for example:
  T: I say.
  S1: I said.
  S2: I didn't say.

Note 3

- Call on a student to read the note and the examples.
- Conduct a transformation drill. Alternate between persons and affirmative / negative, for example:
  T: I was sick yesterday. He.
  Ss: He was sick yesterday.
  T: Negative.
  Ss: He wasn't sick yesterday.
  T: We.
  Ss: We weren't sick yesterday.
- Write a list of adjectives on the board. Put students in pairs or groups. Have them use adjectives and *was / wasn't* to make true sentences about themselves. (Example adjectives: *late, early, absent, sick, tired, worried, happy, cold*)

Note 4

- Say: "I was born on October 10. I was born in Los Angeles."

- Go around the room and have students repeat the sentence with their own birth dates and places.
- Call on a student to read the note and the examples.

Identify the Grammar: Have students identify the grammar in the reading on page 209. For example:
  When the peasant's friends **saw** the horse they **said**, . . .
  Two days later the horse **ran** away.
  And it **brought** three other horses.

Go to **www.myfocusongrammarlab.com** for grammar charts and notes.

Step 3: Focused Practice (pages 212–215)

See the general suggestions for Focused Practice on page 4.

Exercise 1: Discover the Grammar

- Go over the example with the class. Tell students that they can refer to the handout (if you have given them one) and / or the list of irregular verbs in Appendix 11 on page A-11.
- Have students complete the exercise individually.
- Have students make similar statements about a family member's success story. Ask: "Did you or did any of your brothers or sisters do something that surprised your parents?"

Exercise 2: Simple Past: Irregular Verbs

- Ask students: "Who was Abraham Lincoln?"
- Have students complete the exercise individually. Go over answers as a class.
- Ask students if any leaders of their country came from backgrounds similar to Lincoln's.

Exercise 3: Simple Past: Irregular Verbs

- Ask: "Do you know who James Earl Jones is?" "What movies have you seen him in?" Then have students read the paragraphs quickly for meaning. Go over any key vocabulary, such as *stutter, by heart, scholarship, admired*.
- Have students complete the exercise in pairs. Then combine pairs to form groups of four and have students compare answers.
- Have students close their books and tell what they remember from the passage about James Earl Jones.

Exercise 4: Simple Past: Irregular Verbs

- Go over the example with the class. Then call on a student to read the verbs in the boxes.

- Have students complete the exercise individually. Then go over the answers as a class.
- (⏱) Have students close their books and tell what they remember from the passage about Joanne Kathleen.

Exercise 5: Editing
- Go over the example with the class. Point out that they should find eight more mistakes in the paragraph.
- Have students find and correct the mistakes in pairs.
- Combine pairs to form groups of four and have students compare answers. Then call on students to read the corrected passage. Have them explain why the incorrect structures are wrong.

Go to www.myfocusongrammarlab.com for additional grammar practice.

Step 4: Communication Practice (pages 215–217)
See the general suggestions for Communication Practice on page 5.

Exercise 6: Listening

A
- Call on a student to read the sentence and answer choices.
- Play the audio. Have students listen and mark their answers.
- Elicit the answer from the class.

B
- Have students read the sentences quickly for meaning.
- Play the audio. Have students listen and complete the exercise individually.
- Have students compare answers in pairs. Then call on students to read the complete sentences.

Exercise 7: Pronunciation

A
- Play the audio. Have students read along as they listen to the Pronunciation Note.
- Say the / æ / sound several times and have students repeat, first chorally and then individually.

B
- Play the audio. Have students listen and repeat.
- Call on individual students to say the target words.

C
- Highlight the contrast between the two sounds. Say both sounds in isolation and have students repeat. Then elicit words that contain each sound.
- Play the audio. Have students listen and complete the exercise individually.
- (⏱) Have students make sentences using the target words and then say them for the class.

Exercise 8: A Memory Game
- Go over the example with the class.
- Form small groups. Have students in each group play the game.
- This game can also be played as a ball-toss activity. Bring a medium-sized soft ball or bean bag to class. Have students stand in a circle. After the first student says a sentence, he or she throws the ball to the next student, who says a sentence and then tosses the ball to another student, and so on.

Exercise 9: Discussion
- Call on students to read the instructions and the examples.
- You may want to give students some time to make notes about what happened on their wonderful and terrible days.
- Have students work in groups of three or four.
- Have students take turns sharing their stories.
- Call on students to report on another group member's day.

Exercise 10: Writing

A
- Have students read the questions quickly for meaning. Then go over the example with the class.
- To help them as they begin to write, have students make notes as they think about the questions.
- Have students complete the exercise individually.

B
- Have students correct their work using the Editing Checklist.
- Then have students exchange papers and check their partner's work.
- (⏱) Have students read their autobiographies to the class or in small groups. Alternatively, play a guessing game. Collect the papers and remove the students' names. Then hand them out randomly. Have students read the autobiography and have the class guess the author.

OUT OF THE BOX ACTIVITIES

Speaking

- Have students play a charades game called What Happened? with past tense irregular verbs.
- Make a set of cards with the following phrases on them:
  You broke your leg.
  You lost your wallet.
  You ate something spicy.
  You went fishing and caught a big fish.
  You found some money.
  You got an A+ on your English test.
  You saw a ghost.
  A friend gave you a present.
- Have a student come up to the front and choose one card to mime for the class. The student should mime the action as though it has just happened to him or her.
- The rest of the class tries to guess the sentence on the card.

Go to **www.myfocusongrammarlab.com** for additional listening, pronunciation, speaking, and writing practice.

Note:
- See the *Focus on Grammar Workbook* for additional in-class or homework grammar practice.

Unit 19 Review (page 218)

Have students complete the Review and check their answers on Student Book page UR-4. Review or assign additional material as needed.

Go to **www.myfocusongrammarlab.com** for the Unit Achievement Test.

Grammar: SIMPLE PAST: *Yes / No* AND *Wh-* QUESTIONS

Unit 20 focuses on the structure and use of the simple past in *yes / no* and *wh-* questions, and long and short answers to simple past questions.

Theme: INTERVIEWS

Unit 20 focuses on language and expressions used to conduct interviews and respond to questions during an interview.

Step 1: Grammar in Context (pages 219–221)

See the general suggestions for Grammar in Context on page 1.

Before You Read

- Books closed. Write the two quotations on the board and call on a student to read them. Ask: "Do you know these lines?" "Who wrote them?" If students give the correct answer, ask: "What play are they from?"
- Have students open their books. Call on a student to read the information below the quotes.
- Elicit any additional information they know about Shakespeare, such as where he was from, what plays he wrote, and so on. Ask: "Many people say Shakespeare is the greatest writer in the English language. Do you agree?"

Read

- Have a student read the interview. Elicit the meaning of the glossed words.
- To encourage students to read with a purpose, write these questions on the board:
  1. Why does Professor Gibbons say that Shakespeare's life is a mystery? *(There are many things we don't know about him.)*
  2. What are some of the examples of things we do *not* know about Shakespeare? *(his exact birthdate, how he knew about royal life, whether he wrote all of his own plays)*
  3. What does it mean when a writer uses a pen name? *(He / She uses a different name.)*
- Have students read the text. (OR: Play the audio and have students follow along in their books.) Then call on students to share their answers to the questions on the board.

After You Read

A. Practice
- Have students complete the exercise in pairs.
- Call on a pair to read the interview.

B. Vocabulary

- Read the words in the box and have students repeat.
- Have students find the words in the interview. Elicit the sentences in which the words are used.
- Have students complete the exercise individually. Then go over the answers as a class and have students explain how they decided on the answers.

C. Comprehension

- Have students read the questions and answer choices quickly for meaning.
- Have students complete the exercise individually. Encourage them to do so without looking back at the text.
- Have students compare answers in pairs. Have them point out the information in the text that answers the questions.

Go to **www.myfocusongrammarlab.com** for an additional reading, and for reading and vocabulary practice.

Step 2: Grammar Presentation (pages 222–223)

See the general suggestions for Grammar Presentation on page 2.

Grammar Charts

- Call on students to read the examples of *yes / no* questions and answers.
- Write the examples of the target grammar on the board. Ask: "How do we form *yes / no* questions in the simple past?" (Did + *subject* + *verb*) "How do we answer a *yes / no* question in the simple past in the affirmative?" (Yes, + *subject* + did) "In the negative?" (No, + *subject* + didn't)
- Call on a student to read the examples of *wh-* questions and answers. Ask: "What is the word order in *wh-* questions about the object?" (wh- *word* + did + *subject* + *verb*)
- Have students look at the last grammar chart. Ask: "What's the word order of *wh-* questions about the subject?" (wh- *word* + *verb* + *object*) Point out that the *wh-* word is the subject in these questions.
- Remind students that questions have the same word order in the present and in the past. Write contrasting sentences on the board:
  Does he have a dog? / Did he have a dog?
  Where do you live? / Where did you live?

Grammar Notes

Note 1

- Call on a student to read the notes and the examples.
- To drill the form of *yes / no* questions, provide a statement and have students transform it into a question. Use a mix of regular and irregular verbs, for example:
  T: I made a cake.
  Ss: Did you make a cake?
  T: Alice lived in Sydney.
  Ss: Did Alice live in Sydney?
- Repeat the drill with sentences with *be*, for example:
  T: We were cold.
  Ss: Were you cold?
  T: The teacher was late.
  Ss: Was the teacher late?
- Have students write the name of their favorite English book or movie on an index card. Put all the cards in a box, bag, or hat.
- Have a student draw one card out of the box, read it, and make a statement and question. (Example: *I didn't see* Twilight. *Candace, did you see* Twilight?)
- The student should answer truthfully, for example:
  Yes, I did. / No, I didn't.
  Yes, I saw it, but I didn't like it.
  No, I didn't see it, but I want to.
- Then the next student should draw another card out of the box and ask the next question.
- Continue until all students have asked and answered a question.

Notes 2 and 3

- Call on a student to read the notes and the examples.
- Before class, arrange for one student to help you with this part of the lesson. Ask this student to pretend to have been in an accident. The student can limp, or you can tie up the student's arm in a bandage.
- To begin, write *who, what, when, where, why, how, whom, how long* on the board.
- Say: "Poor [Alex]. He had an accident. [Alex,] come up here." Alex should then limp up to the front of the class.
- Ask Alex *wh-* questions about the accident. (Example: *What happened? Where did it happen? Who was with you?*)
- Have students ask additional questions.
- Have a pair of students role-play a similar situation. Again, encourage students to ask questions.

- In pairs, have students interview each other about a true event that happened to them. (Example: *a time when they got hurt or when something funny or embarrassing happened to them*)
- Walk around the room and note any errors you hear. When students finish, write sentences on the board with the errors you heard. Have students copy them and then correct them for homework.

Note 4
- Point out that short answers are the same in the present and past tenses, except for the form of *do*:
  Do you live with your parents? *(Yes, I do. / No, I don't.)*
  Did you live with your parents? *(Yes, I did. / No, I didn't.)*
- You may want to teach students other (more informal) expressions often used by native English speakers to mean *yes* or *no*, for example:
  Yes: yeah, yup, uh-huh, mm-hmm
  No: nope, nah, uh-uh, mm-mm
- Have students ask you some simple *yes / no* and *wh-* questions. Answer them.
- Have students in pairs do the same. Encourage them to have fun with the questions and answers, for example:
  S1: Jana, did you study English last night?
  S2: Yup! How about you?
  S1: Nope.

⏱ **Identify the Grammar:** Have students identify the grammar in the conversation on page 219, for example:
  . . . why did you write the book?
  . . . was his education good enough?
  How did Shakespeare learn to write so well?

Go to **www.myfocusongrammarlab.com** for grammar charts and notes.

Step 3: Focused Practice (pages 223–226)

See the general suggestions for Focused Practice on page 4.

Exercise 1: Discover the Grammar

A
- Have students complete the exercise individually.
- Have students compare answers in pairs.
- Elicit the base forms of the verbs from the class. Then have them give answers to the questions.

B
- Have a student read the answers from the box. Then have students read the questions quickly for meaning.
- Have students complete the exercise in pairs.
- Call on pairs to read the completed conversations.

Exercise 2: Simple Past: *Yes / No* Questions
- Go over the example with the class. Then ask: "What will the first word of every question be?" *(did)*
- Have students complete the exercise individually. Then have them compare answers in pairs.
- Have students write the questions on the board. Correct any errors.

Exercise 3: Simple Past: Short Answers
- Go over the example with the class. Remind students that the information given at the end of the question will tell them whether they should answer in the affirmative or the negative.
- Have students complete the exercise individually.
- Have students compare answers in pairs. Then call on pairs to read the questions and answers.

Exercise 4: Simple Past Questions
- Go over the example with the class. Then have students read the interview quickly for meaning.
- Have students complete the exercise in pairs. Then go over the answers as a class.
- ⏱ Have pairs come up with three or four additional interview questions to include in the interview and then role-play the interview for the class.

Exercise 5: Editing
- Go over the example with the class. Point out that they should find nine more mistakes in the questions and answers.
- Have students find and correct the mistakes in pairs.
- Combine pairs to form groups of four and have students compare answers. Then call on students to read the corrected passage. Have them explain why the incorrect structures are wrong.

Go to **www.myfocusongrammarlab.com** for additional grammar practice.

Step 4: Communication Practice (pages 227–229)

See the general suggestions for Communication Practice on page 5.

Exercise 6: Pronunciation

A

- Play the audio. Have students read along as they listen to the Pronunciation Note.
- Say the two sounds in isolation and have students repeat, first chorally and then individually.
- Write the following rhyming pairs of words (minimal pairs) on the board in two columns. Then have students practice saying them.

/dʒ/	/y/
jam	yam
Jack	yak
jewel	yule
Jess	yes

B

- Play the audio. Have students listen and repeat.

C

- Model the first item with a student. Say one of the sentences from Part A and prompt the student to choose the appropriate response.
- Have students complete the exercise in pairs.
- Call on pairs to say the sentences and responses.

D

- Go over the example with the class. Then have students read the sentences quickly for meaning.
- Play the audio. Have students listen and complete the exercise individually.
- Have students compare answers in pairs. Then call on students to read the sentences, focusing on careful pronunciation of the target sounds.

Exercise 7: Listening

A

- Have students read the questions and answer choices quickly for meaning.
- Play the audio. Have students complete the exercise individually.
- Have students compare answers in pairs. Then call on pairs to give answers.

B

- Have students read the text quickly for meaning.
- Play the audio. Have students complete the exercise in pairs.

- ⏱ If you or any of the students have seen the movie *Shakespeare in Love*, extend the practice by having the rest of the class ask you questions about the actors, plot, and other details of the movie.

Exercise 8: Describing a Performance or Event

- Go over the instructions with the class.
- Call on two students to read the model conversation.
- Before students interview one another, you may want to give students time to think and make notes about their event, for example, when and where it was, who they were with, what happened, etc.
- Have pairs take turns interviewing their partner. Encourage them to take notes on their partner's answers.
- Combine pairs to form groups of four and have students take turns telling about their partner's event. Encourage students to ask questions to find out more information.
- Call on students to report on one very interesting or exciting event from their group.

Exercise 9: Writing

A

- Form small groups. Have students in each group work together to complete the chart.
- Brainstorm as a class a few additional names for each column of the chart.

B

- Go over the example with the class.
- Have students complete the exercise individually.

C

- Have students correct their work using the Editing Checklist.
- Then have students exchange papers and check their partner's work.
- ⏱ Have students use the Internet or the library to find the answers to their questions.

OUT OF THE BOX ACTIVITIES

Reading and Speaking

- Have students work in pairs. Have them choose one of the famous people from the chart in Exercise 9.
- Tell students they will role-play a TV talk show interview. Have students choose the role of the celebrity or the talk show host.
- Have students brainstorm interview questions and answers. You may want to have them use the Internet or the library to research answers to their questions. Alternatively, have them be creative and make up funny or outrageous answers.
- Have pairs practice their role-play and then perform it for the class.

Go to **www.myfocusongrammarlab.com** for additional listening, pronunciation, speaking, and writing practice.

Note:
- See the *Focus on Grammar Workbook* for additional in-class or homework grammar practice.

Unit 20 Review (page 230)

Have students complete the Review and check their answers on Student Book page UR-4. Review or assign additional material as needed.

Go to **www.myfocusongrammarlab.com** for the Unit Achievement Test.

From Grammar to Writing (pages 231–232)

See the general suggestions for From Grammar to Writing on page 9.

Go to **www.myfocusongrammarlab.com** for an additional From Grammar to Writing Assignment, Part Review, and Part Post-Test.

PART VII OVERVIEW

VERB REVIEW AND CONTRAST AND EXPANSION

UNIT	GRAMMAR FOCUS	THEME
21	Simple Past Review	Biographies
22	Gerunds and Infinitives	Careers and Abilities
23	Simple Present, Present Progressive, and Simple Past	Creativity

Go to **www.myfocusongrammarlab.com** for the Part and Unit Tests.

Note: PowerPoint® grammar presentations, test-generating software, and reproducible Part and Unit Tests are on the *Teacher's Resource Disc*.

UNIT 21 OVERVIEW

Grammar: SIMPLE PAST REVIEW

Unit 21 provides a review of all aspects of the simple past, including affirmative and negative statements and *yes / no* and *wh-* questions.

Theme: BIOGRAPHIES

Unit 21 focuses on language and expressions used to ask questions about life events and give biographical information.

Step 1: Grammar in Context (pages 234–235)

See the general suggestions for Grammar in Context on page 1.

Before You Read
- Read the list of words in the box and have students repeat. Then go over the example with the class.
- Have students complete the exercise in pairs.
- Tell the class which of the qualities describe you. Give examples: "I think I'm very loyal. I am always there to help my friends." Ask: "Do any of these words describe you?" and elicit responses and examples from several students.

Read
- Introduce the article. Ask: "Has anyone heard of the famous dog named 'Hachiko'?" Elicit any information students may know about the dog. Then go over the glossed vocabulary at the end of the article.

- Have students read the text. (OR: Play the audio and have students follow along in their books.)
- Have students close their books and have the class give you a brief summary of the article in their own words.

After You Read

A. Practice
- Have students work in pairs and take turns reading the article.
- Call on students to read paragraphs of the article to the class.

B. Vocabulary
- Have students complete the exercise individually. Then have them compare answers in pairs.
- Go over the answers as a class and have students explain how they decided on the answers.

C. Comprehension
- Have students complete the exercise individually. Encourage them to do so without looking back at the text.
- Have students compare answers in pairs.
- Call on students to give answers. After each answer, ask: "What are some other details that you remember from the article?" Try to elicit several more details for each item.

Go to **www.myfocusongrammarlab.com** for an additional reading, and for reading and vocabulary practice.

Step 2: Grammar Presentation (pages 236–237)

See the general suggestions for Grammar Presentation on page 2.

Grammar Charts
- Before class, prepare a handout that includes the following headings. (Alternatively, write the headings on the board and have students copy them into their notebooks.) Leave space after each heading for students to write example sentences underneath.
  Simple Past:
  Affirmative Statements
  Affirmative Statements with *Be*
  Negative Statements
  Negative Statements with *Be*
  Yes / No Questions
  Yes / No Questions with *Be*
  Wh- Questions
  Wh- Questions with *Be*
  Wh- Questions About the Subject
  Wh- Questions About the Subject with *Be*

- Have students work in pairs to write two sentences for each heading. One sentence must be an example from the Student Book, either from the unit opener text or from any of the exercises in Units 18 through 21. The other sentence must be the student's own original sentence.
- Do not go over the sentences yet, as students will use them in the next step.

Grammar Notes

Notes 1–7
- Draw attention to the *Be Careful!* note.
- Write the 10 headings from the previous steps on slips of paper and put the slips in a hat.
- Form small groups. Then have a member of the first group choose a slip from the hat and read the heading. The group must then find a corresponding sentence in the Notes.
- If the chosen sentence is correct, the group gets a point. If it is incorrect, the other teams may each try and receive 1 point for their correct sentence.
- Continue until all of the slips have been taken from the hat.
- Have students turn to the charts on page 236 and have them check and correct their sentences from the previous exercise.

🕐 **Identify the Grammar:** Have students identify the grammar in the reading on page 234. For example:
  Hachiko **was** an Akita Inu dog.
  Hachiko **was born** in 1923.
  Every morning Uyeno and Hachiko **walked . . .**

Go to **www.myfocusongrammarlab.com** for grammar charts and notes.

Step 3: Focused Practice (pages 238–242)

See the general suggestions for Focused Practice on page 4.

Exercise 1: Discover the Grammar
- Go over the example with the class. Then have students read the conversation quickly for meaning.
- Have students complete the exercise individually. Then have them compare answers in pairs.
- Call on students to write the statements on the board. Have the rest of the class check and correct them as necessary.

Exercise 2: Affirmative and Negative Statements
- Go over the example with the class. Then have students read the conversation quickly for meaning.

- Have students complete the exercise individually. Then have them compare answers in pairs.
- (!) Have students work in pairs to create an interview role play. Have them use the text to develop interview questions for Pierre Omidyar, for example:
  Where were you born?
  What did your parents do?
  Where did you go to college?

Exercise 3: Affirmative and Negative Statements
- Have students complete the exercise individually. Then have them compare answers in pairs.
- (!) To extend the practice, have pairs write quiz questions for which the answers can be found in the article, for example:
  Did Anne Schreiber have many close friends?
  Where did she live?
  What did she wear?
  How much money did she make from investing?
- Books closed. Have pairs take turns asking another pair their quiz questions. Teams get 1 point for each correctly answered question. The aim is to get more points than the other pair.

Exercise 4: Simple Past: Questions and Answers
A
- Have students read the text quickly for meaning. Then go over the example with the class. Ask: "Since these questions are asking for information, what type of word will be at the beginning of each sentence?" (a wh- word)
- Have students complete the exercise in pairs. Then call on pairs to write their questions on the board.
- Books closed. Call on students to select a question from the board, read it, and give the answer from the text.

B
- Have students complete the exercise. Then have them compare answers in pairs.
- Go over answers as a class.

Exercise 5: Editing
- Go over the example with the class. Point out that they should find ten more mistakes.
- Have students find and correct the mistakes in pairs.
- Combine pairs to form groups of four and have students compare answers. Then call on students to read the corrected passage. Have them explain why the incorrect structures are wrong.

Go to **www.myfocusongrammarlab.com** for additional grammar practice.

Step 4: Communication Practice (pages 243–246)
See the general suggestions for Communication Practice on page 5.

Exercise 6: Pronunciation
A
- Play the audio. Have students read along as they listen to the Pronunciation Note.

B
- Play the audio. Have students listen and repeat.

C
- Play the audio. Have students listen and repeat.
- (!) Have students practice asking the following questions in pairs. They should give true answers for themselves. Encourage them to ask for repetition if they don't understand the verb.
  Did you work last week?
  How long did you walk this morning?
  Did you walk fast or slow today?
  Did you ever work all night?
  Why didn't you work yesterday?

Exercise 7: Listening
A
- Have students read the question and answer choices silently.
- Play the audio. Have students circle their answer.
- Go over the answer as a class.

B
- Have students read the text quickly for meaning.
- Play the audio. Have students listen and complete the exercise individually. Alternatively, you may want to play the audio once and have students just focus on the questions. Then play it again for them to write the answers.
- Have students compare answers in pairs. Then elicit the questions and answers from the class.

Exercise 8: A Quiz Show
- Go over the example with the class. Then brainstorm categories to help guide students. (Example: *movies and actors, books, world history, famous artists*)
- Form small groups. Have groups write their questions and choose a host.

- Call on a group to start the quiz show. The host stands and asks a question. Students raise their hands and try to answer.

Exercise 9: What Were You Like as a Child?

- Go over the example with the class. Then review the vocabulary for personal qualities by asking questions to elicit the vocabulary. (Example: *What does an athletic person like to do? What do you do a lot if you are talkative?*)
- Have students complete the exercise in pairs.
- Call on students to report on their partner's answers. (Example: *When Tina was a child, she wasn't athletic. She studied very hard.*)

Exercise 10: Information Gap: Guess the Musician

- Have students work in pairs and have students choose A and B roles.
- Have Students B turn to page 246.

1.
- Have Students A read their paragraphs.
- Have Students B write questions to ask Students A. Students A answer.
- You may want to encourage Students B to take notes on the answers to help them figure out who the person is.

2.
- Have Students B read their paragraphs.
- Have Students A write questions to ask Students B. Students B answer.
- You may want to encourage Students A to take notes on the answers to help them figure out who the person is.

Exercise 11: Writing

A
- To help them begin to write, have students make some notes about what to include in their biography. (Example: *where and when the person was born, who discovered them, what their first popular song was*)
- You may want to prepare some selected music websites to suggest to students and have students do Internet research on their musicians, print photos, and so on.
- Have students complete the exercise individually.

B
- Have students correct their work using the Editing Checklist.
- Then have students exchange papers and check their partner's work.
- Have students present their biographies to the class.

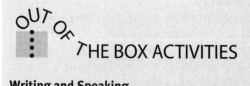

OUT OF THE BOX ACTIVITIES

Writing and Speaking
- Have students interview a family member, preferably an older one such as a grandparent, to find out about their lives.
- Have them make a timeline showing significant events in the person's life: when they were born, when / where they went to college, when they got married, when they had children, and any other important events.
- Have students present their timelines to the class.

Go to **www.myfocusongrammarlab.com** for additional listening, pronunciation, speaking, and writing practice.

Note:
- See the *Focus on Grammar Workbook* for additional in-class or homework grammar practice.

Unit 21 Review (page 247)

Have students complete the Review and check their answers on Student Book page UR-4. Review or assign additional material as needed.

Go to **www.myfocusongrammarlab.com** for the Unit Achievement Test.

UNIT 22 OVERVIEW

Grammar: GERUNDS AND INFINITIVES

Unit 22 focuses on the structure and use of gerunds and infinitives and common verbs used with gerunds, infinitives, or both.

Theme: CAREERS AND ABILITIES

Unit 22 focuses on language and expressions used to express career interests and job preferences.

Step 1: Grammar in Context (pages 248–250)

See the general suggestions for Grammar in Context on page 1.

Before You Read

- Have students look at the pictures. Ask: "What are these people doing?" "What are their jobs?"
- Read the questions and lead a class discussion about fashion industry jobs. Ask: "What skills or qualities do people need for these jobs?" "What do you think you would like or dislike about these kinds of jobs?"

Read

- Encourage students to consult their peers about any unfamiliar vocabulary. Then go over any remaining unknown words.
- To encourage students to read with a purpose, write these questions on the board:
  1. What is a good job for a person who likes to learn? (scientist, anthropologist, writer, teacher)
  2. Do chefs enjoy working with their hands? (Yes, they do.)
  3. Do many musicians have unpredictable lives? (Yes, they do.)
  4. How is an attorney similar to a professional athlete? (They are both competitive.)
  5. Which jobs require casual clothes? (carpenter, auto mechanic, farmer, child care worker)
  6. Which jobs are good if you enjoy working with people? (doctor, police officer, attorney, politician, child care worker, teacher, guidance counselor, psychologist or social worker, physical therapist, hotel manager)
- Have students read the text. (OR: Play the audio and have students follow along in their books.) Then call on students to share their answers to the questions on the board.

After You Read

A. Practice
- Have students read the exercise in pairs.
- Then call on pairs to read paragraphs aloud.

B. Vocabulary
- Have students complete the exercise individually. Then have them compare answers in pairs.
- Elicit the answers from the class and have students explain how they decided on the answers.

C. Comprehension
- Have students complete the exercise in pairs. Encourage them to do so without looking back at the text.
- Go over the answers as a class.

Go to **www.myfocusongrammarlab.com** for an additional reading, and for reading and vocabulary practice.

Step 2: Grammar Presentation (page 251)

See the general suggestions for Grammar Presentation on page 2.

Grammar Charts
- Write the following example sentences from the reading on the board:
  I like to learn . . .
  I hope to continue learning . . .
  I enjoy working with my hands.
  I expect to do something different . . .
  I hate losing.
  I can't stand wearing a suit.
  I avoid wearing formal clothes.
- Underline the verb in each example.
- Call on students to read each example sentence. In each case, ask: "What comes after the underlined verbs?" (verb + -ing or to + verb) Use two different colors to underline the gerund or infinitive in each example. Introduce the terms infinitive and gerund.
- Ask: "What part of the sentence are the gerunds and infinitives?" (direct object) Help students understand that in these examples the gerunds and infinitives are nouns even though they look like verbs.
- Call on students to read the examples in the charts.
- Have students work in pairs to divide the verbs in the examples into two groups: those followed by gerunds and those followed by infinitives. (gerund: enjoy, hate, can't stand, avoid; infinitive: like, hope, expect)
- Ask: "Which verbs in the examples can be followed by both?" (hate, like)

Grammar Notes

Note 1
- Call on students to read the note and the examples.
- Direct students to the left column of the previous chart of verbs. Provide an example sentence for each verb to clarify the meanings of the verbs.
- Give the class a context, such as housework. Then go down the list of verbs and elicit a sentence about each, for example:
  T: Avoid.
  S: I avoid washing dishes.

Note 2

- Repeat the procedure for Note 1.
- Have students work in pairs. Have them use the target pattern and as many of the verbs as possible to write a short dialogue about a vacation. You may want to write the first line or two on the board, for example:
  FLORA: Do you intend to go on vacation this year, Avi?
  AVI: Yes, I hope to go to Spain.

Note 3

- Have students read the note and the examples. Then have them look at the right column of the verb chart at the top of the page of the Student Book.
- Have students do a transformation drill. Cue them with verbs and have them form sentences with gerunds and infinitives, for example:
  T: Hate.
  S1: I hate to run.
  S2: I hate running.
  T: Like.
  S3: I like to eat.
  S4: I like eating.
- Have students sit in pairs or small groups. Have them form sentences with contrasting ideas using a gerund in one part and an infinitive in the other, for example:
  I hate washing dishes, but I love to cook.
  I like to go to the movies, but I don't like watching TV.
- Go around the room and have each student say one sentence.

(ᵀ) **Identify the Grammar:** Have students identify the grammar in the reading on pages 248–249. For example:
  I like **to learn new things**.
  I **enjoy working** with my hands.
  I **hate losing**.

Go to **www.myfocusongrammarlab.com** for grammar charts and notes.

Step 3: Focused Practice (pages 252–254)

See the general suggestions for Focused Practice on page 4.

Exercise 1: Discover the Grammar

- Go over the example with the class. Ask: "How do you know this is a gerund?" (-ing) "What will tell you if it's an infinitive?" (to + base form)
- Have students complete the exercise individually. Then have them compare answers in pairs.

- Ask: "Which verb in this list is followed by both the infinitive and the gerund?" (prefer)

Exercise 2: Infinitives

- Go over the example with the class. Say: "You are going to use the infinitive for this exercise. Are the forms of these verbs going to change?" (no) "What are you going to add?" (to).
- Have students complete the exercise individually.
- Call on students to read the completed sentences.

Exercise 3: Gerunds

- Go over the example with the class. Ask: "What are you going to do to make these verbs gerunds? (add -ing) Then go over the spelling rule: Before adding -ing, drop the silent -e. Elicit the verbs that this will apply to. (leave, take)
- Have students complete the exercise individually. Then have them compare answers in pairs.
- Ask: "Can any of these sentences be formed with infinitives?" (number 4)

Exercise 4: Gerunds and Infinitives

- Go over the example with the class. Then have students read the text quickly for meaning.
- Have students complete the exercise in pairs. Then call on pairs to give answers.
- (ᵀ) Have students practice the conversation, substituting other verbs and careers besides acting / actor. Give them some ideas. (Example: *studying law / lawyer, playing computer games / game designer*) Have them change and adjust the rest of the conversation appropriately. Call on pairs to present their new conversations to the class.

Exercise 5: Gerunds and Infinitives

- Go over the example with the class.
- Have students complete the exercise individually.
- Have students compare answers in pairs. Then call on students to read the completed sentences.

Exercise 6: Editing

- Go over the example with the class. Point out that they should find six more mistakes in the letter.
- Have students find and correct the mistakes in pairs.

- Combine pairs to form groups of four and have students compare answers. Then call on students to read the corrected passage. Have them explain why the incorrect structures are wrong.

Go to **www.myfocusongrammarlab.com** for additional grammar practice.

Step 4: Communication Practice (pages 254–256)

See the general suggestions for Communication Practice on page 5.

Exercise 7: Pronunciation

A
- Play the audio. Have students read along as they listen to the Pronunciation Note.

B
- Play the audio. Have students listen and repeat.

C
- Model the first item with a student.
- Have students complete the exercise in pairs.
- Call on pairs to say the sentences and responses.

Exercise 8: Listening

A
- Call on a student to read the question and answer choices.
- Play the audio. Have students listen and mark their answers.
- Go over the answers as a class.

B
- Have students read the statements quickly for meaning.
- Play the audio. Have students listen and complete the exercise individually.
- ⏲ Hand out the audioscript and have students practice the conversation in pairs.

Exercise 9: Discussion: Likes
- Go over the example with the class.
- Have students complete the categories with things they like or enjoy.
- Have students complete the exercise in pairs.

Exercise 10: Game: What Do I Do?
- Go over the example with the class.
- Form small groups. Give groups time to think of an occupation and at least six to eight hints.
- Call on a group to begin giving their hints. Each group member should participate in giving the hints. Other groups try to guess the job. Continue until all groups have given hints.

Exercise 11: Problem Solving: Finding the Right Job
- Have students read the questions quickly for meaning.
- Have pairs interview each other. Encourage students to ask additional questions to get more information and to take notes on their partner's answers. Then have pairs discuss possible future jobs for each person, based on their answers to the questions.
- Call on pairs to report on the jobs they discussed and why. (Example: *Carla would be a good artist. She likes to do her own thing. She can't stand wearing a suit. She enjoys working with her hands.*)

Exercise 12: Writing

A
- Go over the example with the class.
- To help them begin to write, have students make some notes about what to include in their paragraph. (Example: *things they enjoy doing, things they can't stand, their special talents and skills*)
- Have students complete the exercise individually.

B
- Have students correct their work using the Editing Checklist.
- Then have students exchange papers and check their partner's work.

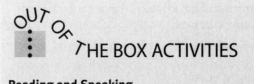

OUT OF THE BOX ACTIVITIES

Reading and Speaking
- Bring in the help-wanted section from the newspaper, or have students browse job search websites online.
- Have students review the qualifications for different jobs and discuss whether each job would be appropriate for them and why or why not. Remind them to use gerunds or infinitives in their answers.

Go to **www.myfocusongrammarlab.com** for additional listening, pronunciation, speaking, and writing practice.

Note:
- See the *Focus on Grammar Workbook* for additional in-class or homework grammar practice.

Unit 22 Review (page 257)

Have students complete the Review and check their answers on Student Book page UR-5. Review or assign additional material as needed.

Go to **www.myfocusongrammarlab.com** for the Unit Achievement Test.

UNIT 23 OVERVIEW

Grammar: SIMPLE PRESENT, PRESENT PROGRESSIVE, AND SIMPLE PAST

Unit 23 reviews and contrasts the structures and uses of the simple present, present progressive, and simple past tenses.

Theme: CREATIVITY

Unit 23 focuses on language and expressions used to talk about creativity, inventions, and innovative ideas and approaches to doing things.

Step 1: Grammar in Context (pages 258–259)

See the general suggestions for Grammar in Context on page 1.

Before You Read

A
- Have students look at the words.
- Choose one item and have the class brainstorm ideas for ways to use it. Encourage them to be creative and humorous. (Example: *You can use a hairdryer to keep away insects, clean papers off your desk, and fly a kite indoors.*)
- Form small groups. Have students complete the exercise in groups.

B
- Call on groups to give their answers.
- Have the class vote on the most interesting / clever idea for each item.

Read
- Before students read, elicit a definition of *creativity. (looking at something in a new or unusual way)* Say: "In the previous exercise, you all used creativity to think of new uses for everyday objects."
- Have students read the online article. (OR: Play the audio and have students follow along in their books.)
- To follow up, lead a brief class discussion. Ask: "What are some examples of other creative ideas?" Discuss any famous inventors or inventions from students' cultures.

After You Read

A. Practice
- Have students complete the exercise in pairs.
- Then call on pairs to read paragraphs.

B. Vocabulary
- Have one student read the words from the box aloud.
- Have students complete the exercise individually and compare answers in pairs.
- Go over the answers as a class and have students explain how they decided on the answers.

C. Comprehension
- Have students complete the exercise individually. Encourage them to do so without looking back at the text.
- Have students compare answers in pairs. Have them point out the information in the text that supports their answers.
- Call on students to read the questions and give the answers. Have students correct the false statements to make them true.

Go to **www.myfocusongrammarlab.com** for an additional reading, and for reading and vocabulary practice.

Step 2: Grammar Presentation (pages 260–261)

See the general suggestions for Grammar Presentation on page 2.

Grammar Charts
- Write the following chart on the board and have students copy it into their notebooks, leaving space to write in each column:

	Affirmative	**Negative**
Simple Present		
Present Progressive		
Simple Past		

- Starting with the simple present, dictate two or three verbs for each tense and have students write one affirmative and one negative sentence for each verb in the chart. For the present progressive, use at least one verb ending in silent -e. (Example: *take, make, drive*) For the simple past, select regular verbs with different endings (Example: *play [-ed], use [-e], hurry [-ied]*) as well as an example or two of irregular verbs.
- Have students compare their sentences in pairs.
- Call on students to write their sentences on the board. Correct any errors as necessary.
- Say the following time markers and have students give you a sentence in the appropriate tense (example answers are given in parentheses):
  a week ago (*I played tennis a week ago.*)
  right now (*We're cooking right now.*)
  usually (*She usually walks to work.*)
  every Tuesday (*John works every Tuesday.*)
  last month (*They went on vacation last month.*)
  sometimes (*Sometimes we have dinner at a restaurant.*)
  this very minute (*The plane is arriving this very minute.*)
  yesterday morning (*I saw Tim yesterday morning.*)

Grammar Notes

Notes 1–3
- Use the descriptions in the notes to create a cloze review handout. Retype the notes, leaving key information blank. Then have students work in pairs to complete the exercise, for example:
  Use the _____ to tell about **things that happen again and again** or to **tell facts**.
  Use the simple present with _____ **verbs**.
- Have students check their answers on page 261. Then call on students to read the example sentences.
- Answer any questions students may have about the structures, meanings, or uses of the verbs.

(!) **Identify the Grammar:** Have students identify the grammar in the reading on page 258. For example:
  Krazy Glue® **is** a new kind of glue.
  In fact, it can **glue** your fingers together.
  Nowadays doctors **are** still **using** a kind of Krazy Glue during surgery.

Go to **www.myfocusongrammarlab.com** for grammar charts and notes.

Step 3: Focused Practice (pages 261–263)
See the general suggestions for Focused Practice on page 4.

Exercise 1: Discover the Grammar
- Have students read the text quickly for meaning.
- Have students complete the exercise individually. Then have them compare answers in pairs.
- Make three columns on the board with the three verb tenses as headings. Then call on students to write the verbs in the correct columns.

Exercise 2: Simple Present and Simple Past
- Go over the example with the class. Then have students read the text quickly for meaning.
- Have students complete the exercise individually. Then have them compare answers in pairs.
- Call on pairs to read the conversation, inserting the answers. Have the rest of the class listen and make corrections as necessary.

Exercise 3: Simple Present, Present Progressive, and Simple Past
- Have students read the text quickly for meaning, underlining any time markers they find. Then go over the example with the class.
- Have students complete the exercise in pairs. Then combine pairs to form groups of four and have students compare answers.
- (!) To extend the practice, lead a brief class discussion. Ask: "What information in this article was interesting to you? What surprised you?"

Exercise 4: Editing
- Go over the example with the class. Point out that they should find six more mistakes in the paragraph.
- Have students find and correct the mistakes in pairs.
- Combine pairs to form groups of four and have students compare answers. Then call on students to read the corrected passage. Have them explain why the incorrect structures are wrong.

Go to **www.myfocusongrammarlab.com** for additional grammar practice.

Step 4: Communication Practice (pages 263–266)

See the general suggestions for Communication Practice on page 5.

Exercise 5: Listening

A

- Have students read the text quickly for meaning.
- Play the audio. Have students listen and circle their answer.
- Elicit the answer from the class.

B

- Have students read the questions and answer choices quickly for meaning.
- Play the audio. Have students listen again and complete the exercise in pairs.
- Go over the answers with the class.

Exercise 6: Pronunciation

A

- Play the audio. Have students read along as they listen to the Pronunciation Note.

B

- Play the audio again. Have students listen and repeat.

C

- Go over the example with the class. Then have students complete the exercise in pairs.
- Have the class brainstorm additional compound nouns and write them on the board, for example:
  taxi driver
  bus stop
  department store
  computer bag
  coffee maker

Exercise 7: Information Gap

- In pairs, have students choose A and B roles.
- Have Students B turn to page 266.

1.

- Have Students A ask Students B questions to complete their charts.

2.

- Have Students B ask Students A questions to complete their charts.

3.

- Form small groups. Have students in each group discuss the questions.

Exercise 8: Writing

A

- Go over the example with the class. Make sure students understand that they should imagine they are writing in a future time about things that are happening in the present and things that happened in the past.
- Have students complete the exercise individually.

B

- Have students correct their work using the Editing Checklist.
- Then have students exchange papers and check their partner's work.
- Encourage students to make corrections before handing in their papers.

OUT OF THE BOX ACTIVITIES

Reading, Writing, and Speaking

- Have students choose a modern invention they are interested in. (Example: *cell phone, PDA, Internet, GPS*) Have students research the history of the invention, who invented it and where, how it became popular, how it has changed over the years, how it's used now, and so on.
- Have students write a report on the invention and present it in class.

Go to **www.myfocusongrammarlab.com** for additional listening, pronunciation, speaking, and writing practice.

Note:

- See the *Focus on Grammar Workbook* for additional in-class or homework grammar practice.

Unit 23 Review (page 267)

Have students complete the Review and check their answers on Student Book page UR-5. Review or assign additional material as needed.

Go to **www.myfocusongrammarlab.com** for the Unit Achievement Test.

From Grammar to Writing (page 268)

See the general suggestions for From Grammar to Writing on page 9.

Go to **www.myfocusongrammarlab.com** for an additional From Grammar to Writing Assignment, Part Review, and Part Post-Test.

PART VIII OVERVIEW

THE FUTURE

UNIT	GRAMMAR FOCUS	THEME
24	*Be Going to* for the Future	City and Campus Planning
25	*Will* for the Future; Future Time Markers	Predicting the Future
26	*May* or *Might* for Possibility	Weather

Go to **www.myfocusongrammarlab.com** for the Part and Unit Tests.

Note: PowerPoint® grammar presentations, test-generating software, and reproducible Part and Unit Tests are on the *Teacher's Resource Disc*.

UNIT 24 OVERVIEW

Grammar: *Be Going to* FOR THE FUTURE

Unit 24 focuses on the structure and meaning of *be going to* for the future, including affirmative and negative statements, *yes / no* and *wh-* questions, and short and long answers.

Theme: CITY AND CAMPUS PLANNING

Unit 24 focuses on language and expressions used to describe and express reactions to future plans for changes and improvements to public places.

Step 1: Grammar in Context (pages 270–271)

See the general suggestions for Grammar in Context on page 1.

Before You Read

- Introduce the "Letters to the Editor" section of the newspaper. If possible, bring in an English newspaper and show an example. Ask: "What kinds of letters do people write?" (*letters expressing opinions about current events*) Read one or two examples to the class.
- Go over the example with the class.
- Have students complete the exercise in pairs. Then call on pairs to give their answers.

Read

- Introduce the letters. Say: "You're going to read letters from two college students about the same issue." Then go over the glossed vocabulary at the end of the letters.
- To encourage students to read with a purpose, write these questions on the board:
  1. Where did these letters appear? (*in a college newspaper*)
  2. What are they about? (*a new fitness center*)
  3. Which writer is against it? (*the first one*)
  4. Why is this person against it? (*It's going to cost a lot of money, so tuition is probably going to increase.*)
  5. How does the other writer feel? (*She loves the idea.*)
  6. Why is she in favor of it? (*The gym will help students relax. Also, if they use the gym, they will not gain weight.*)
- Have students read the text. (OR: Play the audio and have students follow along in their books.) Then call on students to share their answers to the questions on the board.

After You Read

A. Practice
- Have students complete the exercise in pairs.
- Then call on pairs to read the paragraphs.
- ⏱ Lead a class discussion. Ask: "Which writer do you agree with?" If your school has a fitness center, ask: "Do you use the fitness center? How often? What do you do there?" If not, ask: "Would you like to have a fitness center on campus? Even if it meant paying higher tuition?"

B. Vocabulary
- Have students complete the exercise individually.
- Have students compare answers in pairs.
- Go over the answers as a class and have students explain how they decided on the answers.

C. Comprehension

- Go over the words *for* and *against* in this context (agreeing and disagreeing). Then go over the example with the class.
- Have students complete the exercise in pairs.
- Combine pairs to form groups of four and have students compare answers. Then call on students to give answers.

Go to **www.myfocusongrammarlab.com** for an additional reading, and for reading and vocabulary practice.

Step 2: Grammar Presentation (pages 272–273)

See the general suggestions for Grammar Presentation on page 2.

Grammar Charts

- Call on students to read the statements in the first chart. Have them identify the subject and the verb in each sentence.
- Ask the following questions to focus students' attention on the form:
  Which form of *be* is used with *going to* if the subject is singular? *(is)* If the subject is plural? *(are)*
  Does the phrase *going to* change? *(no)*
  What comes after *going to*? *(the base form of the verb)*
  Where do we place the word *not* in negative statements? *(after the verb* be, *before* going to)
- Call on students to read the questions and short answers. Ask: "In both *yes / no* and *wh-* questions, where do we place the verb *be*?" *(before the subject)*
- On the board, prepare a chart like the one below. Give students cues and elicit the forms. Have students copy the chart in their notebooks and fill it in, for example:
  T: Buy a new car. Affirmative.
  S: I'm going to buy a new car.
  T: Negative.
  S: I'm not going to buy a new car.

		Short answers
Affirmative		
Negative		
***Yes / No* question**		
***Wh-* question**		

- When all the correct forms have been filled in, use the chart to drill each pattern separately, for example:
  T: Eat dinner. I.
  S1: I'm going to eat dinner.
  T: You.

S2: You're going to eat dinner.
T: We.
S3: We're going to eat dinner.
- To make the drill more challenging, mix patterns and persons, but change only one element each time, for example:
  T: We're going to be late. *Yes / no.*
  S1: Are we going to be late?
  T: Short answer, affirmative.
  S2: Yes, we are.
  T: Negative statement.
  S3: We're not going to be late.
  T: She.
  S4: She's not going to be late.
  T: Study tonight.
  S5: She's not going to study tonight.

Grammar Notes

Note 1
- Call on students to read the note and the examples.
- Inform students that they will learn about *will* in the next unit.

Note 2
- Call on students to read the note and the examples.
- Model the examples of uncontracted and contracted forms for the students.
- To make sure students can hear the differences, alternate saying sentences with contracted and uncontracted forms. Have students hold up one finger if they hear a contracted form and two fingers if they hear an uncontracted one.
- Do a transformation drill. Say sentences with uncontracted forms and have students produce the contracted form, for example:
  T: It is going to rain.
  Ss: It's going to rain.
- Have students work in pairs. Have them take turns saying sentences with contracted and uncontracted forms. Their partners should hold up fingers to indicate what they heard.
- To illustrate the incorrect *(not)* sentences, write a mix of correct and incorrect sentences on the board and have students identify and correct the errors.

Note 3
- Have students read the note and the examples, matching each example with its meaning.
- Form small groups. Have students in each group write two sentences for each meaning (facts, predictions, plans).
- Have groups share their sentences with the class.

Note 4

- Have students read the note and the examples. Then model a few sentences about your plans for the evening or the weekend.
- Go around the room and have each student make one sentence about what he or she will probably do this evening or this weekend.

Note 5

- Have students read the note and the examples.
- Copy the time markers from the chart onto the board.
- Have students work in pairs for a role play. Have them imagine that one student is a fortune-teller. The other student is a client. The fortune-teller makes predictions about the other student's future, using the time markers on the board. (Example: *Tomorrow you're going to make a new friend. Next week you're going to have a small accident.*) Then have students switch roles.

Note 6

- Read the note and the examples. Reinforce the conditions where the present progressive is possible: with *go* and with words of movement and transportation. You may wish to list common pairs of verbs that are often coupled with the present progressive with future meaning, for example:
  arrive / depart
  come / go
  take off / land (for planes)
  leave / arrive
- Write sentences with *be going to* on the board. Instruct students to change the verb tense to the present progressive if possible. Include a mix of action and non-action verbs, for example:
  It's going to rain later tonight. *(not possible)*
  My brother's train is going to leave at 8 P.M. *(possible)*
  They're going to buy a new TV. *(not possible)*
  I'm going to go to the supermarket. *(possible)*
  The boss is going to leave early today. *(possible)*
  The new furniture is going to arrive next Wednesday. *(possible)*

- ⏱ **Identify the Grammar:** Have students identify the grammar in the reading on page 270. For example:
  It**'s going to have** a beautiful gym . . .
  But this fitness center **is going to cost** a lot of money.
  Where is the money **going to come** from?

Go to **www.myfocusongrammarlab.com** for grammar charts and notes.

Step 3: Focused Practice (pages 273–278)

See the general suggestions for Focused Practice on page 4.

Exercise 1: Discover the Grammar

A
- Go over the example with the class.
- Have students work individually to underline the examples of *be going to*. Then have them compare answers in pairs.

B
- Have students complete the exercise in pairs. Then go over the answer as a class.

Exercise 2: *Be going to* for the Future

- Go over the example with the class. Then have students read the conversation quickly for meaning.
- Have students complete the exercise individually. Then have them compare answers in pairs.
- ⏱ Have students practice the conversation, changing partners and roles several times.

Exercise 3: *Be going to* for the Future: *Wh-* Questions

- Have students read the news announcement and sentence cues quickly for meaning. Then go over the example with the class.
- Have students complete the exercise individually. You may want to have them focus first on the questions and then move to the answers.
- ⏱ Have pairs use the questions and answers to role-play a reporter interviewing the mayor about the new high school.

Exercise 4: *Be going to* for the Future

- Go over the example with the class. Then have students complete the exercise individually.
- ⏱ To extend the practice, elicit the points against the new building and write them on the board, for example:
  The building isn't going to look good.
  There aren't going to be enough parking spaces.
- ⏱ Have students imagine they are Mr. Romp and they are going to write a response letter. Elicit Mr. Romp's points for the new building, for example:
  The building is going to have a parking garage.
  There are going to be more jobs in the area.

Exercise 5: Simple Past, Simple Present, *Be going to*

- Go over the example with the class. Then have students read the conversations quickly for meaning.
- Have students complete the exercise in pairs. Then combine pairs to form groups of four and have students compare answers.
- ⏱ To extend the practice, have groups of six role-play the conversation, changing roles several times.

Exercise 6: Present Progessive for the Future

- Have students look at the schedule. Elicit some sentences about the mayor's plans using the present progessive, for example:
  She is going to give two speeches on Monday.
  She is going to fly to Los Angeles on Tuesday morning.
- Go over the example with the class. Then have students read the sentence cues quickly for meaning.
- Have students complete the exercise individually. Then have them compare answers in pairs.

Exercise 7: Editing

- Go over the example with the class. Point out that they should find four more mistakes in the newsletter article.
- Have students find and correct the mistakes in pairs.
- Combine pairs to form groups of four and have students compare answers. Then call on students to read the corrected passage. Have them explain why the incorrect structures are wrong.

Go to **www.myfocusongrammarlab.com** for additional grammar practice.

Step 4: Communication Practice (pages 279–281)

See the general suggestions for Communication Practice on page 5.

Exercise 8: Pronunciation

A

- Play the audio. Have students read along as they listen to the Pronunciation Note.
- Read the examples with careful pronunciation of *going to* and have students repeat. Then have them repeat with the reduced pronunciation.

B

- Play the audio. Have students listen and complete the exercise individually.
- Go over the answers as a class.

C

- Play the audio. Have students listen and repeat.
- ⏱ To extend the practice, write the following questions on the board. Then have students ask and answer them in pairs. Have them use the reduced pronunciation for *going to* + verb and the careful pronunciation for *going to* + place.
  What are you going to do this afternoon?
    (gonna)
  Are you going to the library this evening?
    (going to)
  What time are you going to go home? *(gonna)*
  Is your teacher going to give a test tomorrow?
    (gonna)
  Are you going to watch TV tonight? *(gonna)*
  Is your family going to a restaurant for dinner? *(going to)*

Exercise 9: Listening

A

- Have students read the question and answer choices quickly for meaning.
- Play the audio. Have students listen and circle their answer.
- Go over the answer as a class.

B

- Call on students to read the questions.
- Play the audio. Have students listen and complete the exercise in pairs.
- Play the audio again. Have students listen and confirm their answers.

Exercise 10: Conversation: Changes in Your Life

- Go over the example with the class.
- Have students make notes about a future change in their own lives or in a friend's or family member's life.
- Have students complete the exercise in pairs.

Exercise 11: Writing

A

- Go over the example with the class.
- To help students with their discussions, provide some phrases for giving and asking opinions, for example:
  I think . . . / I don't think . . .
  I agree. / I disagree.
  In my opinion . . .
  Personally . . .
  What do you think?
  Do you agree?
- Form small groups. Have students complete the discussion in groups. Have students take notes on the ideas in their discussions so that they can use them in their letters in Part B.

B
- Go over the example with the class.
- Have students complete the exercise individually.

C
- Have students correct their work using the Editing Checklist.
- Then have students exchange papers and check their partner's work.
- Have students present their letters to the class.

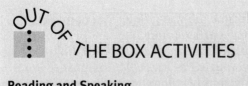

OUT OF THE BOX ACTIVITIES

Reading and Speaking
- Bring in a selection of letters to the editor. Choose letters about issues that will be interesting to students and about which they are likely to have opinions.
- Have students read the letters and discuss them in groups. Have them describe the issue and the writer's opinion. Then have them discuss their own opinions about the issue.

Listening
- Follow the procedure above but use clips from radio talk shows or radio or TV news stories about a current issue.

Go to **www.myfocusongrammarlab.com** for additional listening, pronunciation, speaking, and writing practice.

Note:
- See the *Focus on Grammar Workbook* for additional in-class or homework grammar practice.

Unit 24 Review (page 282)

Have students complete the Review and check their answers on Student Book page UR-5. Review or assign additional material as needed.

Go to **www.myfocusongrammarlab.com** for the Unit Achievement Test.

Grammar: *Will* FOR THE FUTURE; FUTURE TIME MARKERS

Unit 25 focuses on the structure of *will* for the future, including affirmative and negative statements, *yes / no* questions, short answers, and future time markers, as well as meanings of *will*, including predictions, offers, requests, and expressing refusal.

Theme: THE FUTURE

Unit 25 focuses on language and expressions used to make predictions about what life on Earth will be like in the future.

Step 1: Grammar in Context (pages 283–284)

See the general suggestions for Grammar in Context on page 1.

Before You Read
- Introduce the themes of change and the future. Have the class brainstorm some examples of modern systems or technology that are readily available to the public now that were not available 15 or 20 years ago. (Example: *hybrid cars, social networking sites, global positioning systems [GPS], Internet telephone, video chat, e-books*)
- Have students discuss their ideas about the questions in pairs. Encourage them to think beyond the scope of technology. Write some topics on the board to help them. (Example: *food, housing, energy and fuel, travel and transportation, education, clothing*)
- Elicit predictions from the class. Do not correct grammatical errors at this stage, but write students' predictions on the board in full sentences using *will*. (Example: *More people will grow their own food.*)

Read
- Call on a student to read the instructions.
- Go over the glossed vocabulary at the end of the predictions.
- Have students read the text. (OR: Play the audio and have students follow along in their books.)

After You Read

A. Practice
- Have students complete the exercise in pairs.
- Then call on pairs to read the predictions.

- Lead a brief class discussion about the predictions. Ask: "Which predictions do you think are most likely to happen?" "Which ones do you think are probably not going to happen?"

B. Vocabulary
- Read the words and phrases in the box and have students repeat. Then have students read the sentences quickly for meaning.
- Have students complete the exercise individually.
- Have students compare answers in pairs. Then go over the answers as a class and have students explain how they decided on the answers.

C. Comprehension
- Have students read the sentences quickly for meaning. Say: "Some items may have more than one possible answer."
- Have students complete the exercise in pairs.
- Combine pairs to form groups of four and have students compare answers. Then go over the answers as a class. Have students tell you where they found the information in the text.

Go to **www.myfocusongrammarlab.com** for an additional reading, and for reading and vocabulary practice.

Step 2: Grammar Presentation (pages 285–286)
See the general suggestions for Grammar Presentation on page 2.

Grammar Charts
- Call on students to read the affirmative and negative examples in the chart.
- Ask: "What form comes after *will*?" *(base form)* "Does *will* change if the subject is singular or plural?" *(no)* "Where do we place *not* in negative statements?" *(after* will)
- Drill the affirmative and negative statements in the charts. Say the first-person singular form, then cue students with the other pronouns, for example:
  T: I will leave tomorrow. You.
  Ss: You will leave tomorrow.
- For *yes / no* questions, model the first question. Indicate with your head whether the answer should be yes or no, and have the class provide the short answer. After that, cue students with the remaining pronouns and have them form the questions, for example:
  T: Will I arrive tomorrow?
  Ss: Yes, you will.
  T: You.
  Ss: Will you arrive tomorrow? (Indicate *no*.)

Ss: No, I won't.
T: He.
Ss: Will he arrive tomorrow? (Indicate *yes*.)
Ss: Yes, he will.
- Read the chart of future time markers and have students repeat.

Grammar Notes

Notes 1–3
- Have students read the notes and the examples.
- Have students work in groups of four or five. Instruct them to take turns rereading the predictions from the opening reading, transforming them into the negative and question forms and answering the questions according to their real opinion of what will happen, for example:
  S1 [reading]: Robots will cook our meals.
  S2: Robots won't cook our meals.
  S3: Will robots cook our meals?
  S4: Yes, they will. / No, they won't.
- Draw attention to the *Be Careful!* notes. Remind students not to use contractions for short answers.

Note 4
- Have students read the note and the examples.
- Pretend to be upset about things students have done. They should respond by promising to do or not to do those things in the future, for example:
  T: Diana, you forgot to write your name on your paper.
  Diana: Next time I'll write my name on my paper. / I won't forget next time.
  T: Class, you didn't speak only in English during the whole class.
  Ss: We'll speak only in English next time.
  T: Olivier, Sandra fell asleep in class.
  Olivier: She'll go to bed early tonight.

Note 5
- Have students read the note and the examples.
- Write the situations below on slips of paper:
  You are carrying a load of books and cannot open the door.
  You dropped your pencil on the floor.
  You spilled coffee on your shirt.
  You want to open the window, but it's stuck.
  You dropped all of your papers on the floor.

- Have students work in pairs. Give a slip to a student in each pair. The student with the slip should pantomime the situation and ask for help and the other should respond, for example:

  You don't have an eraser.
  S1: Will you please lend me your eraser?
  S2: Sure. Here it is.

Note 6
- Have students read the note and the examples.
- Elicit negative statements about tomorrow's weather in a variety of cities, for example:
  T: Bangkok.
  S1: It won't snow tomorrow.
  S2: It won't be cold.
  T: New York.
- Go around the room and have each student name a food or drink he or she will not eat or drink, for example:
  S1: I won't eat liver. I hate it.
  S2: I won't eat cheese. It's fattening.
  S3: I won't eat seaweed. It's too salty.

Note 7
- Have students read the note and the example.
- Have students say what they will probably do next weekend.

Note 8
- Read the examples. Have students explain the difference between the first two sentences (future) and the third one (past). Explain that time expressions with *this* can have two meanings, depending on the time of speaking. (Example: *At 7 P.M., "this morning" is in the past. At 8 A.M., "this morning" is in the present or future.*)
- Practice by having students use expressions with *this* to form real past and future sentences. Note that the expressions will vary depending on the time your class is held, for example, if your class is in the morning:
  This morning, I saw Kento on the bus.
  This morning, we will finish class at 10:30.

⏱ **Identify the Grammar:** Have students identify the grammar in the reading on page 283. For example:

  More people **will be** vegetarians.
  They **won't eat** any meat or fish.
  Robots **will cook** our meals.

Go to **www.myfocusongrammarlab.com** for grammar charts and notes.

Step 3: Focused Practice (pages 287–289)
See the general suggestions for Focused Practice on page 4.

Exercise 1: Discover the Grammar
- Have students read the text quickly for meaning. Then go over the example with the class.
- Have students complete the exercise in pairs.
- Call on pairs to read the sentences and the uses. Ask the rest of the class to confirm or correct as necessary.

Exercise 2: *Will* for the Future
- Have students read the conversations quickly for meaning. Then go over the example with the class. Ask: "Will the form of the verbs in parentheses change?" *(no)*
- Have students complete the exercise individually. Remind students to use contractions where possible. Then have them compare answers in pairs.
- ⏱ Have students practice the conversations in pairs, changing partners and roles.

Exercise 3: *Will* for the Future
- Have students read the conversations quickly for meaning. Then go over the example with the class.
- Have students complete the exercise in pairs. Remind them to use contractions where possible.
- Combine pairs to form groups of four and have students compare answers. Then call on pairs to read the completed conversation.

Exercise 4: *Will* for the Future
- Go over the example with the class.
- Have students complete the exercise individually, using contractions where possible. Then call on pairs of students to read the questions and answers.
- ⏱ Have students answer the questions about their own country, city, or town.

Exercise 5: Review of Present, Past, Future
- Go over the example with the class.
- Have students complete the exercise in pairs, using contractions where possible. Then assign the roles in the conversation to pairs of students and have them read the conversation, inserting the answers.
- ⏱ To extend the practice, elicit the predictions in the conversation and write them on the board:
  By the year 2100 there will be cities in the ocean.
  We'll take trips to the moon, and we'll learn everything from computers.
  2100? We'll all be gone by then.
- Have the class discuss whether they agree or disagree with the predictions.

Exercise 6: Editing

- Go over the example with the class. Point out that they should find five more mistakes in the conversation.
- Have students find and correct the mistakes in pairs.
- Combine pairs to form groups of four and have students compare answers. Then call on students to read the corrected conversation. Have them explain why the incorrect structures are wrong.

Go to **www.myfocusongrammarlab.com** for additional grammar practice.

Step 4: Communication Practice (pages 290–292)

See the general suggestions for Communication Practice on page 5.

Exercise 7: Pronunciation

A
- Play the audio. Have students read along as they listen to the Pronunciation Note.

B
- Play the audio. Have students listen and repeat the contractions.

C
- Play the audio. Have students listen and repeat the sentences.
- To extend the practice, say sentences with noun subjects and have students change the subjects to pronouns, for example:
  T: The weather will be nice tomorrow.
  Ss: It'll be nice tomorrow.
  T: Fatima will be late for dinner.
  Ss: She'll be late for dinner.

Exercise 8: Listening

A
- Have students read the question and answer choices quickly for meaning.
- Play the audio. Have students listen and circle their answer.
- Go over the answer as a class.

B
- Call on students to read the questions aloud.
- Play the audio, pausing a few times for students to write their answers. Alternatively, you may want to play the audio once and have students take notes and then write their answers to the questions afterwards.
- Have students compare answers in pairs. Then play the audio again to confirm the answers.

Exercise 9: Class Survey

- Go over the example with the class.
- Form small groups. Have students in each group choose one member to write down group members' opinions and one member to report back to the class.
- Have students discuss the predictions. Make sure that all group members have a chance to give their opinions for each prediction.

Exercise 10: Survey: In the Future

A
- Have students complete the exercise individually.

B
- Have students complete the questions individually.
- Have students stand and walk around the class to survey five classmates. Remind them to take notes on their classmates' responses, as they will need to report back to the class.

C
- Go over the example with the class.
- Call on students to report on their results to the class.

Exercise 11: Making Predictions

A
- Go over the example with the class. Then call on a student to read the topics. Elicit additional topics from the class and write them on the board.
- Hand out three or four strips of paper to each student and have them write one prediction on each one.
- Have students tape their predictions on the wall.

B
- Have students number their predictions.
- Have students circulate around the classroom, reading their classmates' predictions.
- Call on students to choose four predictions and say whether they agree or disagree with them.

Exercise 12: Writing

A
- Go over the example with the class.
- Form small groups. Have students discuss the topics in groups.

B
- Have students complete the exercise individually.
- Have students compare answers in pairs.

C
- Have students correct their work using the Editing Checklist.
- Then have students exchange papers and check their partner's work.

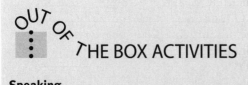

OUT OF THE BOX ACTIVITIES

Speaking
- Have students work in pairs to role-play one or more of the following situations, showing the different meanings of *will*.
  1. Student A is upset because Student B (example: *spouse, roommate, relative*) hasn't done his or her share of the housework. (Example: *He or she was supposed to wash the dinner dishes and hasn't done it.*) Student A confronts Student B and complains. Student B promises to do the work later.
  2. Student A asks Student B for help with something. (Example: *homework, moving into a new apartment, getting to a doctor's appointment, buying a gift for someone*) Student B agrees to help.
  3. Student A (a parent) agrees to lend the family car to Student B (the teenage son or daughter). As the child is leaving, the parent reminds the teenager of many things. (Example: *Don't forget to lock the car.*) Each time the teenager patiently responds, "I won't . . ."
  4. Student A (a pet owner) is telling Student B (a veterinarian) why he or she is worried that his or her pet (Example: *dog, cat, bird, horse*) is sick. (Example: *He won't eat.*) The vet gives advice.

Listening
- Print out the lyrics for "All My Loving" by The Beatles, but leave blank spaces in place of *will* + base form of verb.
- Have students listen one time through and read along. Then have students listen and try to fill in the verbs.
- Have students listen and check their work.
- Play the song for students to sing along.

Go to **www.myfocusongrammarlab.com** for additional listening, pronunciation, speaking, and writing practice.

Note:
- See the *Focus on Grammar Workbook* for additional in-class or homework grammar practice.

Unit 25 Review (page 293)
Have students complete the Review and check their answers on Student Book page UR-5. Review or assign additional material as needed.

Go to **www.myfocusongrammarlab.com** for the Unit Achievement Test.

UNIT 26 OVERVIEW

Grammar: *May* OR *Might* FOR POSSIBILITY

Unit 26 focuses on the structure of and use of *may* and *might* to express possibility in affirmative and negative statements.

Theme: WEATHER

Unit 26 focuses on language and expressions used to discuss predictions and possibility related to the weather and its effects on upcoming plans.

Step 1: Grammar in Context (pages 294–296)
See the general suggestions for Grammar in Context on page 1.

Before You Read
- Introduce the theme of weather. Ask: "What is the weather report for tomorrow?" Elicit responses from several students.
- Have students complete the exercise individually.
- 🕐 Lead a brief class discussion. Ask students for examples of instances they remember when the weather report was wrong.

Read
- Have students look at the photo of the weather report. Ask: "What kind of weather do you think the report will be about?" (Example: *bad, cold, rainy, snowy*) Elicit predictions from several students.
- Go over the glossed vocabulary at the end of the conversation.

- Have students read the text. (OR: Play the audio and have students follow along in their books.)

After You Read

A. Practice

- Form groups of three. Then have students take turns reading the conversation, changing roles so that everyone has a chance to play all three roles.
- Call on groups to read the conversation.
- Ask any or all of the following questions:
  How will the weather be tomorrow? *(cold and windy)*
  Is it going to rain? *(yes)*
  Why should people use public transportation to go to work? *(There will be flooding on the highways.)*
  How will the weather be on Wednesday and Thursday? *(rainy on Wednesday and milder on Thursday)*
  Will it be sunny on Thursday? *(maybe)*
  Is Alex going to play soccer tomorrow? *(maybe)*
  How was the weather last Friday? *(awful)*
  Does Alex enjoy playing in the mud? *(yes)*

B. Vocabulary

- Read the words and phrases in the box and have students repeat. Then have students read the text quickly for meaning.
- Have students complete the exercise individually.
- Have students compare answers in pairs. Then go over the answers as a class and have students explain how they decided on the answers.

C. Comprehension

- Have students complete the exercise individually.
- Have students compare answers in pairs.

Go to **www.myfocusongrammarlab.com** for an additional reading, and for reading and vocabulary practice.

Step 2: Grammar Presentation (pages 296–297)

See the general suggestions for Grammar Presentation on page 2.

Grammar Charts

- Call on students to read the example sentences.
- Do a substitution drill with affirmative statements and *may* or *might*. Give a base sentence, then cue students with different pronouns, for example:

T: I may go to a movie tonight. You.
Ss: You may go to a movie tonight.
T: We.
Ss: We may go to a movie tonight.

- Follow the same procedure with a negative sentence and use *might*. (Example: *They might not come.*)
- Continue cueing students with pronouns, sentence type (affirmative or negative), and *may* or *might*, for example:
T: I might go out later. Negative.
S1: I might not go out later.
T: She may.
S2: She may not go out later.
T: Affirmative.
S3: She may go out later.

Grammar Notes

Notes 1 and 2

- Ask a pair of students to read the first two examples. Ask a different student to read the notes.
- Go around the room and ask students what they're going to do this weekend. Students should answer with *may* or *might*.

Notes 3 and 4

- Ask a student to read the Usage Note in Note 3. You may want to simplify it with the following simple rule: "Don't use *may* or *might* in questions about the future."
- Call on pairs of students to read the examples.
- Have students read Note 4 and the examples.
- Do an error correction exercise based on the incorrect sentences in Notes 2, 3, and 4. Write the following sentences on the board and have students correct them:
Sandra may to get married next year.
Hector mightn't come to the class party.
May Kang graduate this year?
Marta is sure she might go to San Francisco next weekend.
Might you return to your country after the end of this course?
Peter might works for his father next year.

Note 5

- Have students read the examples and transform them from *maybe* to *may / might* and vice versa.
- Drill the transformation, for example:
T: Maybe the president will go to Japan.
Ss: The president might go to Japan.
T: Maybe the class will go to Japan.
Ss: The class might go to Japan.
T: Maybe it won't rain.
Ss: It might not rain.

- Reverse the order. Cue students with *may / might* and have them rephrase the sentences with *maybe*.
- Put students into pairs and have them ask each other about their plans for the weekend or for an upcoming vacation, following the model in Note 1.

🕐 **Identify the Grammar:** Have students identify the grammar in the conversation on page 294. For example:
... there **may be** flooding ...
... the weather **may become** milder ...
We **might** even **see** some sun.

Go to **www.myfocusongrammarlab.com** for grammar charts and notes.

Step 3: Focused Practice (pages 298–300)

See the general suggestions for Focused Practice on page 4.

Exercise 1: Discover the Grammar
- Go over the example with the class.
- Have students complete the exercise individually. Then have them compare answers in pairs.
- 🕐 To extend the practice, give students another verb along with percentages or expressions of possibility and have them form sentences with *will*, *will probably*, *may*, or *might*, for example:
T: Snow, definitely.
S1: It will snow.
T: Fifty percent.
S2: It might snow. / It may snow.
T: Eighty percent.
S3: It'll probably snow.

Exercise 2: Affirmative of *May* or *Might*
- Go over the example with the class. Have students read the text quickly for meaning. Ask: "Will the form of the verbs in the box change?" *(no)* "How about the form of *may* and *might*?" *(no)*
- Have students complete the exercise individually and then compare answers in pairs.
- 🕐 Have students practice the conversations, changing partners and roles several times.

Exercise 3: *May / Might / Will / Will Probably*
- Call on a student to read the weather report. Then go over the example with the class.
- Have students complete the exercise individually. Then call on pairs to read the completed sentences.

- 🕐 Have students use the weather report and the sentences to create a new weather report role play and perform it for the class.

Exercise 4: *Maybe* and *May / Might*
- Go over the example with the class. Highlight that the modal *can* changes to *be able to* when preceded by *may* or *might*. Also point out that with short answers the main verb is dropped, for example:
S1: Is it going to snow tonight?
S2: It might.
- Have students complete the exercise in pairs. Make sure students understand that they should add a subject and / or a verb where necessary.

Exercise 5: Editing
- Go over the example with the class. Point out that they should find five more mistakes in the conversations.
- Have students find and correct the mistakes in pairs.
- Combine pairs to form groups of four and have students compare answers. Then call on students to read the corrected passage. Have them explain why the incorrect structures are wrong.

Go to **www.myfocusongrammarlab.com** for additional grammar practice.

Step 4: Communication Practice (pages 300–302)

See the general suggestions for Communication Practice on page 5.

Exercise 6: Pronunciation
A
- Play the audio. Have students read along as they listen to the Pronunciation Note.

B
- Play the audio. Have students listen and circle the word they hear.
- Go over the answers as a class.

C
- Play the audio. Have students listen and complete the exercise individually.
- Have students practice the conversations in pairs, changing roles and partners several times.

Exercise 7: Listening
A
- Have students read the question and answer choices quickly for meaning.

- Play the audio. Have students listen and circle their answer.
- Go over the answer as a class.

B
- Call on a student to read the list of items. Then go over the example with the class.
- Play the audio, pausing a few times for students to write their answers. Alternatively, you may want to play the audio once and have students take notes and then write their answers afterwards.
- Have students compare answers in pairs. Then play the audio again to confirm the answers.

Exercise 8: Discussion
- Have students read the ideas in the list and add any others they can think of. Then go over the example with the class.
- Have students complete the exercise in pairs. Then combine pairs to form groups of four to discuss their answers.
- Call on students to report on their discussion.

Exercise 9: Writing

A
- Go over the example with the class.
- You may want to allow students to refer to current local weather reports online to help them. Alternatively, have students choose to write about the weather in another city, either domestic or international.
- Have students complete the exercise individually.

B
- Have students correct their work using the Editing Checklist.
- Then have students exchange papers and check their partner's work.
- ⏱ Have students role-play their weather reports in small groups.

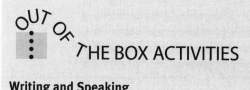

OUT OF THE BOX ACTIVITIES

Writing and Speaking
- Put up a large calendar showing the next week.
- For each day on the calendar, have students use *will*, *will probably*, *may*, or *might* and write their own weather predictions.

- Do a daily update of students' predictions throughout the week. Have students say what their predictions were and whether they were correct.

Speaking
- Write the following on the board:
  Five years from now . . .

100%	will
80%	will probably
50%	may, might, may not, might not
10%	probably won't
0%	won't

- Form small groups. Have students in each group have a conversation about their plans for the future. Have students ask each other questions with *will / be going to*. Their goal should be to use each of the structures above in their answers.

Reading and Speaking
- Bring newspapers to class. Assign stories to pairs of students or let them choose their own.
- Have students read the article and prepare a short summary of what happened or is happening.
- Have students use the expressions above to say three things that will or might happen next.
- Combine pairs and have each pair present their report to the other pair. Alternately, have pairs present their reports to the whole class.

Go to **www.myfocusongrammarlab.com** for additional listening, pronunciation, speaking, and writing practice.

Note:
- See the *Focus on Grammar Workbook* for additional in-class or homework grammar practice.

Unit 26 Review (page 303)
Have students complete the Review and check their answers on Student Book page UR-5. Review or assign additional material as needed.

Go to **www.myfocusongrammarlab.com** for the Unit Achievement Test.

From Grammar to Writing (pages 304–305)

See the general suggestions for From Grammar to Writing on page 9.

Go to **www.myfocusongrammarlab.com** for an additional From Grammar to Writing Assignment, Part Review, and Part Post-Test.

┌─ **UNIT 27 OVERVIEW** ─────────────┐

Grammar: Count and Non-count Nouns, Quantifiers, Articles

Unit 27 focuses on the structure and use of quantifiers such as *some, many,* and *much* and articles *a, an,* and *the* with count and non-count nouns.

Theme: Restaurants and Food

Unit 27 focuses on language and expressions used to talk about food in general and to describe dishes served in restaurants.

└────────────────────────────────────┘

Step 1: Grammar in Context (pages 308–309)

See the general suggestions for Grammar in Context on page 1.

Before You Read

- Introduce the theme of food and restaurants. Ask: "How often do you go out to eat at a restaurant?" "What are some of your favorite restaurants and dishes?" Then call on students to read the instructions and the list of criteria. Go over any unfamiliar vocabulary such as *service, atmosphere, portions*.
- Have students complete the exercise individually.
- 🕐 Lead a brief class discussion. Ask students for other criteria they think are important in a restaurant dining experience.

Read

- Call on a student to read the names of the two restaurants. Ask: "What kind of restaurants do you think these are?" Elicit guesses from several students.
- Go over the glossed vocabulary at the end of the conversation.
- Have students read the text. (OR: Play the audio and have students follow along in their books.)

After You Read

A. Practice

- Have students complete the exercise in pairs.
- Then call on pairs to read paragraphs.
- Ask: "Which restaurant would you prefer? Why?"

B. Vocabulary

- Read the words and phrases in the box and have students repeat.
- Have students complete the exercise individually and then compare answers in pairs.
- Go over the answers as a class and have students explain how they decided on the answers.

C. Comprehension

- Have students complete the exercise individually. Encourage them to do so without looking back at the text.
- Have students compare answers in pairs. Then go over the answers as a class.
- 🕐 Have a few students give a brief review of a restaurant they went to recently.

Go to **www.myfocusongrammarlab.com** for an additional reading, and for reading and vocabulary practice.

Step 2: Grammar Presentation (pages 310–312)

See the general suggestions for Grammar Presentation on page 2.

Grammar Charts

- Begin by saying that English has two types of nouns: count and non-count (or uncountable). Write the two headings on the board.
- Call on students to read the examples in the charts. Ask: "What are the two forms of count nouns?" *(singular and plural)* "How many forms of non-count nouns are there?" *(one)* "Does it look like the singular or the plural form?" *(singular)* "Why?" *(It doesn't end in -s.)*
- Explain that *a* and *an* are called articles. Words that tell how much or how many are called quantifiers.
- Ask: "What kinds of nouns follow the articles *a* or *an*?" *(singular count nouns)* Have students identify the quantifiers in the charts. (Example: *a few, a little, many, much*)
- Elicit that count nouns are items that can be counted. Ask students for some examples from the classroom and write them on the board. (Example: *pens, books, students, desks*) Elicit that non-count nouns are things that can't be counted. Ask for some examples and write them on the board. (Example: *water, air, music, love*)
- Have students go through the opening reading and find additional examples of each category. Call them up to the front to write the examples.
- Elicit additional examples of count and non-count nouns and add them to the board.
- Have students read the chart featuring the definite article *the*.
- Have students find all the examples in the opening reading with *the*. List them on the board and have students identify the type of noun that follows each example: singular, plural, or non-count. Elicit further examples and list them on the board.

Grammar Notes

Note 1

- Have students read the note and the examples.
- In a large box, collect 15 to 20 countable items. Include a few that begin with vowels. (Example: *egg, onion, apple, envelope, umbrella*) Put in one of some items and more than one of other items. Plural items should be kept together in a clear plastic bag or with a rubber band.
- Place the box on your desk and have students come up one at a time, reach in, pull out an object, and say what it is. (Example: *an egg / a wristwatch / two pens*)

- Do a variation of the above activity. Blindfold students before they reach into the box. When they select an item, they should feel it and say what they think it is. (Example: *It's an egg.*) If they're unable to guess, the class can provide hints. (Example: *You can eat it. It comes from a chicken.*)

Notes 2 and 3

- Make a full-page handout like the following. Leave space in each cell for students to add items.

Liquids	Solid foods	Small particles*
milk	cheese	sugar
Natural elements	Natural phenomena and weather	Abstract nouns (feelings or ideas)
wood	rain	love
Gases	Groups consisting of similar items	Activities and recreation
air	jewelry	golf swimming

*Substances made up of many tiny parts, such as dust, sugar, salt, hair, sawdust, grass, chalk, rice.

- Place students into groups. Assign one category of non-count nouns to each. Students must come up with additional nouns to add to the chart.
- Call on groups to share their work with the class. Correct errors.
- Draw attention to the *Be Careful!* note.

Note 4

- Have students read the note and the examples.
- Write the following partial dialogue on the board:
  A: For dinner last night I had _____, _____, _____, and _____.
  B: How was the _____?
  A: It was [spicy / sour / bitter / overcooked / undercooked / not fresh / delicious / sweet / good / fresh / wonderful].
- Model, telling about your own experience, for example:
  T: For dinner last night I had chicken, rice, salad, and ice cream.
  S: How was the chicken?
  T: It was a little dry.
- Have students work in pairs or small groups. Have them follow the model and speak about a recent meal.

Note 5

- Have students read the note and the examples. To help clarify, you may want to put the following chart on the board:

singular count	the apple
plural count	the dogs
non-count	the water

- Have students work in pairs and think of two more examples for each category.

Note 6

- Call on students to read the note and the examples.
- Do a transformation drill. Have students convert sentences with non-count and plural-count nouns from affirmative to negative and vice versa, for example:
  T: I had some orange juice.
  Ss: I didn't have any orange juice.
  T: I didn't have any eggs.
  Ss: I had some eggs.
- Ask: "What did you eat for breakfast?" Elicit affirmative and negative sentences. (Example: *I had some cereal. I didn't have any coffee.*)

Note 7

- Have students read the note and the examples.
- Summarize the information in a chart. Draw the cells and headings on the board. Elicit the quantifiers from the students. Highlight that *many* and *much* are used in negative statements. (Example: *I didn't eat many grapes. There isn't much milk.*)

	Small amounts	Large amounts
Count	[a few]	[a lot of, (not) many]
Non-count	[a little]	[a lot of, (not) much]

- Draw attention to the *Be Careful!* note.
- Form small groups. Have students in each group use the quantifiers above to describe the contents of their refrigerator or closet. They can also use *some / any* and *a / an*. (Example: *some milk, a few apples, a lot of soda, a little cheese, a watermelon, not much ice cream*)

Note 8

- Have students read the note and the examples. Write a few more examples on the board:
  chicken   a chicken
  glass   a glass
  noise   a noise

- This concept may be difficult for students to understand. Explain that the countable item refers to something that is a whole unit (a chicken), a single event (a noise), or an object (a glass). The non-count noun refers to a substance (chicken), phenomenon (noise), or material (glass) in general.
- Put students in pairs and assign one count / non-count noun pair to each pair. Challenge them to compose sentences using both the count and the non-count noun together, for example:
  I love coffee, but my brother hates it. We went to a café and I bought a coffee for myself and a soda for him.
  My son said he wants chicken for dinner tonight, so I went to the supermarket and bought a chicken, some rice, and some broccoli.

⏱ **Identify the Grammar:** Have students identify the grammar in the reading on page 308. For example:
  Rich **spices** are the **draw** at **Al Hambra**.
  The **flavor** of **ginger, garlic, cumin,** and **lemon** make the **chicken** in a **tagine (ceramic pot)** our favorite **choice**.
  There isn't **much beef** on the **menu**, and there isn't **any pork**.

Go to **www.myfocusongrammarlab.com** for grammar charts and notes.

Step 3: Focused Practice (pages 312–316)

See the general suggestions for Focused Practice on page 4.

Exercise 1: Discover the Grammar

A
- Go over the example with the class.
- Have students complete the exercise in pairs. Then combine pairs to form groups of four and have students compare answers.
- Write the three column headings on the board. Call on students to write the nouns in the appropriate columns, including the articles and quantifiers.

B
- Have students complete the exercise individually.
- Have students compare answers in pairs. Then call on students to give answers.

Exercise 2: *A, An, The*

- Review the use of articles. Ask: "What types of nouns can follow each article?" (a, an: *singular count nouns*; the: *singular or plural count or non-count nouns*) "When do we use *the?*" (*when we know which person or thing we mean*) Then go over the example with the class.
- Have students complete the exercise individually. Then have them compare answers in pairs.
- 🕐 Have students practice the conversations, changing partners and roles several times.

Exercise 3: *A, An, The*

- Go over the example with the class. Then have students read the paragraph quickly for meaning.
- Have students complete the exercise in pairs. Then call on pairs to give answers.
- 🕐 To extend the practice, ask the following questions and have students respond with complete sentences:
  Who is Kel Warner? (*He is a college student.*)
  What does he do? (*He is a writer / food critic.*)
  Where can you read his reviews? (*You can read them in the school paper.*)
  Which restaurants does he write about? (*He writes about all the restaurants in town.*)
  Why is his job so wonderful? (*He can take a friend to restaurants and the school newspaper pays the bill.*)

Exercise 4: *Some, Any*

- Go over the example with the class. Then review the uses of *some* and *any*. Write the following on the board and call on students to fill in the blanks with *some* or *any*:
  I don't have _____ fruit. Let's buy _____ bananas.
  Sorry, there isn't _____ coffee. Would you like _____ tea?
  Do you have _____ juice?
- Have students complete the exercise individually.
- Have students compare answers in pairs. Then call on pairs to read the conversation.

Exercise 5: *Many, Much*

- Review the uses of *many* and *much*. Ask: "Which word will you use before a plural noun?" (*many*) "Which word will you use in a negative sentence?" (*much*) Then go over the example with the class.
- Have students complete the exercise individually.
- Have students compare answers in pairs. Then call on pairs to read the conversation.

Exercise 6: *Many, Much*

- Go over the example with the class. Then in pairs have students discuss which quantifier they will use with each noun.
- Have students complete the exercise in pairs.
- Combine pairs to form groups of four and have students compare answers. Then call on pairs to read the completed conversations.

Exercise 7: *A few, A little, Much,* or *Many*

- Review the uses of *a few, a little, much,* and *many*. Ask: "Which words can come before a plural noun?" (*a few, many*) "Which words can be used in negative sentences?" (*much, many*) "Which ones can be used with small amounts?" (*a few, a little*) "With large amounts?" (*much, many*). Then go over the example with the class.
- Have students complete the exercise individually.
- Have students compare answers in pairs. Then call on pairs to read the sentences.

Exercise 8: Editing

- Go over the example with the class. Point out that students should find eight more mistakes in the paragraph.
- Have students find and correct the mistakes in pairs.
- Combine pairs to form groups of four and have students compare answers. Then call on students to read the corrected passage. Have them explain why the incorrect structures are wrong.

Go to **www.myfocusongrammarlab.com** for additional grammar practice.

Step 4: Communication Practice (pages 317–319)

See the general suggestions for Communication Practice on page 5.

Exercise 9: Pronunciation

A
- Play the audio. Have students read along as they listen to the Pronunciation Note.

B
- Play the audio. Have students listen and repeat.

C
- Put students into pairs and have them read the incomplete recipe and try to predict the answers (using the phrases from Part B).
- Play the audio. Have students listen and complete the recipe.
- Play the audio again. Have students listen and repeat.

Exercise 10: Listening

A

- Have students read the list of food items quickly for meaning.
- Play the audio. Have students listen and complete the exercise individually.
- Go over the answers as a class.

B

- Call on a student to read the questions.
- Play the audio. Have students listen and write their answers. Alternatively, you may want to play the audio once and have students take notes and then write their answers afterwards.

Exercise 11: Presentation

A

- To prepare students for this task, you may want to show them a few clips from the introductions to TV or online cooking shows, where the chef introduces the dishes that will be prepared.
- Give students time to make some notes about the meal they will prepare on their show. You may want to specify that students should present three items: an appetizer, a main course, and a dessert.

B

- Call on students to give their presentations to the class and answer their classmates' questions.

Exercise 12: A Restaurant

A

- To help students get started, have them think of a restaurant they go to often, for example, to meet friends or for special occasions such as birthdays, dates, and so on.
- Have students read the ideas in the box. Go over any unfamiliar vocabulary. Have students add any other ideas they can think of.
- Have students complete the exercise individually.

B

- Go over the example with the class.
- Form small groups. Have students in each group discuss their restaurants.

Exercise 13: Writing

A

- Go over the example with the class. Then use the following questions to generate ideas and elicit vocabulary:

What is the name of the restaurant?
Where is it?
What kind of food does it have?
Which dishes are good? Which dishes are not good?
How are the prices?
How is the service?
How is the atmosphere?
Do you recommend this restaurant?

- Give students time to make some notes about the restaurant they have chosen. Point out that the example is a positive review, but, if students wish, they may describe a restaurant that they do not recommend.
- Have students complete the exercise individually.

B

- Have students correct their work using the Editing Checklist.
- Then have students exchange papers and check their partner's work.
- Have students read their restaurant reviews in small groups.

OUT OF THE BOX ACTIVITIES

Speaking and Writing

- Have the class work together to plan a potluck meal.
- Divide the class into groups and assign each group a type of item to bring. (Example: *drinks, appetizer, main dish, side dish, dessert*)
- Groups decide on a dish to bring and work together to research the recipe and make a shopping list.
- Groups create a recipe card for their dish to hand out when the class has the meal.

Listening

- Have students think of a dish they would like to make. Allow them to watch online videos showing how to make the dish.
- Have students take notes as they watch, listing the ingredients and steps.
- Have students teach one other student how to make the dish.

Go to **www.myfocusongrammarlab.com** for additional listening, pronunciation, speaking, and writing practice.

Note:
- See the *Focus on Grammar Workbook* for additional in-class or homework grammar practice.

Unit 27 Review (page 320)

Have students complete the Review and check their answers on Student Book page UR-6. Review or assign additional material as needed.

Go to **www.myfocusongrammarlab.com** for the Unit Achievement Test.

UNIT 28 OVERVIEW

Grammar: *How much / How many,* QUANTIFIERS, *Enough,* ADVERBS OF FREQUENCY

Unit 28 focuses on the structure and use of questions with *how much* and *how many,* quantifiers and quantity expressions with count and non-count nouns, statements of quantity with *enough,* and adverbs and expressions of frequency.

Theme: DESSERTS, COOKING, AND BAKING

Unit 28 focuses on language and expressions used to talk about frequency of cooking and baking certain dishes and to explain recipes, preparation, and procedures for cooking and baking.

Step 1: Grammar in Context (pages 321–322)

See the general suggestions for Grammar in Context on page 1.

Before You Read
- To spark students' interest in the topic, you may want to bring in and post magazine cut-outs or photos from the Internet of delicious-looking desserts.
- To introduce the theme of desserts and baking, tell students about one of your favorite desserts. Explain briefly what the ingredients are and how it is prepared.
- Have students work in pairs to discuss the questions. Encourage them to talk about desserts that are traditional to their culture, or in their own families, with which their partner might not be familiar.

Read
- Call on a student to read the first line of the conversation. Ask: "Have any of you every tried a dessert from Thailand? What was it? What was it like?"
- Have students read the text. (OR: Play the audio and have students follow along in their books.)

After You Read

A. Practice
- Have students complete the exercise in pairs.
- Then call on a pair to read the conversation.
- ⏱ Ask students the following questions to follow up:
  What does Carlos find unusual about the dessert? *(the color; the purple rice)*
  What makes the color of the dessert? *(the black rice)*
  Does Carlos decide to try some? *(yes)*
  What are they going to do? *(make the dessert together)*
  What does Wasana want to learn from Carlos? *(how to make cookies)*

B. Vocabulary
- Read the words and phrases in the box and have students repeat. Then have students read the text quickly for meaning.
- Have students complete the exercise individually. Then have them compare answers in pairs.
- ⏱ Have pairs use the new vocabulary to create new dialogues.

C. Comprehension
- Have students complete the exercise individually. Encourage them to do so without looking back at the text.
- Have students compare answers in pairs. Then go over the answers as a class.
- ⏱ Have students come up with additional false statements about the text and have the class correct them, for example:
  Wasana's mother doesn't make the dessert often.
  Wasana wants to learn how to make a cake from Carlos's country.
  Carlos knows how to make the dessert from his country.

Go to **www.myfocusongrammarlab.com** for an additional reading, and for reading and vocabulary practice.

Step 2: Grammar Presentation (pages 323–325)

See the general suggestions for Grammar Presentation on page 2.

Grammar Charts

- Read the charts showing questions and answers with *how much*. Ask:

  What kind of noun comes after *how much*? *(non-count)*

  How can we answer questions with *how much*? (*a lot of, two quarts of,* etc.)

  Which answer doesn't use the word *of*? (*a little*)

  What kind of noun do we use after *a little*? *(non-count)*

- Read the charts showing questions and answers with *how many*. Ask:

  What kind of noun comes after *how many*? *(plural count)*

  How do we answer questions with *how many*? (*a lot, one bag, a few,* etc.)

  What kind of noun do we use after *a few*? *(plural)*

- Focus on the charts presenting *enough*. Ask: "What kinds of nouns can follow *enough*?" *(count and non-count)*

- To clarify the meaning, write the following sentences on the board:

  1. We have enough food.
  2. We don't have enough food.

- Ask: "Which sentence means we are hungry?" *(2)*

- Further demonstrate by handing out pieces of paper to the class (have fewer pieces than you have students). Ask: "Do I have enough paper?" *(no)* Give another example with *money*: "I want to buy a new camera. It costs $300. I have $325 in my wallet. Do I have enough money?" *(yes)*

- Read the charts showing questions and answers with *how often*. Ask:

  How do we form questions with *how often*? (*do / does + base form of the verb*)

  What are some ways we can answer questions with *how often*? (*two days a week, once in a while,* etc.)

  Where do we place adverbs of frequency? (*before the verb*)

  How about in statements with *be*? (*after the verb*)

- Have students read the charts explaining the adverbs and percentages of frequency. Do a question chain activity with *how often* questions to help clarify the meaning. Write a variety of prompts on the board:

cook dinner	eat fast food	buy ice cream
bake cookies	eat dessert	order dessert at a restaurant

- Example:

  T: Keyana, how often do you cook dinner?

  KEYANA: I often cook dinner. Gregoire, how often do you bake cookies?

  GREGOIRE: I bake cookies once in awhile.

Grammar Notes

Notes 1 and 2

- Have students read the notes and the examples.
- On the board, make two columns labeled *How much* and *How many*. Have students copy them into their notebooks.
- Dictate a variety of count and non-count nouns and have students write them under the appropriate columns in their notebooks. (Example: *eggs, flour, sugar, chocolate, nuts, cream, cake, cookies, cherries*)
- Have students come to the front and write the nouns under the headings on the board. Correct errors as necessary.
- Have students each come up with six more food nouns: three count and three non-count.
- In pairs, have students dictate their words to each other, adding to the columns in their notes.
- Have students change partners and practice the information in Note 2, for example:

  S1: Do you have any cake?

  S2: (referring to list) Yes, I have some cake.

  S1: How much do you have?

  S2: I have a little. Do you have any cherries?

  S1: Yes, I have some.

  S2: How many do you have?

  S1: I have a few.

Note 3

- If possible, bring in real objects (or pictures) illustrating the measurements and containers in the note, such as a quart of milk or a cup of coffee.
- Write the measurement words and containers on the board. Have students say other items that come in these quantities and list those on the board as well.
- Put students into pairs. Have them say which of the items on the board they have used or bought recently, for example:

  Yesterday I bought a quart of milk.

  This morning I had a cup of coffee.

Note 4
- Have students read the note and the examples.
- Tell them they're going on a one-month trip to New York, Paris, London, and Morocco. They can take only one small suitcase, and they can't buy anything during the trip. Ask: "What will you bring?" Have students make their own list, including quantities, for example:
  $500
  One bottle of shampoo
  One tube of toothpaste
  Three shirts
  One suit
  Two pairs of shoes
- Call on a student to read his or her list to the class. The class should respond with "That's enough" or "That's not enough."
- Have students continue the activity in pairs.

Notes 5 and 6
- Have students read the notes and the examples.
- Prepare a Find Someone Who activity with the prompts below or your own ideas. This can be done as a handout, prepared before class, or written on the board.
- Have students walk around and ask their classmates, "How often do you . . . ?" When students find someone who matches an item, they run to the board and write in the person's name next to the item.

  Find someone who . . .
     often cooks Italian food _____
     never eats fast food _____
     rarely bakes cakes _____
     sometimes eats in bed _____
     always skips breakfast _____
     drinks coffee every morning _____
     eats out once a week or more _____
     often watches TV cooking shows _____
     sometimes has dinner parties _____

Notes 7 and 8
- Have students read the notes and examples.
- Draw attention to the *Be Careful!* notes.
- Have students report on their classmates' actions from notes 5 and 6. (*Marta watches TV cooking shows every day.*)

🕐 **Identify the Grammar:** Have students identify the grammar in the conversation on page 321. For example:
   OK, but just **a little**. That's **enough**.
   I don't **usually** eat purple rice. **How often** do you have it?
   My mom **often** makes it when mangoes are in season.

Go to **www.myfocusongrammarlab.com** for grammar charts and notes.

Step 3: Focused Practice (pages 326–328)
See the general suggestions for Focused Practice on page 4.

Exercise 1: Discover the Grammar
A
- Call on students to read the phrases. Then go over the example with the class.
- Have students complete the exercise in pairs. Then combine pairs to form groups of four and have students compare answers.
- Write the three column headings on the board. Call on students to write the nouns in the appropriate columns.

B
- Have students complete the exercise individually. Then have them compare answers in pairs.
- Call on students to first tell you the adverbs of frequency and then the expressions.

Exercise 2: *How much / How many / How often*
- Review the use of *much* and *many*. Ask: "What types of nouns can follow much?" (*non-count nouns*) "How about *many*?" (*plural count nouns*)
- Have students complete the exercise individually. Then have them compare answers in pairs.
- 🕐 Have students practice the conversations, changing partners and roles several times.

Exercise 3: Word Order: Adverbs and Expressions of Frequency
- Review the placement of adverbs of frequency in sentences with *be* (after the verb) and with other verbs (before the verb). Then go over the example with the class.
- Have students complete the exercise individually. Then go over the answers as a class.
- 🕐 Have students use complete sentences to compare themselves to Manny. (Example: *Manny has coffee every afternoon, but I rarely have coffee.*)

Exercise 4: *Enough*
- Go over the example with the class.
- Have students complete the exercise in pairs. Then combine pairs to form groups of four and have students compare answers.
- Call on students to read the completed sentences. Have students tell you how they decided on the answers.

Exercise 5: Containers

- Have students look at the pictures and read the text quickly for meaning. Then go over the example with the class.
- Have students complete the exercise in pairs. Then call on pairs to read the completed conversation. Have the rest of the class listen and make corrections as necessary.
- ⏱ Have students practice the conversations, changing roles and partners several times.

Exercise 6: Editing

- Go over the example with the class. Point out that students should find six more mistakes in the conversations.
- Have students find and correct the mistakes in pairs.
- Combine pairs to form groups of four and have students compare answers. Then call on students to read the corrected conversations. Have them explain why the incorrect structures are wrong.

Go to **www.myfocusongrammarlab.com** for additional grammar practice.

Step 4: Communication Practice (pages 329–332)

See the general suggestions for Communication Practice on page 5.

Exercise 7: Pronunciation

A
- Play the audio. Have students read along as they listen to the Pronunciation Note.

B
- Play the audio. Have students listen and underline the words containing the /aʊ/ sound.
- Have students compare answers in pairs. Then go over the answers as a class.

C
- Play the audio. Have students listen and repeat.
- ⏱ To extend the practice, have students work in pairs and have them use the sentences to create a dialogue. For an added challenge, have them try to use as many words as possible with the /aʊ/ sound, for example:
  S1: It's my sister's birthday, and I need to make a cake.
  S2: That <u>sounds</u> like fun. How much <u>flour</u> do you need?
  S1: <u>About</u> a <u>pound</u>.
  S2: <u>Wow!</u> How much <u>brown</u> sugar?
  S1: <u>Around</u> three cups.

Exercise 8: Listening

A
- Have students read the statements quickly for meaning.
- Play the audio. Have students listen and complete the exercise individually.
- Call on students to say the answers. Have them correct the false statements.

B
- Call on a student to read the list of ingredients.
- Play the audio. Have students listen and complete the exercise individually.
- Have students compare answers in pairs. Then play the audio again so that they can confirm the answers.

Exercise 9: Survey

- Have students read the words in the list. Then go over the example with the class.
- Have students walk around the room and interview five classmates, taking notes on their answers.
- Call on students to report their survey results to the class.

Exercise 10: Information Gap

- Put students into pairs. Have students choose A and B roles.
- Have Students B turn to page 332.
- Have students read their recipes quickly for meaning. If necessary, go over how to say the fractions: 1/2 = half, 3/4 = three-quarters, 2/3 = two-thirds.

1.
- Go over the example with the class.
- Have Students A ask questions and have Students B answer to provide the missing information.

2.
- Go over the example with the class.
- Have Students B ask questions and have Students A answer to provide the missing information.

Exercise 11: Group Presentation

- Go over the example with the class.
- Form small groups. Have students complete the exercise in groups.
- To assist students in making their plans, if possible provide each group with flip chart paper and markers. Have them list each dessert, how much / many they will make, and the ingredients needed.

Exercise 12: Writing

A
- Go over the example with the class.
- Have students complete the exercise individually. Remind them to write quantities where possible.

B
- Have students correct their work using the Editing Checklist.
- Then have students exchange papers and check their partner's work.
- To follow-up, have students read their paragraphs in small groups.

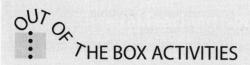

OUT OF THE BOX ACTIVITIES

Writing and Speaking
- Have students type up and exchange recipes for favorite desserts.
- In small groups, have them explain how the dessert is made.

Go to **www.myfocusongrammarlab.com** for additional listening, pronunciation, speaking, and writing practice.

Note:
- See the *Focus on Grammar Workbook* for additional in-class or homework grammar practice.

Unit 28 Review (page 333)

Have students complete the Review and check their answers on Student Book page UR-6. Review or assign additional material as needed.

Go to **www.myfocusongrammarlab.com** for the Unit Achievement Test.

Grammar: *Too Much / Too Many, Too* + ADJECTIVE

Unit 29 focuses on the meanings and uses of the phrases *too much / many*, and *too* + adjective.

Theme: THE RIGHT PLACE TO LIVE

Unit 29 focuses on language and expressions used to talk about the pros and cons of various aspects of cities, towns, and living spaces.

Step 1: Grammar in Context (pages 334–336)

See the general suggestions for Grammar in Context on page 1.

Before You Read
- To introduce the topic, ask students what they like and dislike about living in their town or city. Then have a student read the list of problems.
- Have students complete the exercise individually.
- Take a poll to find out what students think is the best local city or town to live in and why.

Read
- Have students look at the photos. Elicit the names of the three places students will read about: Miami; New York City; Kenai, Alaska.
- Have students predict some of the pros and cons of living in each place.
- Have students read the text. (OR: Play the audio and have students follow along in their books.)

After You Read

A. Practice
- Have students complete the exercise in pairs.
- Then call on pairs to read sections.
- Draw the following chart on the board. Call on students to come up and write a few ideas about each place in the chart.

	Pros (good points)	Cons (problems)
Miami		
New York City		
Kenai		

B. Vocabulary
- Read the words and phrases in the box and have students repeat.

- Have students complete the exercise individually. Then have them compare answers in pairs.
- ⏱ Have students work in pairs to create new sentences using the vocabulary.

C. Comprehension
- Have students complete the exercise in pairs. Encourage them to do so without looking back at the text.
- Elicit the answers from the class.
- ⏱ Lead a brief discussion comparing the three locations in the reading to students' own towns and cities.

Go to **www.myfocusongrammarlab.com** for an additional reading, and for reading and vocabulary practice.

Step 2: Grammar Presentation (page 336)

See the general suggestions for Grammar Presentation on page 2.

Grammar Charts
- Have students read the examples in the charts. Elicit the rules from the class. Ask:
  What kind of noun comes after *too much*? *(non-count)*
  What kind of noun comes after *too many*? *(plural count)*
  What kind of noun comes after *too few*? *(plural count)*
  What kind of word comes after *too* by itself? *(an adjective)*
  What comes after *too little*? *(non-count noun)*
  Are these examples of good things or bad things? *(bad things)*

Grammar Notes

Notes 1–2
- Have students read the notes and the examples.
- Make a handout with the following chart, or write it on the board and have students copy:

too much	
too many	
too few	
too little	
too + adjective	

- Have students work in pairs or small groups. Give them a context and have them complete the chart using the structures given. They should write the nouns or adjectives in the right column, for example:

If you give the context "the school cafeteria," students might write the following in the right column:

too much	*noise*
too many	*students*
too few	*chairs*
too little	*artwork*
too + adjective	*food = too expensive*

- Other contexts to talk about:
  students' apartments or dorm rooms
  the bus or train they take to come to school
  a local restaurant or café
  a local park or public shopping area
  a gym or sports facility
- Have pairs or groups compare sentences.

⏱ **Identify the Grammar:** Have students identify the grammar in the reading on page 334. For example:
  . . . the weather is **too hot** and **humid**, . . .
  There are **too few busses** . . .
  . . . there's **too much traffic**.

Go to **www.myfocusongrammarlab.com** for grammar charts and notes.

Step 3: Focused Practice (pages 337–340)

See the general suggestions for Focused Practice on page 4.

Exercise 1: Discover the Grammar
- Go over the example with the class.
- Have students complete the exercise individually. Then call on students to tell you the full phrases. (Example: *too expensive, too much crime*) Write the phrases on the board.
- ⏱ Have students use the phrases on the board to make new sentences.

Exercise 2: *Too much / Too many*
- Have a student read the words in the box. Then go over the example with the class.
- Review the use of *much* and *many*. Ask: "What types of nouns can follow *much*?" *(non-count nouns)* "How about *many*?" *(plural count nouns)*
- Have students complete the exercise in pairs. Then call on students to read the completed sentences. Have the rest of the class check and correct as necessary.

Exercise 3: *Too + Adjective*
- Go over the example with the class.
- Have students complete the exercise individually. Then have them compare answers in pairs.

- ⏱ Have students discuss places and things in their area that are too expensive, are too small, take too long, etc.

Exercise 4: *Too few / Too little*
- Go over the example with the class.
- Have students complete the exercise in pairs. Then combine pairs to form groups of four and have students compare answers.
- Call on students to read the completed conversations. Have the rest of the class listen and make corrections as necessary.

Exercise 5: *Too much / Too many / Too few / Too little / Too*
- Go over the example with the class. Highlight that, to decide on their answers, students need to pay attention to both the grammar (whether the nouns are count [singular or plural] or non-count) and the overall meaning of the conversation.
- Have students complete the exercise in pairs. Then combine pairs to form groups of four and have students compare answers.
- Call on students to read the completed conversations. Have the rest of the class listen and make corrections as necessary.

Exercise 6: Editing
- Go over the example with the class. Point out that students should find six more mistakes in the conversations.
- Have students find and correct the mistakes in pairs.
- Combine pairs to form groups of four and have students compare answers. Then call on students to read the corrected passage. Have them explain why the incorrect structures are wrong.

Go to **www.myfocusongrammarlab.com** for additional grammar practice.

Step 4: Communication Practice (pages 340–342)
See the general suggestions for Communication Practice on page 5.

Exercise 7: Pronunciation
A
- Play the audio. Have students read along as they listen to the Pronunciation Note.
- Say all three sounds: /t/, /θ/, and /ð/. Have students repeat until the voiced / unvoiced distinction is clear. You may want to bring several small hand mirrors to class and have students use them to see that their tongue comes between their front teeth when they make the latter two sounds.

B
- Play the audio. Have students listen.
- Play the audio again. Have students listen and repeat with their hands on their throats.

C
- Have students read the sentences quickly for meaning.
- Play the audio. Have students listen and complete the exercise individually.
- Go over the answers as a class.

D
- Play the audio. Have students listen and repeat.
- ⏱ To extend the practice, have students work in pairs and have them use one of the sentences from part C to create a dialogue. They should try to include as many words as possible with the /t/, /θ/, and /ð/ sounds. Have pairs perform their dialogues for the class.

Exercise 8: Listening
A
- Have students use *too, too much, many, few,* and *little* to predict some things that people might say about an apartment they are looking at with a real estate agent. (Example: *The rooms are too small. There's too little light.*) Then have students read the question and answer choices quickly for meaning.
- Play the audio. Have students listen and complete the exercise individually.
- Go over the answer as a class.

B
- Have students work in pairs to discuss what they remember about the things the people in part A liked and disliked about the apartments.
- Play the audio. Have students listen and complete the exercise in pairs.
- Go over the answers as a class. Have students tell you the words and phrases from the conversation that helped them decide on their answers.

Exercise 9: Role Play
- For each situation, have the class brainstorm some appropriate phrases with *too, too much, many, few,* and *little* and write them on the board for students to use in their conversations, for example, for the first situation:

The City	The Country
too much traffic	too far
too crowded	too inconvenient
too expensive	too many wild animals

- Have pairs develop their conversations. Encourage them to write the conversation down and then practice it several times.
- Call on pairs to present their role plays for the class.

Exercise 10: Describe Your City
- Go over the example with the class.
- Form small groups. Have each group choose one student to write the group's ideas. Remind students that all group members should contribute ideas as they complete the exercise.

Exercise 11: Writing
A
- Go over the example with the class.
- To help students get started, give them time to make some notes about positive and negative attributes of life in their cities.
- Have students complete the exercise individually.

B
- Have students correct their work using the Editing Checklist.
- Then have students exchange papers and check their partner's work.
- ⏱ Have students read their paragraphs in small groups.

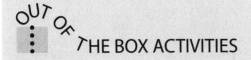

OUT OF THE BOX ACTIVITIES

Speaking
- Have students think of problems and ways to improve particular aspects of their lives. Give them some topic prompts:
  My room / apartment / house
  Our school / campus / classroom
  This textbook
  The mall
  The downtown area
- Have students use the target grammar to write about the problems. Then have them work in pairs or groups to share their problems and help one another brainstorm solutions.

Go to **www.myfocusongrammarlab.com** for additional listening, pronunciation, speaking, and writing practice.

Note:
- See the *Focus on Grammar Workbook* for additional in-class or homework grammar practice.

Unit 29 Review (page 343)

Have students complete the Review and check their answers on Student Book page UR-6. Review or assign additional material as needed.

Go to **www.myfocusongrammarlab.com** for the Unit Achievement Test.

From Grammar to Writing (pages 344–345)

See the general suggestions for From Grammar to Writing on page 9.

Go to **www.myfocusongrammarlab.com** for an additional From Grammar to Writing Assignment, Part Review, and Part Post-Test.

PART X OVERVIEW

MODALS: REQUESTS, ADVICE, NECESSITY

UNIT	GRAMMAR FOCUS	THEME
30	Advice: *Should, Ought to, Had Better*	Dos and Don'ts of the Business World
31	Requests, Desires, and Offers: *Would you, Could you, Can you . . . ?, I'd like . . .*	Neighbors
32	Necessity: *Have to, Don't Have to, Must, Mustn't*	Rules at School

Go to **www.myfocusongrammarlab.com** for the Part and Unit Tests.

Note: PowerPoint® grammar presentations, test-generating software, and reproducible Part and Unit Tests are on the *Teacher's Resource Disc*.

> **Grammar: ADVICE:** *Should, Ought to, Had Better*
>
> Unit 30 focuses on the structure, meaning, and use of modals of advice: *should, ought to,* and *had better*.
>
> **Theme: DOS AND DON'TS OF THE BUSINESS WORLD**
>
> Unit 30 focuses on language and expressions used to give advice about culturally appropriate and inappropriate behaviors in international business settings.

Step 1: Grammar in Context (pages 348–349)

See the general suggestions for Grammar in Context on page 1.

Before You Read

- Model shaking hands. Have students imagine they are meeting you for the first time. Go around the room and have individual students stand. Introduce yourself and shake hands with each student firmly while making eye contact.
- Have students tell you anything they noticed about your handshake. Accept all answers.
- Have students stand and shake hands with one person next to them. Have these pairs of students discuss the question.
- ⏱ Lead a brief class discussion about business greetings in students' own countries. Ask:
  How do people in your country usually greet one another in business situations?
  Do they shake hands?
  What is important to remember when greeting someone from your country in a business situation?

Read

- Before students begin reading, elicit anything students might know about Chile or Egypt. Have students find the two countries on a map. Ask:
  What regions of the world are these countries in? *(Chile: South America; Egypt: North Africa)*
  What do you know about these countries? *(capital cities [Santiago / Cairo], famous landmarks [Easter Island / the Great Pyramid, Sphinx], languages spoken [Spanish / Arabic])*
  Do you know anything else about these countries' cultures?

- Go over the glossed vocabulary at the end of the conversation.
- Have students read the text. (OR: Play the audio and have students follow along in their books.)

After You Read

A. Practice

- Call on pairs to read paragraphs.
- Call on students to give an example or two of a "Do" and a "Don't" for each country.

B. Vocabulary

- Have a student read the words in the box aloud.
- Have students complete the exercise individually.
- Have students compare answers in pairs. Then go over the answers as a class and have students explain how they decided on the answers.

C

- Have students complete the exercise individually and compare answers in pairs.
- Go over the answers as a class.

Go to **www.myfocusongrammarlab.com** for an additional reading, and for reading and vocabulary practice.

Step 2: Grammar Presentation (pages 350–351)

See the general suggestions for Grammar Presentation on page 2.

Grammar Charts

- Call on students to read the examples in the charts. Ask: "What is the general meaning of *should* and *ought to*?" *(advice, or the right thing to do)* "What are the affirmative forms?" *(should, ought to, had better)* "What is the negative form?" *(should not or shouldn't)* *(Ought not* is not used in modern American English.)
- Call on students to read the examples of *yes / no* questions and answers.
- Provide some subjects and verb prompts and have students form questions as follows:
  T: You shake hands.
  Ss: Should you shake hands?
  T: We eat with our right hand.
  Ss: Should we eat with our right hand?
- Point out that we do not generally ask questions with *ought to*.
- Ask questions from the opening reading and elicit the short answers, for example, "Should you keep your hands on the table in Chile?" *(Yes, you should.)* Ask a similar question to elicit a negative response: "Should you eat all the food on your plate in Egypt?" *(No, you shouldn't.)*

- Call on students to read the examples of *wh*-questions.
- Ask questions from the opening reading and elicit the answers, for example, "When should you avoid planning a business trip to Chile?" *(in January)* "In Egypt, which hand should I eat with?" *(the right hand)*
- Call on students to read the statements with *had better* and *had better not*. Ask: "What do these expressions mean?" *(Something bad might happen if you don't follow the advice.)*
- Say a sentence with each of the contracted forms and have students repeat. (Example: *I'd better leave now. You'd better leave now. He'd better leave now.*)

Grammar Notes

Notes 1 and 2
- Call on students to read the notes and the examples.
- Have students give more examples of cultural customs related to flowers; for example, ask them to make sentences about the types, colors, and numbers of flowers that are appropriate for different occasions in their culture. Have them use *should* and *shouldn't*. (Example: *In Iran, you shouldn't give people yellow flowers as a gift. In China, you shouldn't give people white flowers. In Armenia, you should give people uneven numbers of flowers on happy occasions.*)

Note 3
- Have students read the note and the examples. Make sure students understand that we use *ought to* only in affirmative statements. In questions and negatives, we use *should*.
- Put students into small groups. Give them the following list of problems (or write your own). Have them talk about what people ought to do or shouldn't do in these situations.

1. An American family has invited you to come to their house for Christmas dinner. You don't know what kind of gift to bring.
2. Your American teacher often touches your shoulder or arm when he or she is talking to you. This makes you uncomfortable.
3. Your neighbor has a big dog that barks late at night and early in the morning. This wakes you up.
4. You are renting a room in a house that belongs to an American family. You are sure that someone is listening to your phone conversations and going into your room when you are not home.

5. You always bring your lunch to work and put it in the office refrigerator. Your lunch has disappeared from the refrigerator three times in the past two weeks. This has also happened to one of your coworkers.

Notes 5 and 6
- Prepare the prompts in the following boxes on separate strips of paper or index cards.
- Call on students to read the notes and the examples.
- Have students work in pairs and have each student look at a different box (below). Have students take turns reading the items in their boxes. Partners respond with "had better" or "had better not" using an appropriate subject pronoun, for example:

S1: They just washed the floor, and it's still wet.
S2: We'd better not walk on it. / We'd better be careful.

STUDENT 1

1. You have a bad cold.
2. My midterm exam in grammar is tomorrow. I haven't started studying.
3. Coffee makes Mary nervous.
4. John has very white, sensitive skin.
5. The chicken in your refrigerator smells bad.

STUDENT 2

1. It is raining very hard, and you need to go to work.
2. Juan smokes, and he knows that smoking is very bad for his health.
3. You're late for an important appointment.
4. Blanca's car is almost out of gas.
5. You forgot to pay your cell phone bill.

Identify the Grammar: Have students identify the grammar in the reading on page 348. For example:
  . . . you **should not plan** a business trip . . .
  . . . how **should** you greet people . . . ?
  . . . you **ought to greet** and **shake hands** with everyone.

Go to **www.myfocusongrammarlab.com** for grammar charts and notes.

Step 3: Focused Practice (pages 352–355)
See the general suggestions for Focused Practice on page 4.

Exercise 1: Discover the Grammar

- Go over the example with the class. Then have students read the text quickly for meaning.
- Have students complete the exercise in pairs. Then call on pairs to read the questions and answers.
- 🕐 Have students form sentences explaining the dos and don'ts of exchanging business cards in Japan, for example:

   You should present your business card right after you shake hands or bow.

   You shouldn't start your business before you exchange cards.

Exercise 2: *Should*: Affirmative and Negative

- Go over the example with the class. Then have students read the text quickly for meaning.
- Have students complete the exercise in pairs. Then call on pairs to read the questions and answers.
- 🕐 To extend the practice, lead a brief class discussion. Have students compare the customs described in the exercises to their own. (Example: *In my country, it's the same as in Korea. You shouldn't blow your nose at the table.*)

Exercise 3: *Should*: Affirmative and Negative

- Read the verbs in the box and have students repeat. Then go over the example with the class.
- Have students complete the exercise individually. Then call on students to read the completed sentences.
- 🕐 Have students write sentences comparing the statements about Hungary to their own culture.

Exercise 4: *Ought to*

- Call on a student to read the verbs in the box. Ask: "Will the form of these verbs change?" *(no)* Then go over the example with the class.
- Have students complete the exercise individually.
- Have students compare answers in pairs. Then call on pairs to read the completed sentences.

Exercise 5: *Had better*: Affirmative and Negative

- Go over the example with the class.
- Have students complete the exercise individually.
- To check answers, ask questions to elicit the responses, for example:

   Should I show the soles of my feet in Thailand or Saudi Arabia?

   Which hand should I eat with in Hindu and Islamic countries?

Exercise 6: *Had better*

- Go over the example with the class. Make sure students understand that different answers and ideas are possible. They should use the information given to give advice about what people had better or had better not do. Remind them to use the contracted form where possible.
- Have students complete the exercise in pairs. Then combine pairs to form groups of four and have students compare answers.
- 🕐 Have groups make sentences about their own culture, using *had better* or *had better not*.

Exercise 7: Editing

A

- Go over the example with the class. Point out that students should find five more mistakes in the conversations.
- Have students find and correct the mistakes in pairs.

B

- Have students find three mistakes in the conversations.
- Call on students to read the corrected conversations.
- Have students explain why the incorrect structures are wrong.

Go to **www.myfocusongrammarlab.com** for additional grammar practice.

Step 4: Communication Practice (pages 356–358)

See the general suggestions for Communication Practice on page 5.

Exercise 8: Pronunciation

A

- Play the audio. Have students read along as they listen to the Pronunciation Note.

B

- Play the audio. Have students listen and repeat.

Exercise 9: Listening

A

- Have students read the questions quickly for meaning.
- Play the audio. Have students listen and complete the exercise individually.
- Go over the answers as a class.

B

- Have students read the text quickly for meaning.
- Play the audio. Have students listen and complete the exercise individually.
- Have students compare answers in pairs. Then play the audio again to confirm the answers.

Exercise 10: Discussion: Gift Giving

A

- Have students read the text quickly for meaning.
- Have students complete the exercise in pairs.

B

- Use the questions to lead a class discussion about gift giving. If you have students from different countries, compare and contrast gift-giving customs, including when it's important to give gifts, types / colors / numbers of gifts that should / shouldn't be given, and so on.

Exercise 11: Conversation: Body Language

A

- To help students get started, model some examples of body language, for example, nodding or shaking your head, shrugging shoulders, hand or finger gestures meaning "Come here," "OK," "Great!" and so on. Have students guess the meanings. You may want to write some verbal expressions of common gestures to give students some ideas. (Example: *I don't know, be quiet, money, go away, come here, OK, great!*)
- Form small groups. Have students complete the exercise in groups.

B

- Have students in each group discuss body language in their cultures. Ask: "What kinds of things can be expressed with body language? What gestures do you know from other cultures?"

C

- Lead a class discussion about body language. Have students compare and contrast body language and gestures in their cultures.

Exercise 12: Writing

A

- Go over the example with the class. Call on different students to read the topics.
- Give students time to make some notes to help them get started.
- Have students complete the exercise individually.

B

- Have students correct their work using the Editing Checklist.
- Then have students exchange papers and check their partner's work.
- To follow-up, have students read their advice in small groups.

OUT OF THE BOX ACTIVITIES

Speaking

- Tell students that they're going to discuss "culture bumps"—mistakes they have made in this culture because they were not aware of the local customs or traditions.
- Give an example of a mistake you made while traveling or living abroad. Use the target structures from this unit, for example: When I went to France, I wanted to mail a letter to my family, so I went to the post office. When I got there, I was very confused because there weren't any lines. I saw a big crowd of people and I couldn't understand how to get to the window to buy some stamps. I was there for 15 minutes, and finally I just left. Later, somebody explained to me that in France, people don't stand in lines at the post office. If you want to buy stamps, you shouldn't stand there patiently. You should just push your way to the front like everybody else.
- Have students from different countries sit together in small groups and tell their stories. Finally, have students share stories about culture bumps with the class.

Writing and Speaking

- Have students gather information about customs and traditions individually or in groups.
- Each student or group is given (or selects) one topic about customs or traditions to research (e.g., using names).
- Encourage them to survey students from different countries, collect the responses, and write them on a poster. For example:

Using Names	
United States	You shouldn't call older people by their first names without permission.
Korea	You should use a person's title with his or her name.
China	You shouldn't call a woman by her husband's name.

- Have students or groups write their findings on posters. Then display them in the classroom.

Go to **www.myfocusongrammarlab.com** for additional listening, pronunciation, speaking, and writing practice.

Note:
- See the *Focus on Grammar Workbook* for additional in-class or homework grammar practice.

Unit 30 Review (page 359)

Have students complete the Review and check their answers on Student Book page UR-6. Review or assign additional material as needed.

Go to **www.myfocusongrammarlab.com** for the Unit Achievement Test.

> **UNIT 31 OVERVIEW**
>
> **Grammar:** REQUESTS, DESIRES, AND OFFERS: *Would you, Could you, Can you . . . ?, I'd like . . .*
>
> Unit 31 focuses on the structure of and use of the phrases *would you, could you, can you . . . ?, I'd like . . .* in making offers and requests and expressing desires.
>
> **Theme:** NEIGHBORS
>
> Unit 31 focuses on language and expressions used to talk about asking favors and making and responding to requests from others.

Step 1: Grammar in Context (pages 360–361)

See the general suggestions for Grammar in Context on page 1.

Before You Read
- Introduce the theme of neighbors. Elicit a definition for the word *neighbor* (a person who lives very near you, in the same building or on the same street).
- Ask students about their neighbors: "Are they friendly?" "How well do you know them?" "What kind of relationships do you have with them?"
- Have students complete the exercise individually.

Read
- Call on a student to read the introduction.
- Have students read the messages silently.

After You Read

A. Practice
- To get students to read with a purpose, write these questions on the board:
  1. What is Jade asking for advice about? *(She did many favors for her friend, Gina, but when she asked Gina for a favor, Gina did not help.)*
  2. How does Jade feel? *(angry and hurt)*
  3. Do you think she should feel that way?
  4. What advice did Luz give to Jade? *(tell Gina how she feels)*
  5. Do you agree with the advice?
- Have students read the text. (OR: Play the audio and have students follow along in their books.) Then call on students to share their answers to the questions on the board.

B. Vocabulary
- Read the words and phrases in the left column and have students repeat.
- Have students complete the exercise individually.
- Have students compare answers in pairs. Then call on students to give answers and explain how they decided on them.

C. Comprehension
- Call on students to read the statements in the chart.
- Have students complete the exercise individually. Encourage them to do so without looking back at the text.
- Have students compare answers in pairs. Then go over the answers as a class.

Go to **www.myfocusongrammarlab.com** for an additional reading, and for reading and vocabulary practice.

Step 2: Grammar Presentation (pages 361–362)

See the general suggestions for Grammar Presentation on page 2.

Grammar Charts

- Have students read the examples in the charts.
- Ask the following questions to draw students' attention to the target structures in the opening text:

  Which questions can you use to ask for a favor? (*Can you drive . . . , Could you help . . . , Would you help me?*)

  Which question can you use to offer to help someone? (*Would you like me to . . . ?*)

  What are some ways of agreeing to do someone a favor? (*I'd be glad to, sure, of course*)

  How can you say that you refuse to do someone a favor? (*I'd like to, but . . .*)

- Call on students to read the Polite Requests chart. Have them write three requests using *would you*, *could you*, and *can you*. Encourage them to write silly or unusual requests, such as *Could you give me a bag of turtles?*
- Put students into pairs and have them take turns reading their requests. Partners should respond with short answers from the chart.
- Have students read the Desires and Contractions charts silently. Then model the contracted forms and have students repeat. (Example: *I'd like to help. You'd like to help.*)
- Call on students to read the last two charts. To practice, have students pretend some friends have come to their home for dinner. Set up a drill like the following:

  T: Blueberries.
  S1: Would you like some blueberries?
  S2: Yes, thank you.
  T: Coffee.
  S2: Would you like some coffee?
  S3: No, thanks.
  T: Tea.
  S3: Would you like some tea?
  S4: Yes, I would.

Grammar Notes

Note 1

- Read the first line of the examples column: *Would you (please) help me carry these books?* Ask pairs of students to read the next two examples.
- Ask: "What are the three new ways of making requests? How can you agree to a request? How can you say 'no' politely?"

- To practice, make a diagram of an empty bedroom similar to the following:

	door		
			closet
window		window	

- Then give students a list of items like the following:

bed	television	2 large framed
desk	nightstand	posters
computer	dresser	bicycle
	floor lamp	shoes

- Have students form groups of three. Have students imagine they're moving into a new apartment with the help of classmates. Right now the bedroom is empty. They should use polite requests and short answers to tell their friends where to put their belongings, for example:

  S1: Would you please put my shoes in the closet?
  S2: Sure.

Note 2

- Call on students to read the note and the examples.
- Have students form small groups. Say: "Would you like some ice cream?" Have students imagine they are at an ice-cream shop and have them describe the ice-cream cone they'd like to order. They should say what kind of cone they want (plain, sugar, waffle), the kind of ice cream, how many scoops, and what kind of topping. (Example: *I'd like a sugar cone with one scoop of mint chip and one scoop of vanilla, and I'd like a cherry on top.*)

Note 3

- Call on students to read the notes and the examples.
- Have students do mini role plays. Give students a list of the contexts like the ones below. Have them take turns offering services or help and accepting or rejecting the offers, for example:

  1. A flight attendant and a passenger on an airplane
     ATTENDANT: Would you like a pillow?
     PASSENGER: Yes, thank you.

2. A server taking an order from a customer at a coffee bar
3. Two neighbors; one has an orange tree full of ripe oranges
4. Two female friends; one has some clothes that don't fit her anymore, but they fit her friend
5. An older person and a younger person on a bus; the younger person is seated, and the older one is standing
6. A person standing outside a supermarket with a box of free kittens; the person offers to give away the kittens to shoppers as they exit the market

⏱ **Identify the Grammar:** Have students identify the grammar in the reading on page 360. For example:

. . . **can you do** me a favor? **Can you drive me** to the airport tonight?

"**Sure**, Gina. **I'd be glad to. Would you like** me to pick you up at 7:00?"

. . . **could you help** me . . .

Go to **www.myfocusongrammarlab.com** for grammar charts and notes.

Step 3: Focused Practice (pages 363–365)

See the general suggestions for Focused Practice on page 4.

Exercise 1: Discover the Grammar
• Have students look at the instructions. Ask: "Which types of sentences are questions?" *(requests and offers)* "Which are statements?" *(desires)*
• Have students complete the exercise individually. Then have them compare answers in pairs.
• ⏱ Have students work in pairs to create mini-dialogues from the statements by adding a response, for example:
S1: Would you give me a ride?
S2: Sorry, I can't. I have to work.

Exercise 2: Requests, Offers, Desires, and Responses
• Go over the example with the class. Then have students read the text quickly for meaning.
• Have students complete the exercise individually. Then call on pairs to read the conversation, inserting the answers. Have the rest of the class listen and correct any errors as necessary.
• ⏱ Have students practice the conversations, changing partners and roles several times.

Exercise 3: Responses to Requests and Offers
• Call on students to read the requests and offers.
• Have students complete the exercise individually. Then have them compare answers in pairs.
• ⏱ Have students stand and walk around the class making the offers and requests to different classmates.

Exercise 4: Requests, Offers, Desires
• Go over the example with the class. Ask: "Which expression sounds more polite?" (Example: *Could you please . . .*) Highlight that *I would like* sounds more polite than *I want.*
• Have students complete the exercise in pairs.
• Call on pairs of students to read the conversation. Have the rest of the class listen and check and correct as necessary.

Exercise 5: Editing
• Go over the example with the class. Point out that there are four more mistakes in the conversations.
• Have students find and correct the mistakes in pairs.
• Combine pairs to form groups of four and have students compare answers. Then call on students to read the corrected passage. Have them explain why the incorrect structures are wrong.

Go to **www.myfocusongrammarlab.com** for additional grammar practice.

Step 4: Communication Practice (pages 366–368)

See the general suggestions for Communication Practice on page 5.

Exercise 6: Pronunciation
A
• Play the audio. Have students read along as they listen to the Pronunciation Note.

B
• Play the audio. Have students listen and repeat.

Exercise 7: Listening
A
• Have students read the sentence and answer choices quickly for meaning.
• Play the audio. Have students listen and complete the exercise individually.
• Go over the answer as a class.

B

- Have students read the questions and answer choices quickly for meaning.
- Play the audio. Have students complete the exercise individually.
- Have students compare answers in pairs. Then ask the questions and call on students to say the answers.

Exercise 8: Survey

A

- Go over the scenarios and the example with the class.
- Have students read the requests and add any others they can think of.
- Form groups of four. Students in each group discuss the requests. Remind them to expand and explain their answers.

B

- Have students take notes on their groups' responses.
- Lead a class discussion about whether these reports are appropriate.

Exercise 9: Making Polite Requests

- Go over the example with the class. Point out that the example uses *can you*. Elicit other ways of beginning a polite request. (Example: *Would you [please], Could you [please]*) Then have students read the situations quickly for meaning.
- Have students complete the exercise in pairs.
- Call on pairs to give their answers. Call on other pairs who have come up with different ways to make and answer the same requests.

Exercise 10: Extending Invitations

- Go over the example and the activities in the box with the class. Then brainstorm with the class additional activities or events to which they would like to invite their classmates. You may also want to have students brainstorm reasons for declining an invitation. (Example: *I have to study for a test. I have a date. I have a doctor's appointment.*)
- Have students complete the exercise in pairs.
- To follow up, call on pairs of students to stand. One student invites the other, who accepts or declines.

Exercise 11: Role Play

- Go over the example with the class. Then have students read the situations quickly for meaning.
- Have students complete the exercise in pairs.
- Call on pairs to present their role plays to the class.

Exercise 12: Writing

A

- Have students read the situations quickly for meaning. Then go over the examples with the class.
- Brainstorm with the class other situations that might lead them to email requests to their neighbors.
- Have students complete the task individually.

B

- Have students correct their work using the Editing Checklist.
- Then have students exchange papers and check their partner's work.
- ⏱ Have students type their emails and send them to a classmate. Classmates respond to the requests in the role of the neighbor.

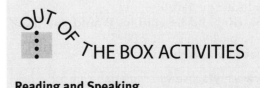

OUT OF THE BOX ACTIVITIES

Reading and Speaking

- Bring in copies of newspapers.
- Have students go through the newspapers. The aim is to find the following:
  — An event to invite a classmate to
  — An advertisement for something that a classmate might like to buy
  — Something expensive that they would like to buy
- Have students ask questions in pairs about the newspaper items. For example:
  Would you like to go to a concert on November 5?
  Would you like to buy a new computer? They're on sale at the mall.
  I'd like to buy this car. Could you lend me $10,000?

Go to **www.myfocusongrammarlab.com** for additional listening, pronunciation, speaking, and writing practice.

Note:
- See the *Focus on Grammar Workbook* for additional in-class or homework grammar practice.

Unit 31 Review (page 369)

Have students complete the Review and check their answers on Student Book page UR-6. Review or assign additional material as needed.

Go to **www.myfocusongrammarlab.com** for the Unit Achievement Test.

UNIT 32 OVERVIEW

Grammar: NECESSITY: *Have to, Don't have to, Must, Mustn't*

Unit 32 focuses on the structure and use of modals of necessity: *have to, don't have to, must, mustn't.*

Theme: RULES AT SCHOOL

Unit 32 focuses on language and expressions used to talk about requirements and rules in various school settings.

Step 1: Grammar in Context (pages 370–371)

See the general suggestions for Grammar in Context on page 1.

Before You Read

- Introduce the theme of school rules. Ask: "What are some of the rules that schools have?" You may want to give some topic prompts to help students. (Example: *clothing, homework, dormitory life, cheating*) Then explain that something you *have to* do is like following a rule; it is something you need to do.
- Have students complete the exercise individually. Then call on students to give answers.
- ⏱ Elicit other activities students have to do for this class or for other classes.

Read

- Explain that course requirements are the things students need to do to pass a course. (Example: *coming to class, completing homework, quizzes, tests, and projects*) Ask: "What are some of the requirements for this class?"
- Go over the glossed vocabulary at the end of the conversation.
- Have students read the text. (OR: Play the audio and have students follow along in their books.)

After You Read

A. Practice

- Have students complete the exercise in pairs.
- Then call on pairs to read paragraphs aloud.

B. Vocabulary

- Read the words and phrases in the box and have students repeat. Then have students read the text quickly for meaning.
- Have students complete the exercise individually.
- Have students compare answers in pairs. Then go over the answers as a class and have students explain how they decided on the answers.

C. Comprehension

- Have students complete the exercise individually. Encourage them to do so without looking back at the text.
- Have students compare answers in pairs. Then call on students to tell you the answers in complete sentences. (Example: *Students don't have to take a quiz every week.*)
- ⏱ Have students compare the requirements in Professor Anderson's class to those in their own classes.

Go to **www.myfocusongrammarlab.com** for an additional reading, and for reading and vocabulary practice.

Step 2: Grammar Presentation (pages 372–373)

See the general suggestions for Grammar Presentation on page 2.

Grammar Charts

- Focus on the meaning of the modals. Ask: "What do we mean when we say something is necessary?" (*It is required. We have no choice of whether to do it.*)
- Have students read the charts with the affirmative and negative forms of *have to*. Ask: "If we have to do something, do we have a choice of whether to do it?" (*No. It is required.*) "What is the meaning of *don't have to?*" (*You can do it if you choose, but it is not required or necessary.*)
- Drill the forms by cueing students with the pronouns. For the affirmative forms, you may want to bring back the large letter *-s* you made earlier in the course, when students were learning the present tense. Hold it up to cue students that an *-s* ending is needed, for example:

  T: I have to pay my phone bill today. You.
  Ss: You have to pay your phone bill today.
  T: He.
  Ss: He has to pay . . .

- To build fluency, do a transformation drill. Provide the affirmative form. Students should change it to the negative or vice versa.

- Have students read the charts of *yes / no* questions. Drill by having them transform statements into questions. (Use your *-s* cue card as needed.) Example:
  T: I have to go to the dentist.
  Ss: Do I have to go to the dentist?
  T: You.
  Ss: Do you have to go to the dentist?
- Next, do a chain drill using *yes / no* questions with short answers. Have students read the chart of short answers. Choose a context and provide cues to form questions. Instruct students to answer truthfully, for example:
  T: At home, do you have to make your bed every day?
  S1: No, I don't.
  T: Cook dinner.
  S1: Do you have to cook dinner?
  S2: Yes, I do.
  T: Vacuum the living room.
  S2: Do you have to vacuum the living room?
  S3: Yes, I do.
- Have students read the chart with examples of *must* and *must not*. (**Note:** Do not do a transformation drill with these two forms, as that would wrongly reinforce the notion that these forms are opposite in meaning.) To practice *must*, put students in pairs. Give each pair a handout with one of the following scenarios. Instruct them to use *must* to make sentences about the scenarios. (Example: *On Saturday nights, Dotan must babysit the children.*)

> Dotan lives with an American family.
> He does not pay rent, but he has to do work around the house. These are his responsibilities:
>
> babysit the children on Saturday nights
> mow the lawn every Sunday
> cook dinner three times a week
> take out the trash
> wash the family car
> clean the kitchen after dinner

> To observe good manners while eating, do not:
>
> talk with food in your mouth
> put your elbows on the table
> reach across another person's plate
> throw objects across the table
> blow your nose at the table
> criticize the food
> make noise while eating
> blow on hot food to cool it down
> use your napkin as a handkerchief
> put your fingers into the serving bowls

Grammar Notes

Notes 1 and 2
- Call on students to read the notes and the examples. Clarify the difference between *must* and *have to* as follows: *Have to* is used in both speaking and writing. *Must* is used in writing but rarely in speaking. Encourage students to use *have to* in conversation.
- Point out the *Be Careful!* note.
- Form small groups. Have students in each group use *have to* or *don't have to* to discuss one of the topics below (or choose your own).

> 1. Graduation requirements in a student's major. Example:
> *My major is French. To graduate, I have to take eight courses . . . I have to pass a reading exam . . . I have to write . . . but I don't have to speak fluently.*

> 2. Requirements to get a certain job in your country. Example:
> *To be a doctor in the United States, first you have to get a B.A. You don't have to major in science, but it helps. After that you have to go to medical school . . .*

Notes 3–6
- Call on students to read the notes and the examples.
- Point out the *Be Careful!* note.
- Since *mustn't* is often used when talking to children, have students list five things that a kindergarten teacher might say to young students in small groups. (Examples: *You mustn't push. You mustn't take another child's toys. You mustn't shout indoors.*)
- Put two groups together. Have the groups share their sentences.

⏱ **Identify the Grammar:** Have students identify the grammar in the conversation on page 370. For example:
  You **must score** an average of 65 percent or above . . .
  . . . you **must include** a bibliography.
  You **have to hand** it **in** . . .

Go to **www.myfocusongrammarlab.com** for grammar charts and notes.

Step 3: Focused Practice (pages 374–378)
See the general suggestions for Focused Practice on page 4.

Exercise 1: Discover the Grammar

- Have students predict some of the requirements for entering a school for the arts. (Example: *Students must sing or dance in front of people.*) Then have students read the text quickly for meaning.
- Have students complete the exercise individually. Then have them compare answers in pairs.
- Call on students to read the sentences with modals.

Exercise 2: *Have to / Don't have to / Must*

A
- Have students try to predict some of the requirements for entering the dance and music programs at a performing arts school. Elicit sentences with *have to, don't have to, must,* and *must not* and write them on the board. Then go over the example with the class.
- Have students complete the exercise individually.
- Call on students to read the paragraph, inserting the answers. Have the rest of the class listen and correct as necessary.

B
- Have students complete the exercise individually.
- Call on students to read the paragraph, inserting the answers. Have the rest of the class listen and correct as necessary.

Exercise 3: *Have / Have to / Had to*

- Go over the example with the class.
- Have students complete the exercise individually. Then have them compare answers in pairs.
- ⏱ Have students practice the conversation, changing roles and partners several times.

Exercise 4: *Have to / Don't have to*

- Go over the example with the class. Then call on a student to read the verbs in the box.
- Have students complete the exercise individually. Then have them compare answers in pairs.
- ⏱ Have students use the target modals and the verbs in the box to make true sentences about their educational experiences (past or present). (Example: *In our English class, we have to attend two classes a week. In high school, I had to wear a uniform.*)

Exercise 5: *Have to / Must / Must not*

- Have students look at the signs. For each one, ask: "Where might you see this sign?" "What does it mean?" Then go over the example with the class.
- Have students complete the exercise in pairs. Then combine pairs to form groups of four and have students compare answers.
- ⏱ Hand out paper and markers. Have students draw other signs (real ones or their own creations). Have them note the meaning of the sign, but not write it. Have students form groups. Students take turns showing their signs. The rest of the group guesses the meaning.

Exercise 6: Editing

- Go over the example with the class. Point out that they should find seven more mistakes in the sentences.
- Have students find and correct the mistakes in pairs.
- Combine pairs to form groups of four and have students compare answers. Then call on students to read the corrected sentences. Have them explain why the incorrect structures are wrong.

Go to **www.myfocusongrammarlab.com** for additional grammar practice.

Step 4: Communication Practice (pages 378–380)

See the general suggestions for Communication Practice on page 5.

Exercise 7: Pronunciation

A
- Play the audio. Have students read along as they listen to the Pronunciation Note.
- Say both pronunciations of *have to* in isolation and have students repeat.

B
- Play the audio. Have students listen and repeat.
- ⏱ Have students practice the conversations in pairs, changing roles and partners several times.

C
- Go over the example with the class. Then have students think of three things they have to do this week.
- Have students complete the exercise in pairs.
- Call on students to tell you what their partner has to do this week.

Exercise 8: Listening

A

- Have students read the instructions. Ask: "What are you going to listen for?" *(the type of degree)* As students may be unfamiliar with degree titles and acronyms in English, you may want to elicit a few examples and write them on the board. (Example: *B.A.: Bachelor of Arts, B.S.: Bachelor of Science, M.A.: Master of Arts, Ph.D.: Doctorate*)
- Play the audio. Have students listen and complete the exercise individually.
- Go over the answer as a class and explain that an M.B.A. is a Master of Business Administration, a degree for people interested in becoming business managers.

B

- Play the audio, pausing a few times for students to write their answers. Alternatively, you may want to play the audio once and have students take notes and then write their answers afterwards.
- Have students compare answers in pairs. Then play the audio again to confirm the answers.
- Go over the answers as a class.

Exercise 9: Discussion

- Go over the example with the class.
- Have students form small groups. Have students in each group discuss the topic. Remind them to expand and explain their answers.
- Call on students to report on their group's discussion.

Exercise 10: Survey

A

- Go over the example with the class. Then elicit some ways that you try to prevent cheating in your own classes.
- Have students walk around the class and survey five classmates. Have them take notes on their classmates' answers.

B

- Go over the example with the class.
- Have students complete the exercise as a class, using ideas from Part A as well as new ideas.

Exercise 11: Writing

A

- Go over the example with the class. Then use the following questions to generate ideas and elicit vocabulary:

What do children at your elementary school say when the teacher enters the room?
How must students address the teacher?
What must they wear?
How must they behave in class?
When can they talk? When do they have to be quiet?
Do they have to clean their classroom?

- Give students time to make some notes about their elementary school experiences.
- Have students complete the exercise individually.

B

- Have students correct their work using the Editing Checklist.
- Then have students exchange papers and check their partner's work.
- ⏱ Have students read their paragraphs in small groups. Then call on students to tell you some of the similarities and differences between their elementary school experiences. In a multicultural class, this is a good opportunity to focus on cultural comparison.

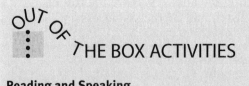

OUT OF THE BOX ACTIVITIES

Reading and Speaking

- Bring in a selection of help-wanted ads from an English-language newspaper or print them from the Internet. If your class is small, bring in one ad per student. If the class is large, plan on groups of four or five students, find four or five ads, and make one set of copies per group.
- In groups, have students describe the requirements for the jobs and then choose a job they would like to have. Choose ads with information that students can use to make sentences with *have to, must,* and *don't have to.* The following is an example of a useful ad:

> **Taxi Drivers**
> Make good money! We provide car.
> 25 or older. Clean driving record.
> Will train. Driving test. 310-555-1857

- This ad lends itself to sentences such as the following:
  — You don't have to have your own car.
  — You must be older than 25.
  — You must have a clean driving record.

- You don't have to have experience. They will train you.
- You have to take a driving test.

- Have students present their ads to the class or to their groups. They should say what kind of job it is and what the job requirements are. (Example: *This is an ad for a taxi driver. If you want this job, you have to be older than 25. You don't have to have a car, but you must have a clean driving record.*)

Go to **www.myfocusongrammarlab.com** for additional listening, pronunciation, speaking, and writing practice.

Note:
- See the *Focus on Grammar Workbook* for additional in-class or homework grammar practice.

Unit 32 Review (page 381)

Have students complete the Review and check their answers on Student Book page UR-7. Review or assign additional material as needed.

Go to **www.myfocusongrammarlab.com** for the Unit Achievement Test.

From Grammar to Writing (pages 382–383)

See the general suggestions for From Grammar to Writing on page 9.

Go to **www.myfocusongrammarlab.com** for an additional From Grammar to Writing Assignment, Part Review, and Part Post-Test.

COMPARISONS

UNIT	GRAMMAR FOCUS	THEME
33	The Comparative	Comparing Cities
34	Adverbs of Manner	Public Speaking
35	*Enough, Too / Very, As + Adjective + As, Same / Different*	Proms and Parties
36	The Superlative	Penguins

Go to **www.myfocusongrammarlab.com** for the Part and Unit Tests.

Note: PowerPoint® grammar presentations, test-generating software, and reproducible Part and Unit Tests are on the *Teacher's Resource Disc.*

UNIT 33 OVERVIEW

Grammar: THE COMPARATIVE

Unit 33 focuses on the structure and use of the comparative, including the comparative form of adjectives with one, two, and more than two syllables; irregular comparatives, such as *far* and *farther*; and questions with *which*: *Which is bigger?*

Theme: COMPARING CITIES

Unit 33 focuses on language and expressions used to describe and compare features of different cities.

Step 1: Grammar in Context (pages 386–387)

See the general suggestions for Grammar in Context on page 1.

Before You Read

- Introduce the theme of comparing cities. Have students think about the city where your school is located. Elicit the name of another town or city nearby. Ask: "What are some of the differences between [this city / town] and [other city / town]?"
- Call on a student to read the discussion questions. Then model the task by briefly giving your own answers to the questions.

- Have students discuss the questions in pairs. Then call on pairs to share their ideas with the class. Alternatively, do this as a class discussion.

Read
- If possible, point out or have students point out Portland, Oregon, and Portland, Maine, on a U.S. map. If any students have visited either Portland, ask them to briefly describe the experience.
- Have students read the text. (OR: Play the audio and have students follow along in their books.)
- In pairs, have students discuss which Portland they would prefer to live in. Remind them to expand on and explain their answers.

After You Read

A. Practice
- Call on students to read sentences aloud.
- ⏱ Ask students any or all of the following questions to follow up:
  Where is Maine? Where is Oregon? *(East Coast; West Coast)*
  Why are the two cities named Portland? *(Portland, Maine, because it has a port and Portland, Oregon, because it was named after Portland, Maine)*
  Where is Portland, Maine, located? *(on the coast, 45 minutes from the mountains)*
  Where is Portland, Oregon, located? *(on a river)*

B. Vocabulary
- Read the words and phrases in the box and have students repeat.
- Have students complete the exercise individually. Then have them compare answers in pairs.
- ⏱ Have students use the vocabulary to create new sentences in pairs.

C. Comprehension
- Have students complete the exercise in pairs. Encourage them to do so without looking back at the text.
- Combine pairs to form groups of four and have students compare answers. Then go over the answers as a class.
- ⏱ Have students work in pairs to come up with additional quiz questions from the reading about the two cities. (Example: *Which city has a higher elevation? Which city is close to the mountains and the sea? Which city is located on a river?*)

Go to **www.myfocusongrammarlab.com** for an additional reading, and for reading and vocabulary practice.

Step 2: Grammar Presentation (pages 388–389)
See the general suggestions for Grammar Presentation on page 2.

Grammar Charts
- Write a few comparative sentences from the opening reading on the board. Have students read them. Ask: "What are we comparing?" *(Portland, Maine, and Portland, Oregon)* "Which words form the comparison?" (be + *comparative* + than) "For each comparative form, what is the base form of the adjective?" *(big, mild, diverse)* "Name adjectives that have one syllable." (Example: *big, mild*) "How do we form the comparative?" (*add* -er) "What is an adjective that requires a spelling change in the comparative?" (Example: big; *double the* g) "What is an adjective that has two syllables?" (Example: *diverse*) "How do we form the comparative?" (more + *adjective*)
- Have students look at the first chart. Ask: "For each comparative form, what is the base form of the adjective?" *(big, busy, crowded)* "How do you spell *busy*? How do we form the comparative of an adjective that ends in -*y*?" (*change* y *to* i, *then add* -er)
- Repeat the same procedure for the second chart. Elicit the base forms of the comparatives *better (good), worse (bad),* and *farther (far).*
- Make a handout of the following adjectives. Put students in pairs or small groups and have them write the comparative forms of the adjectives.

good	bad	far
interesting	pretty	long
mild	temperate	funny
formal	sweet	dangerous
famous	old	friendly

- Have students read the chart of questions with *which*. Model questions using the adjectives in the chart above. Have students answer with their opinions, for example:
  T: Which is better, coffee or tea?
  S1: I think coffee is better.
  T: Which is worse, hot weather or cold weather?
  S2: I think hot weather is worse.
- Form small groups. Have students in each group continue asking and answering questions in the same way.

- Write any incorrect sentences you hear on the board. When students finish talking in groups, have them correct the errors.

Grammar Notes

Notes 1–4
- Have students read all the notes and examples. Then have them work in pairs to make true sentences about themselves and their partners using the adjectives in these notes.
- Walk around and monitor students' sentences. Note errors.
- Write the errors on the board and have students correct them.

Note 5
- Using the adjectives in Note 4, have students transform their earlier sentences into sentences with *less*. Go around the room and have each student form a pair of sentences. (Example: *Sheila is quieter than Jonathan. Jonathan is less quiet than Sheila.*)

Notes 6 and 7
- Have students read the notes and the examples.
- To practice *good–better* and *bad–worse,* have students name the last movie they saw. Write the names of the films on the board. Call a student to the board and have him or her point to two films. Ask who has seen both of them. Call on a student who raises his or her hand and ask: "Which film was better? Why?" Encourage other students who saw the same films to use the words *better* and *worse* in sentences to agree or disagree.
- To practice *farther,* ask several students how far they live from the school. Call on other students to form comparative sentences. (Example: *Kim lives farther from school than Yoshi.*)

Note 8
- Have students read the note and the examples.
- Draw attention to the *Be Careful!* notes. Have students read the first two (correct) examples. Ask: "What are we comparing here?" *(John's home and William's home)* Then have someone read a "not" sentence and ask the same question. Help students see the error.
- Write pairs of phrases like the following on the board. Then have students form incorrect sentences on purpose and write them on the board.

Carla's hair	Jin's hair	(Carla's hair is longer than Jin.)
Richard's car	Sato's car	(Richard's car is newer than Sato.)
American food	Chinese food	(American food is worse than China.)

- Call other students to the board to correct the errors.
- Choose two students for the class to compare. Write several adjectives on the board. Have students make formal and informal comparisons between the two people, for example:
  Domingo is taller than he [Diego] is.
  Domingo is taller than him.

Note 9
- Have students read the note and examples. Then have them work in pairs to make true sentences about themselves and their partners using the adjectives in these notes.
- Walk around and monitor students' sentences. Note errors.
- Write the errors on the board and have students correct them.

⏱ **Identify the Grammar:** Have students identify the grammar in the reading on page 386. For example:
  . . . Portland, Oregon, is **farther from** the ocean.
  . . . it is also **higher** in elevation.
  It's much **more diverse than** the other Portland.

Go to **www.myfocusongrammarlab.com** for grammar charts and notes.

Step 3: Focused Practice (pages 390–394)
See the general suggestions for Focused Practice on page 4.

Exercise 1: Discover the Grammar
A
- Have students read the text quickly for meaning.
- Have students complete the exercise individually.
- Have students compare answers in pairs. Then call on students to read the comparative adjectives.

B
- Have students complete the exercise individually. Then have them compare answers in pairs.
- Call on students to give answers. Have them say the base form and then the comparative form.
- ⏱ Have students close their books and make sentences comparing Vancouver and Quebec City.

Exercise 2: Comparison of Adjectives

A
- Go over the example with the class. Then review the general rules for forming comparatives:
  One-syllable adjectives: add *-er + than*
  Two-syllable adjectives ending in *-y* : drop the *y* and add *-ier + than*
  Adjectives with two or more syllables: *more + adjective + than*
- Have students complete the exercise individually. Then have them compare answers in pairs.
- ⏱ Call on pairs to read each conversation, inserting the answers. Have students practice the conversations, changing partners and roles several times.

B
- Have students complete the exercise individually.
- Have students compare answers in pairs.
- Call on students to give answers.

Exercise 3: Comparison of Adjectives
- Have students read the text quickly for meaning. Then go over the example with the class.
- Have students complete the exercise individually.
- ⏱ Have students use the information in the chart to compare their own city with Lakeville or Middletown (they may need to do Internet research to find some of the information about their town).

Exercise 4: Comparison of Adjectives
- Have students read the text quickly for meaning. Then go over the example with the class.
- Have students complete the exercise in pairs.
- Combine pairs to form groups of four and have students compare answers. Then call on students to read portions of the completed paragraph.

Exercise 5: Editing
- Go over the example with the class. Point out that they should find six more mistakes in the sentences.
- Have students find and correct the mistakes in pairs.
- Combine pairs to form groups of four and have students compare answers. Then call on students to read the corrected passage. Have them explain why the incorrect structures are wrong.

Go to **www.myfocusongrammarlab.com** for additional grammar practice.

Step 4: Communication Practice (pages 395–397)
See the general suggestions for Communication Practice on page 5.

Exercise 6: Pronunciation

A
- Play the audio. Have students read along as they listen to the Pronunciation Note.

B
- Play the audio. Have students listen and repeat.
- Call on students to read the sentences.

Exercise 7: Listening

A
- Have students read the instructions.
- Play the audio. Have students listen and write their answers.
- Go over the answer as a class.

B
- Have students read the text quickly for meaning.
- Play the audio. Have students listen and underline their answers. Then call on students to give answers.
- ⏱ Have students compare transportation systems in their own city. (Example: *driving versus taking the bus, train, subway, walking*)

Exercise 8: Comparing Train Systems
- Go over the example with the class. Then have students read the text quickly for meaning. You may want to elicit the comparative adjectives to be used for each section of the chart, for example, year opened = *older*.
- Have students complete the exercise in pairs.

- ⏲ Give students a minute to study the information in the chart. Then divide the class into two teams, have them close their books, and play a quiz game using the information in the text. (Example: *Which system is faster, the Tube in London, or the Moscow Metro?*) The first team to answer correctly gets a point.

Exercise 9: Discussion: Making Comparisons

- Go over the example with the class. Then call on a student to read the categories. You may want to elicit a few pairs of items under each category. (Example: *Clothes: formal clothes or casual clothes; Homes: living in the country, living in the city*)
- Have students complete the exercise in pairs.
- Call on students to report on a few of their partner's preferences.

Exercise 10: Comparing Cities

- Go over the examples with the class.
- Have students complete the exercise.
- ⏲ Ask similar questions about different cities and elicit responses from the class.

Exercise 11: Writing

A

- Go over the example with the class.
- Have students complete the exercise individually. Encourage them to choose methods of transportation that they have used in the past. Give them time to make some notes to help them get started. Remind them to use comparative adjectives where possible.

B

- Have students correct their work using the Editing Checklist.
- Then have students exchange papers and check their partner's work.
- ⏲ Have students read their paragraphs in small groups.

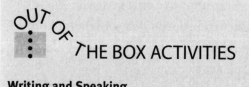

OUT OF THE BOX ACTIVITIES

Writing and Speaking

- Have students write or discuss about how places and aspects of their city or town have changed over the past five or ten years. Give them some adjectives to help them get started:
  crowded
  safe
  dangerous
  expensive
  fun
  convenient
  clean
  dirty

Go to **www.myfocusongrammarlab.com** for additional listening, pronunciation, speaking, and writing practice.

Note:
- See the *Focus on Grammar Workbook* for additional in-class or homework grammar practice.

Unit 33 Review (page 398)

Have students complete the Review and check their answers on Student Book page UR-7. Review or assign additional material as needed.

Go to **www.myfocusongrammarlab.com** for the Unit Achievement Test.

UNIT 34 OVERVIEW

Grammar: ADVERBS OF MANNER

Unit 34 focuses on the structure and use of adverbs of manner, including the form and use of adverbs of manner such as *slowly, hard,* and *carefully;* the difference between adjectives and adverbs ending in -*ly;* and the use of adjectives after linking verbs.

Theme: PUBLIC SPEAKING

Unit 34 focuses on language and expressions used to give tips and advice for successful and effective public speaking.

Step 1: Grammar in Context (pages 399–401)

See the general suggestions for Grammar in Context on page 1.

Before You Read

A

- Introduce the theme of public speaking. Ask: "How many of you have given a speech or a presentation to an audience?" If students raise their hands, have them describe the experience briefly and say how they felt about it. Share any feelings you have about public speaking from the perspective of a teacher.
- Put students into pairs and have them brainstorm jobs that require public speaking.
- Call on students to write their ideas on the board. Then go over the list with students and ask whether students would be interested in any of the jobs in the future.

B

- Call on a student to read the instructions and the chart headings. Explain any unfamiliar vocabulary, such as *confident, miserable, nervous.*
- Model the task by briefly giving your own answers. (Example: *When I speak in front of my friends and relatives, I feel calm and confident, but with 250 people I don't know, I feel nervous and not confident.*)
- Have students complete the exercise individually.

Read

- Call on a student to read the first two sentences of the blog. Ask: "What do you think the author means by the phrase *a bit of a nightmare?*" "What do you think this article will be about?"
- To encourage students to read with a purpose, write these questions on the board:
  1. Where did the speaker give the speech? *(at work)*
  2. How many people were in the audience? *(40)*
  3. What did the speaker include in the speech? *(a lot of facts, big words, long sentences)*
  4. How did she speak? *(quietly)*
  5. What was the response of the audience? *(polite applause)*
  6. What did she do the next time she had to give a speech? *(asked a friend for help)*
  7. How many ideas did her second speech have? *(three)*

8. How did she speak? *(slowly, clearly, and honestly)*
9. How did the audience respond this time? *(The applause was long and loud.)*

- Have students read the text. (OR: Play the audio and have students follow along in their books.) Then call on students to share their answers to the questions on the board.

After You Read

A. Practice

- Have students complete the exercise in pairs.
- Then call on pairs to read paragraphs.

B. Vocabulary

- Read the blue words and have students repeat.
- Have students complete the exercise individually. Then have them compare answers in pairs.
- ⏱ Have students write their own sentences using the vocabulary.

C. Comprehension

- Have students complete the exercise in pairs. Encourage them to do so without looking back at the text.
- Combine pairs to form groups of four and have students compare answers.
- ⏱ Lead a class discussion about memorable speeches students have heard. Ask: "What did the speaker say or do that made the speech memorable?" "In your culture, is it customary to tell jokes in a speech?" "What advice would you give to someone giving a speech in English for the first time?"

Go to **www.myfocusongrammarlab.com** for an additional reading, and for reading and vocabulary practice.

Step 2: Grammar Presentation (pages 401–402)

See the general suggestions for Grammar Presentation on page 2.

Grammar Charts

- Explain that adverbs of manner tell *how* we do something. Elicit the adverbs used in the opening reading to describe how the speaker spoke during her first *(quickly, not loudly enough)* and second presentations *(slowly, clearly).*
- Call on students to read the examples in the charts. Ask: "What part of speech do adverbs modify?" *(verbs)* "Do all adverbs end in *-ly?*" *(no)* "Where do adverbs of manner appear in the sentence?" *(after the verb)*

- Write the following template on the board: *Subject + Verb + Adverb*.
- Divide the class into pairs or small groups. Assign a few adverbs from the chart to each group. Their task is to form sentences that use the adverbs and follow the template.
- Call on students to share their sentences.

Grammar Notes

Notes 1 and 2
- Call on students to read the notes and the examples.
- Draw attention to the *Be Careful!* note.
- Do a paired transformation drill. Students hear sentences with adjectives and change them to sentences with adverbs. Make two handouts with the sentences from the following chart and model the drill, for example:
  T: He's a fast talker.
  Ss: He talks fast.

Student A	Student B
She's a beautiful singer.	He's a quiet eater.
She's a bad speller.	He's a loud speaker.
He's a careful worker.	She's a serious reader.
She's a clear writer.	He's a slow writer.
He's a fluent French speaker.	The cat is a soft walker.
She is a loud talker.	The teacher is an early riser.
She's a neat typist.	The salesman is a fast talker.
He's a nervous speaker.	On weekends they are late sleepers.
He's a quick walker.	

- Circulate and note errors. Write them on the board. When students finish talking, call on students to correct the errors.

Note 3
- Have students read the note and the example.
- Write the following words on the board: *hard, early, fast, late*.
- Put students in pairs and have them make sentences about themselves like the example. (Example: *I don't like to get up early.*)
- Have several students write their sentences on the board. Call on others to read them and correct any errors.

Note 4
- Write the following exchange on the board:
  A: How do you feel?
  B: I feel well.

- Ask students if they have ever heard this exchange. Chances are they will say no. It's more likely that they have heard "I feel fine" or "I feel good," which are now established phrases in American conversational English. Tell students that in formal situations they should use *well* or *fine*, but in casual situations *good* is acceptable.
- Have students read the note and the examples.
- In pairs, have students compose three sentences:
  a sentence with *good* used as an adjective (*This is good cake.*)
  a sentence with *well* used as an adverb (*She speaks English well.*)
  a sentence with *well* used as an adjective (*I don't feel well today.*)
- Call on students to share their sentences with the class.

Note 5
- Write the linking verbs on the board.
- Bring in some photos or magazine pictures showing people eating in a place, such as a restaurant or at a picnic. Pictures of you and your friends or family are ideal.
- Tell a story (true or false) to fit the picture(s) and use as many linking verbs as possible. (Example: *Here is a picture of me and my friends at my 30th birthday party. I remember it was a warm day. The air smelled fresh, and I felt great. My parents were there, and they looked happy.*)
- When you finish telling the story, ask the class questions and have them retell the story using the linking verbs, for example:
  "How did the air feel?" (*It felt warm.*)
  "How did my parents look?" (*They looked happy.*)
- Explain the grammar. Ask students if they noticed the use of the adjective form after the linking verbs. Have them read the note and examples. Focus their attention on the incorrect sentence: *The grapes taste well.*
- If possible, show another, similar picture to the class and have them make sentences using linking verbs.
- Have students work in small groups to talk about their last birthday party. They should give the facts—who was there, where the party was held, and so on—and use the linking verbs on the board to describe the people, the food, and the ambiance.

⏱ **Identify the Grammar:** Have students identify the grammar in the reading on page 399. For example:

. . . I had to prepare **fast** . . .
. . . I spoke **quickly** . . .
I thought **carefully** . . .

Go to **www.myfocusongrammarlab.com** for grammar charts and notes.

Step 3: Focused Practice (pages 403–404)

See the general suggestions for Focused Practice on page 4.

Exercise 1: Discover the Grammar

- Have students read the text quickly for meaning.
- Have students complete the exercise individually.
- Have students compare answers in pairs. Then call on students to read the sentences that have adverbs of manner.

Exercise 2: Adverbs of Manner

- Go over the example with the class.
- Have students complete the exercise individually. Then call on them to write the answers on the board. Check and correct spelling as necessary.
- ⏱ To focus on common verb–adverb collocations, have students say each sentence again, changing the adverb, for example:
He spoke quickly → He spoke quietly.
She writes well. → She writes clearly.

Exercise 3: Adverbs of Manner and Adjectives

- Go over the example with the class. Ask: "How will you know whether to choose the adjective or the adverb?" *(check whether it modifies a noun or a verb)*
- Have students complete the exercise in pairs. Then call on pairs to read the completed conversations. Have the rest of the class listen and check and correct as necessary.
- ⏱ Have students practice the conversations, changing roles and partners several times.

Exercise 4: Editing

- Go over the example with the class. Point out that they should find five more mistakes in the conversations.
- Have students find and correct the mistakes in pairs.
- Combine pairs to form groups of four and have students compare answers. Then call on students to read the corrected passage. Have them explain why the incorrect structures are wrong.

Go to **www.myfocusongrammarlab.com** for additional grammar practice.

Step 4: Communication Practice (pages 405–406)

See the general suggestions for Communication Practice on page 5.

Exercise 5: Listening

A
- Have students read the text quickly for meaning. Have them try to predict the missing information.
- Play the audio. Have students listen and write their answers.
- Go over the answers as a class.

B
- Elicit the advice given in the opening reading for effective public speaking.
- Play the audio, pausing a few times for students to write their answers. Alternatively, play the whole conversation and have students take notes. Then have them write their answers afterward.
- Have students compare answers in pairs. Then play the audio again to confirm the answers.

Exercise 6: Pronunciation

A
- Play the audio. Have students read along as they listen to the Pronunciation Note.

B
- Have students look up any words they do not know.
- Play the audio. Have students listen to the speakers' manner.

C
- Play the audio. Have students listen and repeat.

D
- Have students complete the exercise in pairs.
- Call on pairs to present the sentence to the class in a variety of manners.

Exercise 7: Writing

A
- Have students tell their partners about a sports event.

B
- Go over the example with the class.
- Give students time to make some notes about the sports event they told their partners about in Part A.

- Have students complete the exercise individually.

C
- Have students correct their work using the Editing Checklist.
- Then have students exchange papers and check their partner's work.
- 🕐 Have students read their paragraphs in small groups.

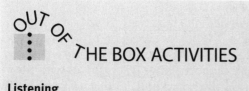

OUT OF THE BOX ACTIVITIES

Listening
- **Note:** Many great historical speeches can be heard on the Internet. A search will yield numerous sites with audio. For example, the History Channel website allows students to listen to short segments of historical speeches.
- If you have access to a listening lab, take your students and allow them to choose the speeches they want to listen to. (OR: Have them do this for homework.)
- Have students complete a listening report similar to the following.

Listening Report
1. Website title:
2. Address:
3. Speaker:
4. Date of speech:
5. Audience:
6. Topic:
7. Main idea:
8. Length:
9. Two facts I learned:
10. Two new words I learned:
11. How did the speaker sound or speak? (Use adverbs of manner.)

- Have students print out the report and submit it as homework. (OR: Have them discuss the reports in small groups.)

Go to **www.myfocusongrammarlab.com** for additional listening, pronunciation, speaking, and writing practice.

Note:
- See the *Focus on Grammar Workbook* for additional in-class or homework grammar practice.

Unit 34 Review (page 407)

Have students complete the Review and check their answers on Student Book page UR-7. Review or assign additional material as needed.

Go to **www.myfocusongrammarlab.com** for the Unit Achievement Test.

UNIT 35 OVERVIEW

Grammar: *Enough, Too / Very, As + Adjective + As, Same / Different*

Unit 35 focuses on the structure, meaning, and use of the following:
- Adjective + *enough*: *It's warm enough to go swimming.*
- Adjective + *too*: *It was too cold to go swimming.*
- *Very* + adjective: *It was a very warm day.*
- *As* + adjective + *as*: *Today is as warm as yesterday.*
- *The same as*: *Today's weather is the same as yesterday's.*
- *Different from*: *Seattle's weather is different from Atlanta's.*

Theme: Proms and Parties

Unit 35 focuses on language and expressions used to discuss proms and parties.

Step 1: Grammar in Context (pages 408–410)

See the general suggestions for Grammar in Context on page 1.

Before You Read
- Call on a student to read the discussion questions.
- Have students discuss in pairs or small groups.

Read
- Tell students they will read a conversation between two high school students. Then preview the glossed vocabulary at the bottom of the conversation.
- Have students read the text. (OR: Play the audio and have students follow along in their books.)

After You Read

A. Practice
- Have students complete the exercise in pairs.
- Then call on pairs to read paragraphs.

B. Vocabulary
- Read the words in blue and have students repeat.
- Have students complete the exercise individually. Then call on students to give answers and explain how they decided on the answers.
- (!) Have students write their own sentences using the vocabulary.

C. Comprehension
- Have students complete the exercise in pairs. Encourage them to do so without looking back at the text.
- Combine pairs to form groups of four and have students compare answers.
- Go over the answers as a class.

Go to **www.myfocusongrammarlab.com** for an additional reading, and for reading and vocabulary practice.

Step 2: Grammar Presentation (pages 410–411)

See the general suggestions for Grammar Presentation on page 2.

Grammar Charts
- Have students read the examples in the charts.
- To reinforce the pattern, bring in items of clothing of various sizes (including some very large and very small), fruit and vegetables (ideally, a melon, a green banana, a yellow banana, and an overripe banana; you can also use pictures with the bananas colored accordingly).
- Have students examine the items. (If your class is large, call up a few representative students to do this.)
- Write adjectives on the board. (Example: *big, small, long, short, ripe, soft, hard*)
- Once again, go through all the charts and have students form sentences about the items you brought in, for example:
  This melon is ripe enough to eat.
  This banana isn't ripe enough.
  This shirt is too big.
  This skirt is very long.
  This banana is the same color as that one.
  This sweater isn't as soft as that one.

Grammar Notes

Note 1
- Call on students to read the note and the examples. Explain that it's usually a good thing if you have *enough* and a negative thing if you *don't have enough* of something.
- Write the following on the board:
  ride a train by myself
  drive a car
  vote
  live alone
  get married
  retire
- Have students work in pairs to make true sentences (affirmative or negative) with the verbs on the board and *enough*. (Example: *I'm old enough to drive, but I'm not old enough to vote. I'm old enough to drive, and I'm also old enough to vote.*)
- This can also be done as a circle drill. Go around the room and have each student make one sentence.

Notes 2 and 3
- Call on students to read the notes and the examples.
- Draw a chart like the following on the board. (Select topics to match the interests of your students.)

Movies	Singers	Restaurant	Cities

- Have students come up to the board and, in the appropriate columns, write the names of items that they do / did not like or enjoy.
- Point to the items. Have students who didn't like them raise their hands. When you call on them, they should make sentences with *too* or *not* + adjective + *enough* to explain why they didn't like the items. (Example: *I didn't like Million Dollar Baby because it was too violent and too sad. I don't like Gary's Grill because the service isn't fast enough.*)

Note 4
- Illustrate this grammar point by drawing cartoon figures on the board. (If you cannot draw well, ask a student to do it for you.) Draw the following:
  a very tall, thin person (male or female)
  the same tall person squeezed into an airplane seat
  a very short person with a basketball hoop way above the person's head

- Point to the tall person and say: "He's / she's very tall." Point to the picture of the tall person on the plane and say: "He's too tall to fit in an airplane seat." Point to the short person and say: "She's very short." Point to the basketball hoop and say: "She's too short to reach the basketball hoop."
- Point to the pictures in turn and have the class repeat the sentences.
- Call on students to read the note and the examples. Draw attention to the *Be Careful!* note.
- Write the following nouns and adjectives on the board. Put students in pairs. Have them make one sentence with *very* and another with *too* and an infinitive, for example:

soup—hot   (This soup is very hot.)
                   (This soup is too hot to eat.)

book—long
weather—cold
weather—hot
sofa—heavy
tea—sweet
I—tired
child—big
homework—difficult

Notes 5 and 6

- To illustrate the grammar in these notes, have several or all of the students line up according to their height.
- Call students out of the line and make model sentences like the ones in the book, for example:
Sally is as tall as Paula.
They're the same height.
Sally is the same height as Paula.
Paru isn't as tall as Fatima.
Fatima is taller.
- Call other pairs of students out of the line and elicit similar sentences from the group. Write one example of each of the structures on the board.
- Have the class sit down. Call on students to read the notes and the examples.
- In pairs, have students make sentences about themselves following the five patterns on the board using these adjectives and nouns:

Adjectives	Nouns
tall	height
short	weight
thin	hair color
heavy	hair length
long	eye color

- Circulate and make notes about errors. Write sentences with mistakes on the board and call on students to correct them.

- 🕐 **Identify the Grammar:** Have students identify the grammar in the conversation on page 408. For example:
. . . he's **too talkative**.
He's in **the same** grade . . .
He's **old enough**, and he's **very** cute.

Go to **www.myfocusongrammarlab.com** for grammar charts and notes.

Step 3: Focused Practice (pages 412–416)

See the general suggestions for Focused Practice on page 4.

Exercise 1: Discover the Grammar

A
- Go over the example with the class.
- Have students complete the exercise individually.
- Have students compare answers in pairs. Then call on students to give answers.

B
- Go over the example with the class.
- Have students complete the exercise individually.
- Have students compare answers in pairs. Then call on students to give answers.

Exercise 2: *Enough, Too*
- Have a student read the words in the box. Then go over the example with the class.
- Have students complete the exercise individually. Then have them compare answers in pairs.
- 🕐 Have students practice the conversation, changing roles and partners several times.

Exercise 3: Word Order Practice; *Enough, Too . . . To*
- Go over the example with the class.
- Have students complete the exercise individually. Then have them compare answers in pairs.
- 🕐 Have pairs use the target grammar and write five more jumbled sentences, as in the exercise. Combine pairs and have them exchange and complete the other pair's jumbled sentences.

Exercise 4: *Too* + Adjective / *The Same ... As*

A

- Read the words in the box. Have students repeat.
- Have students complete the exercise individually.
- Have students compare answers in pairs. Then go over the answers as a class.

B

- Have students look at the driver's licenses. Go over the example with the class. Then ask questions to orient students to the information, for example:
  How tall is Russ Tran?
  How much does Jean Phillippe weigh?
  In what state does Robert Trent live?
  What are their birthdays?
- Have students complete the exercise in pairs.
- Call on students to read the completed sentences.

Exercise 5: *Too / Very*

- Write the following sentences on the board and ask: "What's the difference between the two sentences?"
  This sweater is too big. *(There is a problem: I can't wear the sweater.)*
  This sweater is very big. *(There may not be a problem: The sweater is bigger than the average size.)*
- Go over the example with the class.
- Have students complete the exercise individually. Then call on students to read the completed sentences.

Exercise 6: *As* + Adjective + *As*, *The Same* + Noun + *As*

- Go over the example with the class. Then have students read the text quickly for meaning.
- Have students complete the exercise in pairs.
- Call on pairs to read portions of the conversation, inserting the answers. Have the rest of the class listen and check and correct as necessary.

Exercise 7: Editing

- Go over the example with the class. Point out that they should find seven more mistakes in the sentences.
- Have students find and correct the mistakes in pairs.
- Combine pairs to form groups of four and have students compare answers. Then call on students to read the corrected passage. Have them explain why the incorrect structures are wrong.

Go to **www.myfocusongrammarlab.com** for additional grammar practice.

Step 4: Communication Practice (pages 417–419)

See the general suggestions for Communication Practice on page 5.

Exercise 8: Pronunciation

A

- Play the audio. Have students read along as they listen to the Pronunciation Note.

B

- Have students look at the pictures. Have them brainstorm some phrases with *as* + adjective + *as* that describe each item pictured. (Example: *as small as a mouse, as tall as a horse*)
- Have students read the text quickly for meaning and try to predict the answers.
- Play the audio. Have students listen and complete the exercise individually.

C

- Play the audio. Have students listen and repeat.
- ⏱ Have students talk about people they know who fit the descriptions. (Example: *My sister is as cool as a cucumber. She never gets nervous.*)

Exercise 9: Listening

A

- Have students read the text quickly for meaning. Make sure they understand *promote* (to give someone a higher position in a company).
- Play the audio. Have students listen and complete the exercise individually.
- Go over the answer as a class.

B

- Have students read the text quickly for meaning. Explain that the expressions are idioms; they are difficult to understand without knowing the context. Students should listen carefully to the context to help them decide on the answers.
- Play the audio. Have students listen and complete the exercise individually.
- Have students compare answers in pairs. Then call on pairs to give answers.

Exercise 10: Describing Yourself
- Have a student read the words in the boxes. Then go over the example with the class.
- Have students complete the exercise individually.
- Have students read their sentences to their partners.

Exercise 11: Similarities
- Go over the example with the class. Then have students read the suggestions quickly for meaning and think of some questions to ask their classmates.
- Have students stand and walk around the classroom interviewing classmates. Have them take notes on the answers they hear.
- Have students report to the class. Keep track of who found the most similarities.

Exercise 12: Writing

A
- Go over the example with the class.
- Have students take notes about the friends or events they will write about.
- Have students complete the exercise individually.

B
- Have students correct their work using the Editing Checklist.
- Then have students exchange papers and check their partner's work.
- (🕐) Have students read their paragraphs in small groups.

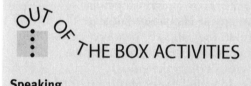

OUT OF THE BOX ACTIVITIES

Speaking
- Have students do a ranking activity.
- Prepare a grid like the following. This example uses cars, but you can make a grid out of any related items, such as foods, hobbies, animals, vacation spots, or jobs. (Note: It is important for some of the items to be similar so that students can form sentences with *as . . . as*.)

	Expensive	Fast	Beautiful	Economical
Ferrari				
Corvette				
Honda Accord				
Toyota Camry				
Mini Cooper				

- Have students work in groups of four. Make copies of the grid and distribute them. The objective of the activity is for students to rank in order the five items from 1 to 5 under each adjective. (Example: *If they agree that a Ferrari is the most expensive car, they would rank it number 1.*) To encourage discussion and to elicit the target structures, students must agree on the rankings. This activity can be repeated with different grids.

Speaking
- Have students alternate roles between a personal shopper and a customer. Personal shoppers work in high-quality department stores. Their job is to help individual customers find items that meet their needs and their budgets.
- Bring in a large variety of catalogs, including clothing, furniture, electronics, cars, shoes, and gifts. Large catalogues (such as the Sears or J.C. Penney catalogues) can be divided into sections.
- Place students work in pairs and explain the task. Distribute the catalogs or let students pick one they want. Model the language you want students to use. (Example: *If the customer likes an item that the personal shopper picked, he or she can say: "I like it. It's very nice / colorful / elegant." If a customer doesn't like an item, he or she can say "It's too large / expensive."*) As students continue talking and the personal shopper shows the customer additional items, the customer might say: "I like this shirt. It isn't as tight as the other one."
- Have the personal shoppers pick at least eight items they think their customer will like. To make the activity livelier, the personal shopper can intentionally choose items he or she knows the customer will dislike.

Go to **www.myfocusongrammarlab.com** for additional listening, pronunciation, speaking, and writing practice.

Note:
- See the *Focus on Grammar Workbook* for additional in-class or homework grammar practice.

Unit 35 Review (page 420)

Have students complete the Review and check their answers on Student Book page UR-7. Review or assign additional material as needed.

Go to **www.myfocusongrammarlab.com** for the Unit Achievement Test.

```
UNIT 36 OVERVIEW

Grammar: THE SUPERLATIVE

Unit 36 focuses on the structure, meaning, and
use of the superlative, including the superlative
forms of regular and irregular adjectives, and
how to use the superlative with one of the.

Theme: PENGUINS

Unit 36 focuses on language and expressions
used to talk about and compare different types
of interesting animals from around the world.
```

Step 1: Grammar in Context (pages 421–423)

See the general suggestions for Grammar in Context on page 1.

Before You Read
- Books closed. Play a guessing game to introduce the theme of penguins. Say: "I'm thinking of a type of animal. It is a bird that can swim. It lives in very cold climates. It eats fish . . ." Continue until students have guessed *penguins*.
- Have students complete the exercise in pairs.
- Go over the answers as a class. On the board, make a list of other facts students know about penguins.

Read
- Go over the glossed vocabulary in the article.
- Have students read the text. (OR: Play the audio and have students follow along in their books.)

- ⏱ Ask: "Have you ever seen a penguin? Where?" "What makes penguins different from other types of birds?"

After You Read

A. Practice
- Have students complete the exercise in pairs.
- Then call on pairs to read paragraphs aloud.

B. Vocabulary
- Read the words in the box and have students repeat.
- Have students complete the exercise individually. Then have them compare answers in pairs.
- ⏱ Have students write their own sentences using the vocabulary.

C. Comprehension
- Have students complete the exercise in pairs. As the information is very specific, you may want to allow them to refer to the text. To help them practice their reading scanning skills, have pairs race to find all of the information. The first pair to finish correctly wins.
- Elicit the answers from the class.
- ⏱ Ask any or all of the following questions: What do penguins look like? *(They have black backs and white bellies. They look fat. They stand upright and waddle.)*
  Where and when did explorers first see penguins? *(South America, 1519)*
  What language does the word *penguin* come from? What does the word mean? *(Spanish / fat)*
  How many kinds of penguins are there? *(17)*
  Where do they all live? *(below the equator)*
  What is another name for little blue penguins? *(fairy penguins)*
  Where do little blue penguins live? *(the warm waters off southern Australia and New Zealand)*
  How tall are emperor penguins? *(4 feet)*
  Where do they live? *(Antarctica)*

Go to **www.myfocusongrammarlab.com** for an additional reading, and for reading and vocabulary practice.

Step 2: Grammar Presentation (pages 423–424)

See the general suggestions for Grammar Presentation on page 2.

Grammar Charts
- On the board, write several sentences from the opening reading with examples of the target grammar, for example:

The penguin is one of the easiest birds to recognize.

They thought this type of bird was one of the strangest birds in the world.

The Little Blue Penguins are the smallest of all.

- For each sentence, ask: "What is the adjective?"
- Elicit the meaning of *one of the strangest birds*. Ask: "Is the penguin the strangest bird, or are there other birds that are very strange?" (*There are other birds that are strange.*) If further clarification is needed, ask three tall students to stand up. Then say: "[Student 1] is the tallest student in the class. [Student 2] is the shortest student."
- Go through the charts. Have students read the sentences. For each sentence, ask students what the adjective is and how many syllables it has. Ask questions to elicit the rules for forming the superlative:

  What do we add to the endings of shorter adjectives to form the superlative? (*-est*)

  What word comes before the adjective? (*the*)

  How do we form the superlative with longer adjectives? (*the most* + adjective)

  What do we do with adjectives ending in *y*? (drop the *y* and add *-iest*)

  What are some examples of irregular superlatives? (*farthest, best, worst*)
- Have students recall the comparative form of each adjective. Have them recite the three forms of each adjective: *big, bigger, the biggest.*
- Repeat the last step for the irregular superlatives.

Grammar Notes

Notes 1–5

- Have students read the notes and the examples.
- Give students a list of adjectives like the following and have them say or write the superlative of each word. Monitor carefully for the use of *the.*

cute	large	far
small	fat	cold
funny	busy	easy
good	strange	exciting
interesting	formal	beautiful

- Do a quick drill. Say an adjective and point to a student. The student gives the three forms of the adjective. (Example: *fat, fatter, the fattest*)

Notes 6–8

- Have students read the notes and the examples.
- Draw attention to the *Be Careful!* note.

- Form students into groups. Give them a list of categories like the following. Their task is to form sentences containing a superlative and the category. They choose their own adjectives, for example:

  Cities: New York is one of the noisiest cities in the world.

animals	singers	movies
restaurants	sports	students
amusement parks	books	cars
desserts	climates	inventions

- Appoint a few students to be monitors. Have the rest of the students work in small groups and say sentences about a category using superlatives. The monitors should correct any errors they hear. (Option: You may want to "plant" some specific errors by arranging with a few students ahead of time to make mistakes on purpose.)

⏱ **Identify the Grammar:** Have students identify the grammar in the article on page 421. For example:

  The penguin is one of **the easiest** birds to recognize.

  . . . this type of bird was one of **the strangest** birds.

  The Little Blue Penguins are **the smallest** of all.

Go to **www.myfocusongrammarlab.com** for grammar charts and notes.

Step 3: Focused Practice (pages 425–428)

See the general suggestions for Focused Practice on page 4.

Exercise 1: Discover the Grammar

A

- Have students complete the exercise individually.
- Have students compare answers in pairs. Then call on students to write the answers on the board.

B

- Have students complete the exercise individually.
- Have students compare answers in pairs. Then call on students to write the answers on the board.

C

- Have students complete the exercise individually. Then have students compare answers in pairs.

- ⏱ Have students work in pairs to make their own superlative sentences about cockroaches. (Example: *I think cockroaches are the most disgusting insects in the world. Cockroaches are probably the most unpopular animal on earth.*)

Exercise 2: Superlative Form of Adjectives
- Call on students to read the animal names in the box. Clarify the meanings of any unfamiliar animal names. Then go over the example with the class.
- Have students complete the exercise individually. Then have them compare answers in pairs.
- ⏱ Have students work in pairs to write similar quiz questions about their classmates. (Example: *She is the tallest girl in the class. He has the best smile in the class.*)

Exercise 3: Superlative Form of Adjectives
- Go over the example with the class.
- Have students complete the exercise individually. Then go over the answers as a class.
- ⏱ Have students explain the forms and spelling rules, for example:
  The adjective *dangerous* has three syllables, so I added *the most.*
  Deadly ends in *y*, so I dropped the *y* and added *-iest.*

Exercise 4: *One of the* + Superlative Adjectives
- Go over the example with the class. Then have students read the text quickly for meaning.
- Have students complete the exercise in pairs. Then combine pairs to form groups of four and have students compare answers.
- ⏱ Have pairs practice the conversations, changing roles and partners several times.

Exercise 5: Comparative and Superlative
- Review the use of the comparative and the superlative. Ask: "How many things are we comparing when we use the comparative?" *(two)* "How about the superlative?" *(three or more)* Then go over the example with the class.
- Have students complete the exercise individually. Then have them compare answers in pairs.
- Call on students to read the completed sentences. Have the rest of the class listen and correct as necessary.

Exercise 6: Editing
- Go over the example with the class. Point out that they should find six more mistakes in the sentences.
- Have students find and correct the mistakes in pairs.

- Combine pairs to form groups of four and have students compare answers. Then call on students to read the corrected sentences. Have them explain why the incorrect structures are wrong.

Go to **www.myfocusongrammarlab.com** for additional grammar practice.

Step 4: Communication Practice (pages 429–431)
See the general suggestions for Communication Practice on page 5.

Exercise 7: Pronunciation
A
- Play the audio. Have students read along as they listen to the Pronunciation Note.

B
- Play the audio. Have students listen and repeat.

C
- Play the audio. Have students listen and repeat.
- ⏱ Have students go back and read the sentences in Exercise 5, focusing on the correct word stress.

Exercise 8: Listening
A
- Have students read the text quickly for meaning.
- Play the audio. Have students listen and complete the exercise individually.
- Have students compare answers in pairs. Then go over the answers as a class.

B
- Have students read the text quickly for meaning.
- Play the audio. Have students listen and complete the exercise individually.
- Have students compare answers in pairs. Then go over the answers as a class.

Exercise 9: Survey
A
- Have students complete the exercise individually.

B
- Go over the example with the class.
- Form groups of four. Have students ask the members of their group the questions. Remind them to ask for reasons and to take notes on their classmates' answers.
- Call on students to report on their survey results.

Exercise 10: Discussion

- Go over the example in the class. Then have students read the text quickly for meaning.
- Have students take notes on the questions. Then have them discuss the topic with their partners.
- 🕐 Have students share their experiences with pests, what happened, and how they reacted. Share some of your own stories.

Exercise 11: Game

A

- Go over the example with the class.
- Have one student come to the board and write while the rest of the class brainstorms types of animals.

B

- Go over the example with the class.
- Have students think of and write a few superlative questions about the animals on the board.
- Form small groups. Have students in each group take turns asking their questions. You may want to have groups appoint one student to write down the questions as they are asked.

C

- Go over the example with the class.
- Have students write their own answers to the questions.
- Have students in each group compare their answers to each question.

Exercise 12: Writing

A

- Go over the example with the class.
- Have students brainstorm details about what they want to write about the topic. Encourage them to think about real-life experiences when they have seen animals in a zoo, in the movies, on TV, or in books. You may want to give some more specific topic prompts to help them get started, for example:
  Amazing animal stories in the news
  Animals in danger
  The pros and cons of zoos
- Have students complete the exercise individually.

B

- Have students correct their work using the Editing Checklist.
- Then have students exchange papers and check their partner's work.
- 🕐 Have students read their paragraphs in small groups.

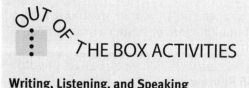

OUT OF THE BOX ACTIVITIES

Writing, Listening, and Speaking

- Play a game of *Jeopardy*, a well-known TV game show in the United States. Contestants are given the *answers* to questions in a category of their choice. The contestants then provide the *questions*, for example:
  In the category of geography, a contestant would read, "the lowest place in the world." The correct answer would be, "Where / What is the Dead Sea?"
- Have students brainstorm general topic categories. (Example: *animals, nature, geography, science, music*) The number of categories and questions you prepare will depend on the size of your class; seven categories with five questions in each is usually enough for 20 students.
- Decide in advance how you will score the game. One option is to give 1 point for each correct question. (Remember: You provide the answers. Contestants provide the questions.) You may also wish to include bonus answers worth 2 points each.
- Have students write superlative statement clues on one side of an index card. (Example: *It's the fastest animal in the world.*) Have them write the questions on the other side. Organize the questions into categories. Write the categories on the board.
- Lay the groups of index cards on a desk or table.
- Divide the class into two teams. Two students at a time will play the game. Toss a coin to decide which team goes first.
- The person whose turn it is chooses a category. The host then reads an answer. The student responds with a question. If the question is correct, the team scores a point. If the question is incorrect, the other team gets a chance to form the correct question. A student who has had a turn goes to the end of the line. The game ends when all the answers have been used or when time is up.

Go to **www.myfocusongrammarlab.com** for additional listening, pronunciation, speaking, and writing practice.

Note:

- See the *Focus on Grammar Workbook* for additional in-class or homework grammar practice.

Unit 36 Review (page 432)

Have students complete the Review and check their answers on Student Book page UR-8. Review or assign additional material as needed.

Go to **www.myfocusongrammarlab.com** for the Unit Achievement Test.

From Grammar to Writing (pages 433–434)

See the general suggestions for From Grammar to Writing on page 9.

Go to **www.myfocusongrammarlab.com** for an additional From Grammar to Writing Assignment, Part Review, and Part Post-Test.

EXERCISE 7 (page 8)

1. She's a talented singer.
2. He's a baseball player.
3. She's a film director.
4. He's a singer.
5. He's a writer.
6. She's my favorite writer.

EXERCISE 8 (page 9)

Hideki Matsui, Lionel Messi, and Kim Yu-na are athletes. Matsui is a baseball player. He's from Japan. Messi is a soccer player. He's from Argentina. And Kim is an ice skater. She's from Korea.

Ang Lee is a movie director. He's from Taiwan.

Rob Pattinson and Olga Kurylenko are in movies. Pattinson is an actor from England. Kurylenko is an actress and a model. She is from Ukraine.

Rihanna is a singer. She is from Barbados.

And finally, Paulo Coelho is a writer. He's from Brazil.

EXERCISE 7 (page 22)

A: Tell me about your class, Hugo. Is your teacher a man?

B: Yes, he is. He's about fifty years old. He's from Canada. I think he's good.

A: What about the students? Are they all from the same country?

B: No. They're from all over the world. They're from Mexico, Chile, Canada, Poland, Korea, and Japan.

A: That's interesting. How's their English?

B: It's hard to say. Some students are good at speaking but not good at writing. Some students are good at writing but not good at speaking.

A: What about you? How are you doing?

B: I don't know. I think I'm good at speaking, but writing and grammar are hard for me. By the way, how's your new job?

EXERCISE 6 (page 31)

MESSAGE 1: Hi, Ella. This is Marta. How was the interview at DB Drugs? Were you happy with the interview? Call me at 917-223-2245.

MESSAGE 2: Hi, Ella. This is Emiko. I'm calling to thank you. The party was great. We were so happy to meet Jay. He's a great guy. We're happy for both of you. My number is 399-090-4444.

MESSAGE 3: Hello, Ella. This is Dave. I'm sorry I wasn't at the party last night. The weather in Ottawa was terrible. All the planes were late. I waited at the airport for four hours. I'm back home now. Please call me at 879-0089.

MESSAGE 4: This call is for Ella Fernandez. This is Sam Hess at DB Drugs. It was a pleasure to meet you. Please call me at 222-989-9029.

MESSAGE 5: Hi, darling. It's Mom. Sorry your dad and I weren't home when you called. We were at a restaurant with Mona. It was her 50th birthday. OK, call me back . . .

EXERCISE 7 (page 32)

1. She wasn't a server.
2. His boss was a bank manager.
3. They were late for the interview.
4. We weren't at work.
5. They were on time.

EXERCISE 7 (page 47)

1. The photos are ready.
2. Her art classes are from 10:00 to 1:00.
3. Be careful. The scissors are sharp.
4. The boxes are full of old photos.
5. The paintings are by different artists.
6. I need my glasses to see the names of the artists.
7. I have some interesting books about Africa in that bookcase.

EXERCISE 8 (page 47)

DOUG: Nice photo.

LILY: Thanks. It's a photo of my family.

DOUG: Was it a holiday?

LILY: Yes. Thanksgiving.

DOUG: Who was the photographer?

LILY: My uncle. He takes photos on all the holidays.

DOUG: He's good. What are all those boxes?

LILY: My gifts.

DOUG: Gifts?

LILY: My birthday's the day before Thanksgiving.

DOUG: What did you get?

LILY: Sunglasses from my brother, jeans from my mom, and a couple of watches—one from my cousin and one from my aunt.

DOUG: What's that?

LILY: My new iPad®. It has all sorts of great features. I can't wait to use it.

UNIT 5

EXERCISE 5 (page 56)

RUSS: Hello?

SUN HI: Hi, it's Sun Hi.

RUSS: Sun Hi! How's your trip? Where are you now?

SUN HI: I'm in Colorado, in Mesa Verde National Park.

RUSS: Wow, Mesa Verde! How is it?

SUN HI: It's awesome. Mesa Verde is so unusual. There are ancient homes in the mountains.

RUSS: What are they?

SUN HI: Very old houses. In the mountains. I'm sending you a photo.

RUSS: It sounds great. Is your hotel nice?

SUN HI: Not really, but it's clean, and it's near the park.

RUSS: How's the weather?

SUN HI: Well, it's cold, but there's one good thing about that. The park isn't crowded.

UNIT 6

EXERCISE 7 (page 67)

1. This country is in Asia. It's between Japan and China. It's near Mongolia. What country is it?
2. This country is in South America. It's between Colombia and Peru. What country is it?
3. This country is in Africa. It's an island. It's near Mozambique. What country is it?
4. This country is in Europe. It's between Portugal and France. What country is it?

UNIT 7

EXERCISE 5 (page 77)

Change your lifestyle. Begin now. Join the Early Morning Spa. It's open from 6:00 to 9:00 weekday mornings.

- Take yoga at 6:00 A.M.
- Then at 7:00 have breakfast with your yoga teacher and partners. Enjoy fresh fruit, whole grain breads, and yogurt.
- Drink freshly squeezed juices and herbal tea.
- At 8:00 get a personal massage,
- Take a shower and go to work.

Join now and get two weeks free.

UNIT 8

EXERCISE 8 (page 88)

ELVIA: I need something new for Bill's party.

PEDRO: Try the Wrap. There's a big sale. What do you want?

ELVIA: A new dress in a bright color. All my clothes are dark-brown, blue, or black. It's spring and I'm tired of dark colors. Can you come with me? The Wrap is just down the block.

PEDRO: OK.

* * * * *

PEDRO: Look at that dress on the mannequin. It's a nice color, and it's on sale.

ELVIA: Yeah. It's bright. I love that red. How much is it?

PEDRO: Forty dollars.

ELVIA: That's all?

PEDRO: Uh-huh.

ELVIA: I think I'll take it.

PEDRO: Wow! You're a fast shopper. I like that.

ELVIA: Oh yeah? My dad thinks I shop too fast. Anyway, if it doesn't fit, I can return it.

UNIT 9

EXERCISE 7 (page 97)

MS. GOLD: So, Andrea, I have just a few more questions.

ANDREA: OK.

MS. GOLD: Tell me Andrea . . . Do you like parties?

ANDREA: Not really. I like to see one friend at a time. I also like to be alone, and I'm a very private person.

MS. GOLD: OK. That's good to know. Do you listen to music?

ANDREA: Yes. I love classical music. I listen to it a lot.

MS. GOLD: How about sports? Are you into sports?

ANDREA: No. Sometimes I go to the gym, but not often.

MS. GOLD: Finally, what time do you study? And where?

ANDREA: I study at night in my room.

MS. GOLD: Thank you. I'll get back to you soon.

UNIT 10

EXERCISE 7 (page 109)

DR. FOX: So Mia. Tell me about your dream.

MIA: OK, Dr. Fox. I have a very important test. I can't find the room it's in. I ask a man, "Where is the room?"

DR. FOX: . . . What does the man say?

MIA: He says, "You're in the wrong building." But I know I'm in the right building. Then I wake up.

DR. FOX: Hmm. Let me see . . . Mia, do you have a lot of stress right now?

MIA: Yes, I do.

DR. FOX: What kind of stress do you have?

MIA: Well, I'm in school and I need to decide my major. I want to be a music major, but my father wants me to be a science major.

DR. FOX: Ah! That's it. In your dream, the two buildings are two paths—music and science. The man in the dream is your father. He wants you to study science. You tell him you want to study music.

UNIT 11

EXERCISE 8 (page 125)

1. The mall is there.
2. There's a parking space behind that car.
3. There are traditional paintings at the Art Gallery.
4. There's an indoor pool at the mall.
5. There are free chocolates on the first level.
6. They're delicious. Here. Have some.

EXERCISE 9 (page 125)

A: Excuse me, is there a mall around here?

B: Uh-huh. There's a big mall up ahead. Follow me. I'm going there.

A: Is there a pizza place at the mall?

B: I don't know, but I know there's a food court. It's on the third level. There are at least ten different places to eat.

A: Sounds good. Thanks.

UNIT 12

EXERCISE 10 (page 139)

1. **A:** Is that Maria's?
   B: I think so.

2. **A:** Is that Maria?
   B: No, it's her sister Carmen. They look alike.

3. **A:** We have two Marias in our class.
   B: It's a popular name.

4. **A:** Is this your partner's phone?
   B: No, it's my phone.

5. **A:** Do you like to work with a partner?
   B: Sometimes.

6. **A:** Sometimes we work with partners, and sometimes we work in small groups.
   B: We do, too.

EXERCISE 11 (page 139)

BORIS: Jasmine, your family's bikes are all the same. How can you tell them apart?

JASMINE: They look the same because we got them at a big sale. But they're not exactly alike. Look. Mine has a basket in the front.

BORIS: Oh, I see it now. But the others are the same.

JASMINE: No. That one is my brother Johnny's bike. His has a small license in the back.

BORIS: Oh yeah. And his has a higher seat. But the other two are the same.

JASMINE: Look carefully. That one, the one next to Johnny's bike is Amy's. She's my sister. Hers has a bag in the back. The rest of ours don't.

BORIS: You're right. Whose is the last one?

JASMINE: That one belongs to my two uncles, Roger and Ted. They don't ride much, so they share the bike. Their bike has a horn.

UNIT 13

EXERCISE 6 (page 149)

1. A zebra can see the color blue, but it can't see the color orange.
2. You can lead a cow upstairs, but you can't lead a cow downstairs.
3. Dolphins can sleep with their eyes open, but dolphins can't sleep on dry land.
4. A pet cat can scare a black bear, but a cat can't scare a jaguar.
5. Dogs can show feelings, but they can't explain them.
6. Elephants can use their trunks to spray water, but they can't jump.

EXERCISE 7 (page 150)

A: What are you looking at?

B: A website about a dolphin named Kelly. She's amazing.

A: Yeah, dolphins are very smart. I saw a dolphin show in Florida. The dolphins could do all kinds of things. They could play basketball. They could catch the ball and throw it. They could even paint pictures.

B: This dolphin is even smarter. Listen to this. Kelly is at a marine institute in Mississippi. All the dolphins there are in pools. Sometimes people throw papers into the pools.

A: That's terrible.

B: I know. But the dolphins hold onto the paper and their trainer gives them a fish for each paper.

A: And all the dolphins can do that?

B: Yup. They're all smart. But Kelly is a genius.

A: Why's that?

B: Kelly saves the paper under a rock. Then she tears the paper and gives a piece of paper to her trainer. He then gives her a fish. She gives him another piece of paper. She gets another fish. So Kelly gets a lot of fish for one piece of paper.

A: Wow. She is smart. She can figure out a way to get more food from her trainer.

B: Yes. In fact, she can also catch a bird with a fish. Then she gives the bird to the trainer and the trainer gives her more fish.

A: You're right; she is a genius.

UNIT 14

EXERCISE 5 (page 159)

JANE: Hello, this is Jane Merrin. May I please speak to Dr. Finkel? I'm calling for the results of an X-ray.

RECEPTIONIST: One moment please.

* * * * *

DR. FINKEL: Hello, this is Dr. Finkel.

JANE: Hi, Dr. Finkel, this is Jane Merrin.

DR. FINKEL: How's the ankle?

JANE: It really hurts.

DR. FINKEL: Well, the X-rays came in. Nothing is broken.

JANE: That's good. But it's still swollen and it really hurts.

DR. FINKEL: Keep your foot up whenever possible. You can also take two extra-strength Tylenol® every four hours.

JANE: Can I go to work?

DR. FINKEL: Yes, you can. You can work. You can drive.

JANE: Can I play tennis?

DR. FINKEL: No, I'm afraid not. No sports for three weeks.

JANE: OK. Thanks, Dr. Finkel.

DR. FINKEL: Bye, Jane.

JANE: Bye.

UNIT 15

EXERCISE 6 (page 171)

JAY: Hello?

MOM: Jay?

JAY: Mom? Where are you?

MOM: I'm on the train. Is Dad there?

JAY: Sure. Hold on. Dad? It's Mom.

DAD: I'm making dinner. Tell Mom I can't talk now.

JAY: Mom, Dad's cooking.

MOM: OK. So how was your day?

JAY: Pretty good.

MOM: Are you doing your homework?

JAY: Well, I was. I'm helping Dad now.

MOM: But you have a test tomorrow.

JAY: Hey, it's math. I'm great at math.

MOM: All right. Oh, I need to talk to Julie. She didn't answer her cell phone. Is she there? Can I talk to her?

JAY: She's not home right now, Mom. I think she's studying at the library with Grace.

MOM: OK. So, what are you and Dad making for dinner?

JAY: Your favorite—chicken and broccoli and a big salad.

MOM: Great. I'm hungry. Tell Dad the train arrives at 7:15.

JAY: OK. Bye Mom.

MOM: Bye Jay.

UNIT 16

EXERCISE 6 (page 181)

A: Dan? Hi. What are you doing here at Goodbuys?

B: I'm looking for a lightweight DVD player.

A: Oh? How come? Is your DVD player broken?

B: It's not for me. It's for my dad. His birthday's next week. He travels a lot by train. I want to buy him a DVD player so he can watch movies on the train. He loves movies.

A: That's a great idea. But get him a Blu-ray. They're not much more. You know, they're having a sale this week.

B: Then I'm in luck.

EXERCISE 7 (page 181)

1. We're buying a new DVD player.
2. That 50-inch flat screen TV is on sale.
3. Do you have an extra CD?
5. Give me the ISBN.
4. We want to get a DVR so we can record shows.
5. He has a BA in film.

UNIT 17

EXERCISE 6 (page 191)

1. Hi Karina. This is Bob. Please send me a copy of the Smith report. Thanks.
2. Hi Mom. This is Lydia. I'm staying late at school. We're practicing for the concert. I'm happy to say we're improving.
3. Hi Karina. It's Natalya. Please call me this evening after 6. I need to make final plans for our trip.
4. Hi Karina. It's me, Grandma Olga. I'm looking for a smart phone and I need your advice. Don't laugh. I know I'm the last to get one. I'll speak to you later. Love you.

EXERCISE 7 (page 191)

WOMAN: What are you buying?

MAN: I'm getting a new motorcycle.

WOMAN: A new motorcycle? You have two other motorcycles.

UNIT 18

EXERCISE 8 (page 205)

A: Any mail?

B: Yes. A postcard from Marta.

A: How is she?

B: Great. She was in Japan for ten days. But she's back in Mexico now.

A: Did she stay with her Japanese friends in Tokyo?

B: She stayed with friends for a week. Then she stayed at a ryokan for two nights. That's a traditional Japanese inn. She loved it, but it was expensive.

A: What else?

B: Well, she visited temples in Kyoto on Saturday and walked all over the city.

A: Did she practice Japanese?

B: Yes. She practiced Japanese with tour guides and shopkeepers. Sometimes they wanted to practice English with her. They didn't realize that English is Marta's second language.

A: That's funny. I'll bet her Japanese is good. How did she travel? Did she rent a car?

B: No. She used public transportation to get around. The trains and subways are easy to use.

A: Sounds like she enjoyed her trip. But there's something I don't understand. Did she write all that in a postcard?

B: No. I called her this afternoon. We talked for a half an hour.

UNIT 19

EXERCISE 6 (page 215)

As a young child I spent a lot of time with my grandparents. My grandfather loved to play with me. I was six when my grandfather died. A few months before he died, he gave me a beautiful blue blanket. I loved that blanket because it reminded me of my grandfather. But after a couple of years, the blanket didn't look good. I didn't want to throw it away, so my mother made it into a book bag. I used it to carry my books to school for a couple of years. Then the book bag tore. I didn't want to throw it away, so my mom made it into a pencil case. One day I lost the case. I felt terrible. My friends said, "Forget about it." I couldn't forget about it. I wrote about it instead. Last week my son found my story in the attic of our house. My son asked about the blanket, and he asked about my grandfather. I felt very good. I felt that my grandfather and his blanket are not forgotten.

UNIT 20

EXERCISE 7 (page 228)

ELENA: What movie did you see last night, Jon?

JON: *Shakespeare in Love*.

ELENA: I heard that was good. Did you like it?

JON: Yes. It was very good.

ELENA: Where did the story take place? In England?

JON: Yes. In London . . . in the late 16th century.

ELENA: What was the story about exactly?

JON: It was about William Shakespeare's true love.

ELENA: Was it a true story? Was it based on Shakespeare's life?

JON: No. The story was made up. In the movie, Shakespeare falls in love. His love gives him the idea for the play *Romeo and Juliet*.

ELENA: I know *Romeo and Juliet*. I read it for class. It was a beautiful tragedy.

JON: I haven't read it. What was the play about?

ELENA: Well, Romeo and Juliet fell deeply in love. But they couldn't marry because of their families. Their families were enemies.

JON: So how did it end?

ELENA: Are you sure you want to know the ending?

JON: Sure.

ELENA: Well, in the last scene, they died in each other's arms.

UNIT 21

EXERCISE 7 (page 243)

TOM: Let's watch *Win a Fortune*. It's on in two minutes.

CAROLINA: OK.

HOST: Good evening and welcome to *Win a Fortune*. With us tonight are Jim daSilva from Naples, Florida, and Amy O'Donnell from Racine, Wisconsin. Jim, Amy, press the button as soon as you know the answer. Then give three more correct answers on that topic and you win $5,000. OK. Now. Our first question is in the field of art. Who painted the famous painting *The Night Watch*?

HOST: OK, Amy?

AMY: Rembrandt.

HOST: Good. Next. In what century did Rembrandt live?

AMY: The seventeenth century.

HOST: Great. You're doing very well. Now where was Rembrandt born? In what country?

AMY: In Holland.

HOST: Good. Now, you have just one more question to answer . . . What is Rembrandt's full name?

AMY: Hmm . . . I . . . uh . . . I don't know.

TOM: It's Rembrandt van Rijn.

HOST: I'm sorry, Amy. It's Rembrandt van Rijn.

CAROLINA: Hey, you're good Tom.

HOST: Our next question is in the field of music. Who married Yoko Ono?

HOST: Jim?

JIM: John Lennon.

HOST: OK. Now. What was the name of John Lennon's group?

JIM: The Beatles.

HOST: Good. Now two more correct answers and you win. Where did the Beatles come from?

JIM: Liverpool, England.

HOST: Right again. Now for our final question. When did the Beatles make their last appearance together?

JIM: 1965?

TOM: He's wrong. It was 1966.

HOST: I'm sorry, Jim. It was 1966. Well, it's time for a new question.

CAROLINA: You're pretty smart, Tom. Why don't you go on the show?

TOM: Maybe I will.

UNIT 22

EXERCISE 8 (page 255)

KEN: Cindy? Cindy Lee?

CINDY: That's me. And you're Ken Walters. It's great to see you again. I heard you became a physical therapist. Is it true?

KEN: Uh-huh.

CINDY: Do you like it?

KEN: I like it a lot. Actually, I intend to go back to school for more training in the fall. What about you? Did you become an accountant?

CINDY: Uh-huh, but I got tired of working for a big company.

KEN: So what are you doing?

CINDY: I decided to start my own business.

KEN: That takes guts. What kind of business?

CINDY: I'm a wedding planner. Here's my card.

KEN: How's it going?

CINDY: Great. I enjoy planning parties, and I like to work with people.

KEN: Terrific.

CINDY: I plan to write a book about it.

KEN: Now I'm really impressed. Listen, I'd love to hear more about your life. Are you free for dinner this Saturday?

CINDY: I'm sorry. I have a wedding.

KEN: Friday?

CINDY: I have a dinner party for the out-of-town guests that night. I guess that's the downside of this business. Any chance we could meet on Monday night?

KEN: Monday? Why not?

UNIT 23

EXERCISE 5 (page 263)

John hurt his hand. He's at the hospital. They're taking an X-ray of his hand. Janet is at the dentist's office. The dentist is taking an X-ray of her teeth. The Smiths are flying to London. The airline is taking an X-ray of their baggage.

X-rays are a big part of our lives. Doctors and dentists use them to look inside the body. Airlines use them to look inside baggage. And scientists use them to study the stars. Do you know who invented them?

A German scientist named Wilhelm Roentgen discovered X-rays in 1895. He took an X-ray photograph of his wife's hand. It showed her wedding ring and her bones. He sent the X-ray and a report about his work to the medical society of his city. Newspapers found out and wrote about his discovery. Six years later he won the Nobel Prize in physics.

Why did Roentgen call them X-rays? He called the rays "X" rays to show the rays came from an unknown type of radiation. In mathematics, the letter "x" is used for unknown quantities. Roentgen's friends wanted him to call them Roentgen Rays, but he didn't. The name X-ray is still the name we use, and X-rays are still important.

UNIT 24

EXERCISE 8 (page 279)

1. I'm going to the park.
2. The mayor is going to give a speech.
3. He's going to talk about the city's future.
4. Bob's going to work.
5. He's going to miss the speech.
6. We're going to a restaurant later.
7. Bob's going to join us.

EXERCISE 9 (page 280)

MAN: Let's get the paper. I wrote a letter to the editor. I want to see if it's in the paper.

WOMAN: What was it about?

MAN: That new twenty-story building on West Street.

WOMAN: Are you for or against it?

MAN: I'm for it.

WOMAN: Why?

MAN: Well, there aren't enough apartments in the area. Many young people are moving away because they can't find a place to live. The new building is going to have two hundred apartments.

WOMAN: Oh.

MAN: And it's going to have a pool.

WOMAN: That's great. Can anyone join it?

MAN: That's what they say. And there are going to be shops on the street level.

WOMAN: But there's going to be more noise and traffic.

MAN: It's not going to be so bad.

WOMAN: It's certainly going to spoil the view for people in nearby homes.

MAN: That's true, but I still think it's going to improve the area.

UNIT 25

EXERCISE 8 (page 290)

REPORTER: Good evening. Here with me now are our two lucky lottery winners, Susan Kerins and Joe Morris. So, Susan, now that you're so rich, what are you going to do?

SUSAN: Well . . . I'll probably leave my job. I'm a waitress. My customers are nice, but after fifteen years . . . I'm ready to see new places.

REPORTER: Will you travel?

SUSAN: I think so. I'll probably go to the moon. But I'll buy a house here on earth with room for my friends and relatives.

REPORTER: Sounds wonderful. How about you, Jim? What will you do with all your money?

JIM: I think I'll give it away.

REPORTER: What was that? You'll give it away?

JIM: That's right. I want it to go to people who really need the money. I'll ask people to write to me and explain why they need the money. And I'll choose the people who need it most.

REPORTER: Wow! That's very unusual . . . and generous. Uh . . . what about your wife and family? Do you have any idea what they'll say?

JIM: I'm sure my wife will want me to keep the money and my family will be angry. But they'll get over it.

REPORTER: Ladies and gentlemen, get out your pens and start writing those letters. A letter to Jim may get you a lot of money.

UNIT 26

EXERCISE 6 (page 300)

B

1. 60 **2.** 30 **3.** 19 **4.** 15 **5.** 80

C

1. A: This tornado has winds of one hundred and fifty miles an hour.
 B: Did you say one hundred and fifteen or one hundred and fifty?
 A: One hundred and fifty.

2. A: It's sixty degrees.
 B: Was that sixty or sixteen?
 A: Sixty.

3. A: There are fourteen inches of snow.
 B: Was that fourteen or forty?
 A: Fourteen.

4. A: It's thirteen degrees below zero.
 B: Did you say thirteen or thirty?
 A: Thirteen.

EXERCISE 7 (page 301)

ALISON: Jack, your suitcase is so heavy. Are you sure you need everything?

JACK: Oh yes. I'm pretty sure I need everything.

ALISON: Boots?

JACK: We may go mountain climbing. Crater Lake has some great trails.

ALISON: Well, in that case I'll take mine, too. What about this raincoat?

JACK: It might rain.

ALISON: Do you need two hats?

JACK: Yes. I have a sun hat because it might be very sunny, and a rain hat in case . . .

ALISON: I know. It might rain. Jack, you packed two heavy books. When are you going to read them?

JACK: At night. Sometimes I wake up during the night. I like to have something to read.

ALISON: And why the sports jacket? You won't need to dress for dinner.

JACK: Just in case we go to a fancy restaurant.

ALISON: Well, you know, these days the airlines are very strict. You may have to pay extra if your suitcase is too heavy.

JACK: Oh, really? . . . You know, I may not need so much. I might not take the jacket. And maybe I'll forget about this book. And maybe . . .

ALISON: That's a good idea.

UNIT 27

EXERCISE 9 (page 317)

1. Put a little butter in a frying pan.
2. Heat the pan and add a few eggs and a little cheese.
3. Scramble the eggs for a few minutes.
4. Remove the eggs from the pan.
5. Add a little salt and a little pepper.
6. Enjoy a delicious dish of scrambled eggs.

EXERCISE 10 (page 317)

THERESA: Hi. You're early. The party isn't until 8:00.

MIGUEL: I know. I'm here to help. I have my car. Can I get you anything?

THERESA: Thanks. Yes. We need soda and chips. And a jar of hot salsa and three cans of tuna fish.

MIGUEL: How about ice?

THERESA: Good idea. Get some ice.

MIGUEL: OK. I'll be back soon.

* * * * *

MIGUEL: Here you are. Here's the soda, the chips, the salsa, the tuna, and the ice.

THERESA: There's a little problem.

MIGUEL: A problem? What's the matter?

THERESA: This is tuna for cats.

MIGUEL: Oh, no.

THERESA: It's OK. I can return it.

MIGUEL: I feel sick.

THERESA: Why? You didn't eat it.

MIGUEL: Not today, but this is the tuna I usually eat. Meow. Meow.

WOMAN: What's going on?

THERESA: Miguel is learning a new language.

UNIT 28

EXERCISE 8 (page 329)

LAURA: These red velvet cupcakes are delicious, Robert.

ROBERT: Thanks. My mom always made them on special occasions.

LAURA: Are you willing to share the recipe?

ROBERT: Sure.

LAURA: Well, I'm taking notes.

ROBERT: OK. First you preheat the oven to 350 degrees. Then mix flour, cocoa powder, baking soda, and salt in a bowl.

LAURA: Wait a second. How much flour?

ROBERT: Two and a half cups.

Laura: How much cocoa powder?

Robert: A half cup. You add a teaspoon of baking soda and a half teaspoon of salt.

Laura: Got it.

Robert: Now set that aside. Then beat the butter and sugar in a large bowl for about five minutes.

Laura: Do I need an electric beater?

Robert: It helps.

Laura: How much butter and sugar do I need?

Robert: One cup of butter and two cups of sugar. Then beat in the eggs, one at a time.

Laura: How many eggs?

Robert: Four. Mix in one cup of sour cream and a half cup of milk.

Laura: OK. Anything else?

Robert: Uh-huh. An ounce of red food color and a teaspoon of vanilla extract. Then bake for twenty minutes.

Laura: Well, thanks. I'll let you know how mine come out.

Robert: No. You'll bring me one to try.

Laura:. Oh, of course.

UNIT 29

EXERCISE 8 (page 341)

Agent: Well, what did you think of the three apartments?

Male: Honestly the first, the one on Maple Street, was too small.

Female: And there were too few closets. It was on a beautiful street, but it really wasn't big enough for us.

Agent: OK. How about the second one, the one across from the park?

Female: That was the right size and had a great view, but it was too noisy. And there were too many people all around.

Agent: Did you like the last apartment?

Male: Yes. I liked it a lot. It was big enough and it wasn't too noisy. I'd like to go there again. How about you, Sandy? What did you think of it?

Female: I agree. The only problem was the kitchen. It had too few cabinets.

Male: That's true, but I can build some cabinets. There was enough room.

Agent: OK. I'll make an appointment to see the apartment again. Is Saturday morning OK?

Male: Yes, that'd be great. Thank you.

UNIT 30

EXERCISE 8 (page 356)

1. You shouldn't call him.
2. You shouldn't send an email.
3. You shouldn't come early.
4. You shouldn't wear shorts.
5. You shouldn't bring a gift.

EXERCISE 9 (page 356)

Max: Kaori, Sho, I just got my plane ticket to Japan. Now I've got a lot of questions.

Kaori: Well, I hope we can help.

Max: First of all, should I bring along cash or can I use a credit card everywhere?

Kaori: You can use credit cards in major stores, but if you shop at small stores, cash is better. So I say bring some cash. Sho, what do you think?

Sho: I agree. Definitely bring cash.

Max: OK. That was easy. Now I know that people bow in Japan. I feel funny bowing, but do you think I should bow when I meet someone?

Sho: No, it's not necessary for you to bow. You're a foreigner and Japanese know that it's not your custom. And a lot of younger Japanese don't bow these days either.

Max: What about when I enter a home? Should I remove my shoes?

Kaori: Yes, you should. You will find some slippers near the door. Put them on and leave your shoes by the door.

Max: OK. Should I learn a few phrases in Japanese? I can't learn very much. Is it worth it?

Sho: I think so. You should learn some phrases because people will appreciate the effort.

Max: Well, I'm sure I'll have more questions before I leave. Thanks so much.

Sho: Wait. There's one important thing you forgot.

Max: What?

Sho: This is really important. Nobody goes to Japan without a translator. You'd better get a ticket for me.

Max: And translators only travel first class, right?

Sho: How did you know?

EXERCISE 7 (page 366)

Ms. Lyons: Hello.

Elena: Hello, is this Ms. Lyons?

Ms. Lyons: Yes. Who's calling?

Elena: Elena Barnes.

Ms. Lyons: Who?

Elena: Elena Barnes. I'm your upstairs neighbor.

Ms. Lyons: Oh, hello. Is everything OK?

Elena: Yes, but I have a favor to ask.

Ms. Lyons: Oh? What is it?

Elena: Could you please turn down your TV?

Ms. Lyons: What was that?

Elena: Would you please lower the volume on your TV?

Ms. Lyons: My TV?

Elena: Uh-huh. You see, I'm taking a very important test next month—I hope to get into medical school, and I can't study with the TV on.

Ms. Lyons: But I didn't think my TV was that loud.

Elena: The walls in this building are thin. Your TV sounds like it's in my living room.

Ms. Lyons: Oh. I'm sorry. I'll lower the volume.

Elena: Thank you.

Ms. Lyons: You're welcome. Bye.

Elena: Bye. Nice talking to you.

Ms. Lyons: What did you say?

Elena: Bye. And thank you.

UNIT 32

EXERCISE 8 (page 379)

Advisor: Hi, Ali, how can I help you?

Ali: I'm planning on getting an MBA after college and I'd like to know what steps to take now.

Advisor: Well, let me see. You're in your second year—and you're majoring in psychology.

Ali: Yes. Is that OK?

Advisor: Yes. You don't have to major in business or economics, but you should take some courses in those areas.

Ali: I plan to take economics next term.

Advisor: Very good. You also have to take the GMAT. It tests your ability in English and math and it's a requirement for all business schools. It's a computer-based test, and it's very important. Any other questions?

Ali: Do I have to go to graduate school right after college or can I work for a while?

Advisor: You don't have to go to business school right after college. Many schools actually prefer students to get some work experience first.

Ali: Really?

Advisor: Yes. I see your grades are high. So keep up the good work.

Ali: Thank you.

UNIT 33

EXERCISE 7 (page 395)

A: Wow. Fogville looks different.

B: You can thank our mayor. He's working very hard to make this a green city.

A: Really? How?

B: Well, it's a lot cleaner than it was.

A: How did that happen?

B: We pay a forty-dollar fine if we drop a piece of paper on the street.

A: It seems to work. The place is spotless. And downtown looks livelier.

B: That's because more people are using the area. And look at the buses. They're bigger and the seats are more comfortable. There are more buses and more bus stops too. These days it's a lot easier to take the bus than a car.

A: Do they run on electricity?

B: Yes, they do.

A: I guess the air is cleaner too.

B: It is. As you can see there aren't many cars around here.

A: How come?

B: It's a lot harder to park here. Actually it's almost impossible. So no one drives. We have bicycle lanes too. And more people are moving downtown and walking everywhere. Remember West Park?

A: I remember it wasn't very safe.

B: You should see it now. It's a lot cleaner and safer. And there are vegetable gardens. People can get a plot of land and do some gardening.

A: How about East Park?

B: Unfortunately East Park is worse. It's more dangerous than ever. It's also dirtier. But in time, I'm sure our mayor will fix it up.

A: You really like the mayor.

B: Yes, I do.

A: Who is he?

B: My uncle, Paul Steiner.

UNIT 34

EXERCISE 5 (page 405)

You're ready to give a speech. You have a good beginning, an introduction that your audience will pay attention to, and a good ending or conclusion. You also have a couple of good jokes. What else should you do? Here are five more tips to help make a good speech a great one.

First of all, remember to look directly at a few people in the audience. Your eyes can make your audience feel involved.

Second, speak confidently. Show your audience that you really believe the words you're saying.

Third, dress appropriately. Remember your audience will be looking at you the entire time.

Fourth, speak freely and use natural language. Don't read your speech or show a PowerPoint® slide with a lot of writing on it.

Finally, summarize your talk and thank your audience sincerely.

UNIT 35

EXERCISE 8 (page 417)

1. She's bright, but she never says a word. She just sits and smiles. She's as quiet as a mouse.
2. I'm sorry I bought that chair. You have to be as strong as an ox to lift it.
3. He never shows his feelings. He's as cool as a cucumber.
4. Her sister is nasty, but she's as sweet as honey.
5. She doesn't weigh much at all. She's as light as a feather.
6. I was very upset when she didn't keep her promise. I thought her word was as good as gold.

EXERCISE 9 (page 418)

JAMES: Colin feels very bad.

VICKIE: I know. He's very bright and he really wanted to be assistant manager, but we couldn't give him the promotion. He's just too critical of others. Nobody's work is good enough for him. It's too bad. But Colin never thinks he's wrong. He always thinks it's the other guy.

JAMES: Yeah. I feel good about Maria, though. She's bright and confident, and she'll bring out the best in others. Also, Maria always does what she says she will do. Her word is as good as gold. Colin is not as reliable as Maria. Maria's a real team player.

UNIT 36

EXERCISE 8 (page 429)

JIM: Good evening and welcome to *How Much Do You Know about Nature?* where guests answer questions and win huge cash prizes. Tonight, back for the third week, is Marsha Williams. You know the rules.

MARSHA: Yes, Jim.

JIM: Five seconds to answer the question. Are you ready?

MARSHA: I'm ready.

JIM: OK. Pick a card. . . . Well, I see you picked the category of animals. Our first question for one thousand dollars is: Which animal has the longest gestation period? In other words, which baby is carried in its mother for the longest time?

MARSHA: I think it's the Asian elephant.

JIM: You're right. The Asian elephant is born after a gestation period of 19 to 22 months. For that answer you win one thousand dollars.

MARSHA: Thank you.

JIM: You're very welcome. . . . Next, for five thousand dollars: What is the fastest land animal?

MARSHA: That's an easy one, the cheetah.

JIM: You're right again. They can run up to 70 miles an hour. You now have six thousand dollars. . . . Now for ten thousand dollars our third question. What's the loudest land animal?

MARSHA: The loudest land animal is the howler monkey. You can hear this monkey from three miles away.

JIM: Excellent. You've just won ten thousand dollars for a total of sixteen thousand dollars.

MARSHA: That's fantastic.

JIM: And our last question is for twenty thousand dollars. . . . This creature kills more than a million people each year.

MARSHA: Is it the mosquito that carries malaria?

JIM: Yes, it is. Fantastic. And for that you win twenty thousand dollars for a grand total of thirty-six thousand dollars. Congratulations, Marsha.

STUDENT BOOK ANSWER KEY

In this Answer Key where the short or contracted form is given, the full or long form is also correct (unless the purpose of the exercise is to practice the short or contracted form). Where the full or long form is given, the contracted form is also correct.

UNIT 1 (pages 2–11)

AFTER YOU READ

B. 1. husband **3.** famous **5.** busy
  2. talented **4.** athlete **6.** exciting
C. 1. b **3.** a **5.** a **7.** b
  2. b **4.** a **6.** b **8.** b

EXERCISE 1

A. 4. aren't **6.** 'm not
B. 1. isn't **4.** aren't **5.** I'm **6.** I'm
C. 1. She isn't single.
  2. She is married to him.
  3. They are athletes.

EXERCISE 2

  2. is **3.** are **4.** is **5.** is **6.** am **7.** are

EXERCISE 3

  2. are   **8.** is not
  3. is   **9.** is
  4. is   **10.** is not
  5. is   **11.** is
  6. are   **12.** am not
  7. are not

EXERCISE 4

  2. He's **4.** It's **6.** She's
  3. We're **5.** They're **7.** They're

EXERCISE 5

Answers will vary.
  2. It's (not) popular in my country.
  3. He's from Spain.
  4. They're talented soccer players.
  5. I'm a student.
  6. I'm (not) from London.
  7. My friends and I are (not) soccer fans.
  8. Soccer is (not) my favorite sport.

EXERCISE 6

My family ⌃ *is* in Mexico. Ɨ *I'm* in Los Angeles. My father is a businessman, and my mother ⌃ *is* a math teacher. Alessandra is my sister. S̶h̶e̶ *She's* an engineer. Marco is my brother. I̶s̶ *He is* in the family business with my father. We all ⌃ *are* soccer fans. Our favorite team is the Club de Fútbol Monterrey. Our team ⌃ *is* on TV very often. I call my family, and we talk about the game on TV. They ⌃ *are* far away, but thanks to email and cell phones, we ⌃ *are* close.

EXERCISE 7

B.

	He's	She's
1.		√
2.	√	
3.		√
4.	√	
5.	√	
6.		√

EXERCISE 8

A. and **B.**

Name	Hideki Matsui	Lionel Messi	Rihanna	Kim Yu-Na
Job	baseball player	soccer player	singer	ice skater
Country of Origin	Japan	Argentina	Barbados	Korea

Name	Rob Pattinson	Olga Kurylenko	Paulo Coehlo	Ang Lee
Job	actor	actress and model	writer	movie director
Country of Origin	England	Russia	Brazil	Taiwan

EXERCISES 9–11

Answers will vary.

AFTER YOU READ

B. 1. Excuse me
  2. room
  3. right
  4. on time
  5. By the way
C. 1. a   **2.** c   **3.** a   **4.** b   **5.** b   **6.** c

EXERCISE 1

2. c   **3.** a   **4.** b   **5.** f   **6.** h   **7.** d   **8.** g

EXERCISE 2

  2. Are we in the right building?
  3. Are you a new student?
  4. Is the teacher from Canada?
  5. Is it ten o'clock?
  6. Are they new computers?
  7. Are two students absent today?
  8. Am I in the right room?

EXERCISE 3

Answers will vary.
  2. A: Is your watch fast?
     B: Yes, it is. OR No, it's not. (No, it isn't.)
  3. A: Is your jacket from Italy?
     B: Yes, it is. OR No, it's not. (No, it isn't.)
  4. A: Is your birthday in the spring?
     B: Yes, it is. OR No, it's not. (No, it isn't.)
  5. A: Is your name easy to pronounce?
     B: Yes, it is. OR No, it's not. (No, it isn't.)
  6. A: Are you and your classmates from different
         cities?
     B: Yes, we are. OR No, we're not. (No, we aren't.)
  7. A: Are your classmates busy now?
     B: Yes, they are. OR No, they're not. (No, they
         aren't.)

EXERCISE 4

  2. Where are the computers?
  3. What's today's date?
  4. Why are you late?
  5. Why is she the teacher?
  6. How's your computer class?

EXERCISE 5

A. 2. A: Is Oscar smart?
       B: Yes, he is.
  3. A: Are Alejandra and Oscar a good pair?
       B: Yes, they are.
  4. A: Who is always late?
       B: Oscar is.
B. *Answers may vary.*
  2. A: Is Oscar a bad boyfriend?
       B: No, he isn't.

  3. A: Is Oscar bad at planning time?
       B: Yes, he is.
  4. A: Is Smartgirl's answer good?
       B: Yes, it is.

EXERCISE 6

  2. A: Is ⌃*it* easy?
       B: No, it's hard.
  3. A: ⌃*Is he* ~~He~~ Korean?
       B: No, he isn't.
  4. A: Excuse me. Where's the office?
       B: ~~Yes, it's~~ *It's* here.
  5. A: Is this English 3?
       B: Yes, I think⌃*so*.
  6. A: ⌃*Are* ~~Is~~ they in room 102?
       B: I don't know.
  7. A: Where ⌃*are* you from?
       B: I'm from Peru.
  8. A: How ⌃*is* your class ~~is~~?
       B: It's very good.
  9. A: What ⌃*'s* your nickname?
       B: Susie.

EXERCISE 7

A. a
B. 1. Canada   **3.** Korea, Japan
   2. fifty years old   **4.** speaking

AFTER YOU READ

B. 1. busy   **3.** a big deal   **5.** boring
   2. make money   **4.** still
C. 1. He was a lifeguard.
   2. He was 16 years old.
   3. Yes, he was. OR Yes.
   4. No, it wasn't. It was boring. OR No. It was boring.
   5. Yes, he was. OR Yes.

EXERCISE 1

As a teen he <u>was</u> an ice cream salesman.

Ray Romano, the comedian, <u>was</u> a bank teller.

Jennifer Aniston and Madonna <u>weren't</u> always stars.
Before they <u>were</u> famous, they <u>were</u> servers in
restaurants.

And Warren Beatty, the actor, <u>was</u> a rat catcher in a
Virginia movie theater.

EXERCISE 2

2. wasn't	**7.** was
3. was	**8.** was
4. was	**9.** was
5. Were	**10.** Were
6. were	**11.** wasn't

EXERCISE 3

3. He was in Seoul
4. it was cold
5. She wasn't in class
6. He was at a job interview
7. was in the swimming pool
8. was busy

EXERCISE 4

1. B: No, he wasn't.
2. A: Where was he?
  B: He was in Vancouver.
3. A: Why was he in Vancouver?
  B: He was there for work.
4. A: How was the weather in Vancouver?
  B: It was terrible.
5. A: Was the airport closed?
  B: No, but all the planes were late.

EXERCISE 5

Hi Victor,

How ~~your week was~~ *was your week?* ~~You were~~ *Were you* busy? I hope things are good at your new job.

I was at a job interview yesterday. It ~~were~~ *was* for a sales job at DB Drugstore.

The interviewer ~~be~~ *was* friendly. The questions ~~no were~~ *weren't* easy, but I think my answers were good.

It's not my dream job, but it's a paycheck.

Write soon.
  Ella

EXERCISE 6

A.

	Friend	Family	Business Call
Message 1	√		
Message 2	√		
Message 3	√		
Message 4			√
Message 5		√	

B. 2. party, were, meet
  3. weather, was terrible
  4. 222-989-9029
  5. at a restaurant

EXERCISE 7

C.

	was	wasn't	were	weren't
1.		√		
2.	√			
3.			√	
4.				√
5.			√	

EXERCISES 8–10

Answers will vary.

PART I From Grammar to Writing
(pages 36–37)

3

1. This is Ms. Herrera.
2. Her address is 4 Riverdale Avenue.
3. I'm her good friend.
4. She was in Bangkok and Taiwan last year.

4

(See graphic at the top of page 173.)

5

Answers will vary.

UNIT 4 (pages 40–49)

AFTER YOU READ

B. 1. a **2.** a **3.** b **4.** a **5.** b **6.** a
C. 1. F **2.** F **3.** T **4.** T **5.** T **6.** F

EXERCISE 1

B. 1. accountant
  2. photo (college, teacher, girl, etc.)
  3. Jasmine, Brazil (New York, India, etc.)
  4. friends, photos

EXERCISE 2

A. 2. a **5.** a **8.** an
  3. a **6.** a **9.** a
  4. an **7.** an **10.** a
B. left (top to bottom): 3, 7, 8, 4, 9, 10
  right (top to bottom): 5, 1, 6, 2

EXERCISE 3

3. an **5.** a, a **7.** a **9.** Ø, Ø
4. Ø **6.** Ø **8.** Ø, Ø **10.** Ø

4

Hi ~~ruth~~ *Ruth*,

~~john and i are in acapulco~~ *John I Acapulco* this week. ~~it's~~ *It's* beautiful here. ~~the~~ *The* people are friendly and the weather is great. ~~it's~~ *It's* sunny and warm.

~~last~~ *Last* week we were in ~~mexico city~~ *Mexico City* for two days. ~~i~~ *I* was there on business. ~~my~~ *My* meetings were long and difficult, but our evenings were fun. ~~hope~~ *Hope* all is well with you.

                        Regards,

                        Ellen
                        ~~ellen~~

To:

Ms. Ruth Holland
~~ms. ruth holland~~
Oldwick St.
~~10 oldwick st.~~
Ringwood New Jersey
~~ringwood, new jersey~~ 07456
U.S.A.
~~u.s.a.~~

EXERCISE 4

2. countries	**8.** earrings
3. museums	**9.** clothes
4. watches	**10.** artists
5. fish	**11.** lives
6. people	**12.** classes
7. flowers	

EXERCISE 5

mike cho = Mike Cho, mike = Mike
phoenix = Phoenix
san francisco = San Francisco
san francisco = San Francisco
india = India
mexico = Mexico
thanksgiving = Thanksgiving
canada = Canada
sam = Sam

EXERCISE 6

2. This is ^ *a* photo of Henri Matisse.

3. Henri Matisse was ^ *a* great artist.

4. Before Matisse was ^ *an* artist, he was ^ *a* lawyer.

5. Matisse's paintings are in ~~museum~~ *museums* all over the world.

6. In this photo Matisse is in the south of ~~france~~ *France*.

7. We see four ~~bird~~ *birds* outside their cages.

EXERCISE 7

B.

	/s/	/z/	/ɪz/
2. classes			√
3. scissors		√	
4. boxes			√
5. artists	√		
6. glasses			√
7. books	√		

EXERCISE 8

A. c
B. 2. b **3.** b **4.** a **5.** a

EXERCISES 9–11

Answers will vary.

UNIT 5 (pages 51–58)

AFTER YOU READ

B. 1. average   **4.** dry
   2. safe   **5.** comfortable
   3. awesome **6.** unusual
C. 1. b **2.** a **3.** b **4.** a **5.** a

EXERCISE 1

1. small		**7.** good	
2. fun		**8.** helpful	
3. old		**9.** friendly	
4. modern		**10.** easy	
5. expensive		**11.** great	
6. delicious			

EXERCISE 2

2. A: The carpets are awesome.

3. B: The prices are reasonable.

4. B: It is warm and sunny. OR It is sunny and warm.

5. B: I'm tired but happy. OR I'm happy but tired.

EXERCISE 3

2. The food is delicious.

3. The waiters are friendly and helpful.

4. The Bilton is a comfortable hotel.

5. The rooms are not expensive.

6. The outdoor market is safe.

7. The carpets are expensive.

8. That is a beautiful carpet.

9. The climate is mild.

10. The weather is comfortable all year round.

EXERCISE 4

new lamp
A: Is that a ~~lamp new~~?

B: Yes, it is. It's from Turkey.

beautiful
A: The colors are ~~beautifuls~~.

_an_
B: Thanks. I got it at ^ old market in Cappadocia.

interesting things
A: Were there many ~~things interesting~~ to buy?

B: Yes. These plates are from the market too.

are
A: The colors ^ unusual. I like them a lot.

B: Here. This one is for you.

EXERCISE 5

A. b

B. 2. b   **3.** a   **4.** b   **5.** b

EXERCISE 6

C.

     •
2. warm (one syllable)

     •
3. unusual (2nd syllable)

  •
4. friendly (1st syllable)

 •
5. modern (1st syllable)

  •
6. cheap (one syllable)

     •
7. unimportant (3rd syllable)

EXERCISES 7–8

Answers will vary.

UNIT 6 (pages 60–68)

BEFORE YOU READ

Possible Answers:

1. Next to the Photographs of India exhibit.

2. Near the Chinese Garden.

AFTER YOU READ

B. 1. cafeteria

   2. sculpture

   3. flight

   4. 'm free

   5. appointment

   6. rest room

C. 1. F   **2.** F   **3.** T   **4.** F   **5.** T   **6.** ?

EXERCISE 1

1. I

2. LOVE

3. ENGLISH

The message is: I LOVE ENGLISH.

EXERCISE 2

2. next to	**5.** at
3. on the, of	**6.** on the
4. between	**7.** under

EXERCISE 3

2. at	**5.** on
3. on	**6.** in / of
4. between	**7.** in

EXERCISE 4

Answers will vary.

EXERCISE 5

1. A: I'm in school until 2:00, but I'm free after that. Let's go to the Modern Art Museum.

   B: OK. Where is it?

_on_   _Eighth_
   A: It's ~~in~~ Fifth Avenue between ~~Eight~~ and Ninth Streets.

_on_
2. A: Excuse me. Are the masks ^ the third floor?

   B: I don't know. Ask at the Information Booth.

   A: Where is that?

B: It's in front *of* the stairs near ~~to~~ the gift shop.

And the sculptures are ~~in~~ *on* the second floor, in

back *of* the paintings.

EXERCISE 6

B. 2. I'm on the first floor. He's on the fifth floor.

3. The museum is on 5th Street. It's not on 5th Avenue.

4. The museum is on 5th Street. The library is on 5th Avenue.

5. Your glasses are on the table. Your gloves are in the drawer.

EXERCISE 7

A. and B.
1. Korea
2. Ecuador
3. Madagascar
4. Spain

EXERCISES 8–10

Answers will vary.

PART II From Grammar to Writing (page 70)

1

1. and	3. and
2. but	4. but

2

1. and	4. but	7. and
2. and	5. and	8. but
3. and	6. and	

UNIT 7 (pages 72–79)

AFTER YOU READ

B. 1. nap 4. advice
2. secret 5. pray
3. dead 6. island
C. 1. sick 4. scientist
2. bridge 5. take it easy
3. Greece 6. Mary

EXERCISE 1

2. A: I, B: A
3. A: S, B: D
4. A: I, B: A
5. A: S, B: D
6. A: I, B: A

EXERCISE 2

2. close	**7.** give
3. don't tell	**8.** Try
4. check	**9.** Don't take
5. Let's walk	**10.** Don't visit
6. Let's not buy	

EXERCISE 3

A. The gym is on Second Avenue between 70th and 71st Street.
B. 72nd Street. Turn left at 72nd Street. Walk two blocks. The library is between 72nd Street and 73rd Street.

EXERCISE 4

JOE: Let's ~~to~~ go to the movies.
MARY: Why ~~we don't~~ *don't we* go to the park first. It's a beautiful day.
JOE: OK. But first ~~let~~ *let's* have lunch. I'm hungry.
MARY: I'm hungry too. Why don't we have a fruit salad with nuts?
JOE: Good idea.
MARY: But ~~you~~ don't use those apples. They're bad. ~~Throws~~ *Throw* them away.
JOE: OK.
MARY: And why ~~you don't~~ *don't you* add honey to the yogurt? It's delicious that way.
JOE: You're right. This is really good.

EXERCISE 5

A. a
B. 4, 6, 8

EXERCISES 7–11

Answers will vary.

UNIT 8 (pages 81–89)

AFTER YOU READ

B. 1. c **2.** b **3.** b **4.** b **5.** a **6.** b **7.** a
C. 1. T **2.** F **3.** T **4.** T **5.** F **6.** F **7.** F

EXERCISE 1

2. doesn't wear, doesn't eat
3. buy
4. makes, 's
5. wears, exercises

EXERCISE 2

1. wears
2. like, wear
3. knows
4. shop
5. means
6. have

EXERCISE 3

2. don't buy
3. don't like
4. don't need
5. doesn't wear
6. doesn't look
7. aren't
8. isn't

EXERCISE 4

2. a. don't need   **b.** need
3. a. wants   **b.** doesn't want
4. a. like   **b.** don't like
5. a. has   **b.** doesn't have
6. a. doesn't go   **b.** goes

EXERCISE 5

A. 2. 's   **9.** think
3. has   **10.** give
4. have   **11.** doesn't have
5. loves   **12.** wants
6. wears   **13.** don't want
7. prefers   **14.** thinks
8. aren't OR 're not
B. 2. agree   **4.** thinks
3. works   **5.** sounds

EXERCISE 6

Miyuki Myagi is a teenager. She ~~live~~ *lives* in Japan. She ~~like~~ *likes* clothes, and she ~~shop~~ *shops* in the Harajuku District in Tokyo. She ~~say~~ *says*, "My friends and I love fashion. We ~~goes~~ *go* to the stores, but we ~~doesn't~~ *don't* always buy much. Clothes are expensive. But we still look good. My friends and I know inexpensive ways to dress *kawaii*.

For example, sometimes we make our own clothes. And we mix styles. Sometimes we put on gothic clothes with punk clothes or schoolgirl uniforms.

Sometimes we ~~wears~~ *wear* lots of makeup. And sometimes we ~~dresses~~ *dress* like dolls, or like anime."

EXERCISE 7

B.

	/s/	/z/	/ɪz/
2. uses			√
3. buys		√	
4. knows		√	
5. costs	√		
6. misses			√
7. watches			√
8. thinks	√		

EXERCISE 8

A. a
B. 2. big sale (sale)
3. a new dress / a bright color
4. $40 (forty dollars)
5. fast shopper

EXERCISES 9–11

Answers will vary.

UNIT 9 (pages 91–100)

AFTER YOU READ

B. 1. messy, neat
2. bothers
3. stay up
4. wakes up
5. easygoing
6. private
7. outgoing
C. 1. T   **3.** F   **5.** T   **7.** T   **9.** T
2. F   **4.** T   **6.** T   **8.** F

EXERCISE 1

2. d   **3.** c   **4.** e   **5.** a

EXERCISE 2

2. Does, have, doesn't
3. Does, wake up, he doesn't
4. Do, stay up, they do
5. Does, bother, it doesn't
6. Does, have, it does
7. Does, rain, it doesn't
8. Do, have, you do
9. Does, go, she doesn't
10. Do, need, we do
11. Do, sell, they do

EXERCISE 3

2. Does, he does   **8.** Do, do
3. Are, are   **9.** Does, doesn't
4. Do, they don't   **10.** Are, are
5. Are, they aren't   **11.** Are, we are
6. Do, they do   **12.** Do, don't
7. Is, she isn't

EXERCISE 4

3. Does he come   **9.** Yes, he does
4. No, he doesn't   **10.** Do you see
5. Does he play   **11.** Yes, I do OR Yes, we do
6. Do you play   **12.** Do you bring
7. No, I don't   **13.** No, I don't
8. Does he have

EXERCISE 5

1. A: Does she ~~goes~~ *go* to school?
   B: Yes, she ~~goes~~ *does*.
2. A: Does he ~~needs~~ *need* help?
   B: Yes, he does.
3. A: Do they ~~are~~ like rock music?
   B: Yes, they do.
4. A: ~~Do~~ *Does* she live near the museum?
   B: Yes, she ~~lives~~ *does*.
5. A: Does he ~~has~~ *have* a roommate?
   B: Yes, he does.
6. A: Are you friends?
   B: Yes, we ~~do~~ *are*.

EXERCISE 7

A. a
B.

parties	doesn't like parties
music	likes classical music
sports	doesn't like sports
study habits	studies at night in her room

C. 1. No
   Answers may vary. Possible answers:
  2. Leyla likes parties and Andrea doesn't.
    They don't like the same kinds of music. OR
    Leyla likes sports but Andrea doesn't.

EXERCISES 8–11

Answers will vary.

AFTER YOU READ

B. 1. author, guest
  2. remember, Unfortunately, nightmares
C. 1. F   **2.** ?   **3.** T   **4.** F   **5.** F

EXERCISE 1

2. b   **3.** e   **4.** d   **5.** a   **6.** c

EXERCISE 2

2. Where does your guest come from?
3. How do they feel at night?
4. Who does he dream about?
5. What does she dream about?

EXERCISE 3

2. Who has nightmares?
3. Who gets up before 6:00 A.M.?
4. Who hates early morning classes?
5. Who needs more than eight hours of sleep?

EXERCISE 4

2. does Sabrina daydream
3. does Sabrina daydream about
4. does Sabrina daydream during math
5. is Sabrina's boyfriend
6. does Sabrina feel
7. has a good job
8. does he do

EXERCISE 5

2. Who meets his boss at a party? Jake does. Who does Jake meet at a party? His boss.
3. Who hits Maya? Two giants do. Who do two giants hit? Maya.

EXERCISE 6

1. Where do they ~~sleeps~~ *sleep*?
2. Why *do* they need two pillows?
3. Who ~~sleep~~ *sleeps* on the sofa?
4. When does she ~~goes~~ *go* to bed?
5. Who ~~wake~~ *wakes* you?
6. Who ~~does~~ *do* you dream about?
7. How *does* he ~~feels~~ *feel* about that?
8. What *do* you dream about?

9. Where ~~does~~ he sleep?

10. How long does she ~~sleeps~~ _sleep_ at night?

EXERCISE 7

A. The room for her test.
B. 2. You're in the wrong building.
   3. He thinks she has a lot of stress.
   4. The buildings symbolize music and science.
   5. Her father wants her to study science.

EXERCISE 8

D.

It was a <u>great</u> <u>dream</u>. Listen. I buy a <u>black</u> <u>dress</u>. The <u>price</u> is only thirty-<u>three</u> dollars. There's a <u>problem</u> with the <u>dress</u>. I <u>bring</u> it back. The salesperson says she's sorry.

She gives me a <u>bright</u> <u>blue</u> <u>dress</u> instead. I <u>try</u> it on. The <u>dress</u> is perfect. I wear the <u>dress</u> to a party. I have a <u>great</u> night out.

EXERCISES 9–10

Answers will vary.

EXERCISE 11

Student A
   1. I'm on an airplane.
   2. A pilot comes to me.
   3. He says, "I need your help."
   4. I go with the pilot. I fly the plane. I land the plane.
   5. I feel good.
   6. I wake up.

Student B
   1. I'm in the third grade.
   2. I see my third grade teacher.
   3. She is very big.
   4. I'm small.
   5. She says, "Your schoolwork is great. You are my favorite student."
   6. I smile. Then I laugh. Then I wake up.

PART III   From Grammar to Writing
(page 114)

2

Example paragraph:

   First, I take a shower. Next, I have breakfast. After that I drive to the train station. Then I take a train to the bus. Finally I get to work.

UNIT 11 (pages 116–128)

AFTER YOU READ

B. 1. one-of-a-kind
   2. include
   3. international
   4. market
   5. attraction
   6. amusement park
   7. indoor
   8. get away
C. 1. c   **2.** c   **3.** b   **4.** b   **5.** a

EXERCISE 1

2. F	**4.** T	**6.** T	**8.** T	**10.** T
3. T	**5.** F	**7.** T	**9.** T	

EXERCISE 2

   2. There's a shoe store on the second level.
   3. correct
   4. correct
   5. There isn't a men's clothing store in the mall.
   6. There aren't any desks in the furniture store.

EXERCISE 3

   2. There aren't
   3. There isn't
   4. There is
   5. There are
   6. They aren't
   7. There isn't
   8. There is
   9. There are
   10. They are

EXERCISE 4

2. There are	**5.** there
3. Yes, they're	**6.** there
4. there's	**7.** there

EXERCISE 5

   2. There's, He's
   3. There are, They're
   4. There's, It's
   5. There are, They're
   6. There's, It's
   7. There are, They're

EXERCISE 6

1. B: Yes, there is. There's a dance performance tonight at 8:00.

2. A: Are there

    B: Yes, there are. (There is a movie at Main Street Cinema on Saturday and there is a concert at Chicago Cultural Center on Sunday.)

3. A: are there

    B: Three. OR There are three showings at 4:30, 6:30, and 8:30.

4. A: Is there

    B: Yes, there is. It's at 4545 West Division. It's on Friday from 8 to 5.

EXERCISE 7

There ~~be~~ *are* pizza places at almost every mall. The pizzas come in all shapes and sizes. ^*There* are traditional pizzas with mushrooms, pepperoni, and broccoli. There ~~is~~ *are* also pizzas with curry, red herring, and coconut. In the United States ~~they~~ *there* are over 61,000 pizza places. ~~There~~ *They* represent 17 percent of all restaurants. ~~There~~ *They* are popular with young and old.

EXERCISE 8

B. 2. b   **3.** b   **4.** b   **5.** a   **6.** b

EXERCISE 9

A. is there a mall around here

B. 2. ?   **3.** ?   **4.** N   **5.** Y

EXERCISE 10

In Picture A there's a man in front of the bakery. In Picture B there isn't a man in front of the bakery. There's a woman in front of the bakery.

In Picture A, there's a hardware store next to the supermarket. In Picture B, there isn't a hardware store next to the supermarket. There's a flower shop next to the supermarket.

In Picture A, there aren't any signs in the supermarket window. In Picture B, there are signs in the supermarket window.

In Picture A, there are many people in front of the supermarket. In Picture B, there aren't many people in front of the supermarket. There's a policeman in front of the supermarket. There is a car in front of the supermarket.

In Picture A, there are shoes in the window of the shoe repair shop. In Picture B, there aren't shoes in the window. There are signs in the window.

EXERCISES 11–12

Answers will vary.

UNIT 12 (pages 130–141)

AFTER YOU READ

B. 1. recognize, handwriting
   2. composition
   3. back
   4. grade

C. 1. Boris   **2.** Kim   **3.** Juan

EXERCISE 1

2. a   **3.** b   **4.** a   **5.** b   **6.** b.   **7.** b

EXERCISE 2

A. Lao's, Hua's, Mei's

B. 1. grandmother
   2. sister's daughter
   3. wife's sister
   4. uncle's
   5. cousins, mothers, sisters
   6. family's

EXERCISE 3

2. her   **4.** his, their   **6.** his   **8.** her
3. Their   **5.** Its   **7.** your

EXERCISE 4

1. b. his   **2. a.** Theirs   **3. a.** hers
  c. Mine   **b.** ours   **b.** Mine

EXERCISE 5

1. b. Yours   **2. a.** Hers   **3. a.** their
  c. her   **b.** Mine   **b.** Their
                              c. yours
                              d. Ours

EXERCISE 6

1. b. me   **c.** I
2. a. he   **b.** him
3. a. Their   **b.** they   **c.** them

EXERCISE 7

1. are
2. Whose, Is
3. Who's, Is
4. Whose, Are, they're
5. Whose, are
6. Who's
7. live

EXERCISE 8

2. I'm	7. We	12. Hers
3. It's	8. It's	13. We
4. My	9. it's	14. our
5. my	10. We	15. we
6. me	11. Mine	16. us

EXERCISE 9

1. **A:** Is that ~~you~~ *your* dictionary?
   B: No. It's his dictionary.
   A: ~~Who's~~ *Whose*?
   B: ~~Dans~~ *Dan's*.
2. **A:** Is ~~Maria~~ *Maria's* sister here?
   B: No, she's not.
   A: Is Maria here?
   B: No, but ~~his~~ *her* brother is.
   A: Where is Maria?
   B: I think she's with ~~his~~ *her* sister. ~~Their~~ *They're* at the movies.

EXERCISE 10

B.
2. Maria	4. partner's	6. partners
3. Marias	5. partner	

EXERCISE 11

A. a
B. 1. Amy 2. Johnny 3. Jasmine 4. Roger and Ted

EXERCISES 12–14

Answers will vary.

UNIT 13 (pages 143–151)

AFTER YOU READ

B. 1. intelligent
2. are surprised
3. genius
4. professor
5. invent
C. 1. F 2. F 3. T 4. ? 5. F 6. T

EXERCISE 1

A. and **B.**
_e_ 1. N'kisi <u>can invent</u> new words.

_b_ 2. We <u>can't understand</u> our professor.

_f_ 3. I'm sorry. I <u>can't help</u> you now.

_g_ 4. I <u>can't hear</u> you.

_a_ 5. He <u>can lift</u> 110 pounds (50 kilos).

_d_ 6. They <u>can't express</u> their love.

_c_ 7. The boy <u>couldn't reach</u> the button.

EXERCISE 2

1. can say
2. can sit, can't bring
3. can catch, can't catch
4. can understand
5. can help

EXERCISE 3

2. **A:** Can he ask questions?
   B: Yes, he can.
3. **A:** Can he make suggestions?
   B: Yes, he can.
4. **A:** Can Aimee buy a car now?
   B: No, she can't.
5. **A:** Can N'kisi ask for things?
   B: Yes, he can.
6. **A:** Can Aimee and N'kisi go in a car now?
   B: No, they can't.

EXERCISE 4

1. Could, open
2. could use, could make
3. couldn't do
4. could bring
5. couldn't talk
6. Could, say, could say

EXERCISE 5

A: Can you ~~coming~~ *come* to my party? It's next Saturday night. You can ⤫ meet my new dog.
B: Yes. I'd love to. How *can* I get to your home?
A: You can ⤫ take the train or a taxi.
B: Can you meet me at the train station?
A: I'm sorry. I can't. I ~~no can~~ *can't* drive. Maybe Bob can ~~meets~~ *meet* you. He has a car, and he can ⤫ drive.

EXERCISE 6

B. 1. can't see
   2. can lead, can't lead
   3. can sleep, can't sleep
   4. can scare, can't scare
   5. can show, can't explain
   6. can use, can't jump

EXERCISE 7

A. catch a ball, paint pictures, play basketball
B. 1. b
   2. a, c, e, f

EXERCISES 8–10

Answers will vary.

UNIT 14 (pages 153–161)

BEFORE YOU READ

Protein: chicken, fish
Carbohydrate(s): cake, pasta, rice
Fat: oil

AFTER YOU READ

B. 1. overweight, lose   **3.** gain
   2. especially   **4.** pounds
C. 1. T **2.** F **3.** T **4.** T **5.** F **6.** ?

EXERCISE 1

A. and B.
_G_ **B:** Yes, you can, but you <u>can</u> only have boiled, grilled, or baked meat.
_A_ **A:** What about fried chicken? <u>Can</u> I have it? I love fried chicken.
_D_ **B:** Sorry, You <u>may not</u> have any fried food on this diet.
_A_ **A:** <u>Can</u> I eat nuts?
_G_ **B:** Yes, you <u>may</u>, but don't eat too many. And remember, there are many things on this diet that you can eat. You <u>may</u> eat as many green vegetables as you want. And you <u>can</u> drink as much green tea as you want.
    A: Well, that sounds good.
_G_ **B:** If you have any more questions, you <u>can</u> call me weekdays between 11:00 and 1:00.

EXERCISE 2

 1. can, drive, Can, eat
 2. May, help, may take, may keep
 3. Can, have, can, see, can look

EXERCISE 3

 2. May I see your health insurance card?
 3. Can I eat snacks?
 4. Can I eat ice cream?
 5. May I call you with questions?

EXERCISE 4

 1. A: Can we ~~paid~~ ^pay in two installments?
    B: Yes, you can ~~pays~~ ^pay half now and half next month.
 2. A: May I ~~speaks~~ ^speak to the doctor?
    B: I'm sorry. He's with a patient. Give me your number and he'll call you back.
 3. A: Can I ~~to~~ use salt?
    B: Yes, but not a lot.
 4. A: Can I drink coffee or tea?
    B: You may drink tea, but you ~~mayn't~~ ^{may not} drink coffee.
 5. A: May I ~~helping~~ you?
    B: Thanks. I'd like to make an appointment for next week.

EXERCISE 5

A. a.
B. 1. keep her foot raised and take two extra-strength Tylenol
   2. She can work. She can drive.
   3. She can't do sports for three weeks.

EXERCISE 6

D.

	/eɪ/	/ɛ/
2. may	√	
3. eggs		√
4. steak	√	
5. weight	√	
6. may	√	
7. west		√

EXERCISE 7

Student A
 1. (You may see the doctor) Monday, Wednesday, and Friday between 8:00 and 4:00.
 2. (You may call the doctor) Weekdays between 11:00 and 12:00.
 3. Yes, you can contact the doctor by email.
 4. In an emergency, you can call 344-3580.
 5. Yes, you can attend free lectures the first Monday of every month.

6. Yes, you can join a support group.

7. You can see suggested meals at
www.greenhealth.com.

EXERCISES 8

Answers will vary.

PART IV   From Grammar to Writing
(pages 163–164)

1

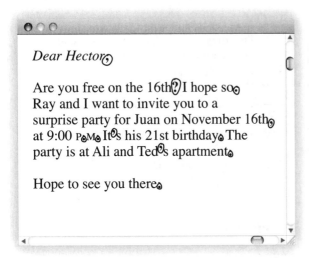

Dear Hector,

Are you free on the 16th? I hope so.
Ray and I want to invite you to a
surprise party for Juan on November 16th,
at 9:00 P.M. It's his 21st birthday. The
party is at Ali and Ted's apartment.

Hope to see you there.

3

Dear Uncle John,

Bob and I want to invite you to a
party for my parents' 25th wedding
anniversary. It's on Sunday,
December 11. The party is at our
home at 23 Main St. It's at three
o'clock. I hope you can make it.

Emily

AFTER YOU READ

B. 1. f   **2.** c   **3.** a   **4.** e   **5.** b   **6.** d

C.

	Mi Young	Julie
1. in school	√	
2. at home		√
3. working hard	√	√
4. hoping to get into a top college	√	√
5. texting a friend		√
6. feeling a lot of pressure	√	√
7. doesn't have a lot of free time	√	√

EXERCISE 1

A. 1. She's <u>putting on</u> her school uniform. Julie <u>is</u> still <u>sleeping</u>.

  2. Mi Young and her classmates <u>are taking</u> the bus to school. Julie <u>is washing</u> her face and <u>combing</u> her hair.

  3. Mi Young <u>is studying</u> English. Julie <u>is swimming</u> at her high school pool.

  4. Mi Young <u>is having dinner</u> with her classmates. Julie <u>is eating</u> at home.

  5. Mi Young <u>is riding</u> home on the bus. Julie <u>is studying</u> physics.

B. 2. put   **6.** comb   **10.** eat
  3. sleep   **7.** study   **11.** ride
  4. take   **8.** swim   **12.** study
  5. wash   **9.** have

EXERCISE 2

  1. She's not eating breakfast.

  2. Julie's taking the bus.

  3. Julie's competing, Julie is not giving up.

  4. She's studying physics.

  5. Julie is hanging out with some friends. They're not studying. They're not competing. They're relaxing and having fun.

EXERCISE 3

1. isn't doing or 's not doing
2. is studying, isn't going or 's not going
3. 's taking, are chatting
4. is worrying, aren't sleeping or 're not sleeping, isn't studying, 's hanging out

EXERCISE 4

2. is meeting
3. is having
4. are eating
5. is learning
6. are spending
7. 'm enjoying
8. 'm earning
9. 'm saving
10. 'm not looking
11. are beginning

EXERCISE 5

I'm ~~sit~~ *sitting* in the park. It's a beautiful day. The leaves ^*are* changing color. Today there are a lot of children in the park. They ^'*re* laughing and are playing. They *aren't* ~~no are~~ studying. They're lucky. It's hard to study on a beautiful day.

I ^'*m* trying to memorize vocabulary words for the SATs. I'm ~~wait~~ *waiting* for my friend Grace. She's in my Saturday SAT prep class. We ^'*re* planning to study together all afternoon and evening.

EXERCISE 6

A. on the train
B. 2. He's helping his father.
   3. She's studying at the library.
   4. She's studying at the library, too.
   5. Her train will arrive at 7:15.

EXERCISES 8–9

Answers will vary.

UNIT 16 (pages 174–183)

AFTER YOU READ

B. 1. scene
   2. catching a cold
   3. fever
   4. coughing
   5. classic
   6. favorite

C. 1. Abby is staying home from work because ~~her daughter~~ *she* has a cold and fever.
   2. Greg is ~~taking care of~~ *talking to* Abby.
   3. ~~Greg and Abby are~~ *Abby is* watching *The Wizard of Oz*.

4. Dorothy is giving the Tin Man ~~water~~ *oil*.
5. The Tin Man is ^*not* talking.
6. Greg's boss, Mr. Brooks, ~~isn't~~ *is* going crazy.

EXERCISE 1

A. 2. Is Dorothy giving the Tin Man oil?
   3. Is he talking?
   4. Is Mr. Brooks going crazy?
B.

Wh-word + be	Subject	Base form of verb + -ing
2. What are	you	watching?
3. What part are	you	watching?

Wh-word + be	Base form of Verb + -ing
4. What's	happening
5. What's	going on (at work)?

EXERCISE 2

_d_ 2. What's Johnny Depp doing now?
_c_ 3. Are you watching it on your DVD?
_a_ 4. Are you taping it for me?

EXERCISE 3

2. Are you feeling any better?
3. Are you taking the medicine?
4. Where are you calling from?
5. Who's she eating with?
6. Are people asking for her autograph?

EXERCISE 4

2. Are, looking for
3. is, looking at
4. are, listening to

EXERCISE 5

1. A: Excuse me, who ^'*s* collecting tickets?
   B: He isn't here now. Wait a minute. He'll be right back.
2. A: What ^*are* you doing?
   B: I'm turning off my cell phone.
3. A: Is Dad ~~buy~~ *buying* popcorn?
   B: Yes, he is.
4. A: What ^'*s* taking him so long?
   B: He's waiting in a long line.

Student Book Answer Key 183

5. A: Excuse me, is someone ~~sits~~ *sitting* here?

B: No, no one 's sitting here. Please sit down.

EXERCISE 6

A. b

B. 2. His dad's birthday. (It's his dad's birthday.)
   3. When he's on the train. (He can use the DVD when he travels by train.)
   4. a Blu-Ray player. (His friend tells him to buy a Blu-Ray.)
   5. There's a sale. (This week there's a sale at Goodbuys.)

EXERCISE 7

C. 1. DVD   **3.** CD   **5.** DVR
   2. TV   **4.** ISBN   **6.** BA

EXERCISES 8–10

Answers will vary.

UNIT 17 (pages 185–193)

AFTER YOU READ

B. 1. b   **2.** a   **3.** a   **4.** a   **5.** a   **6.** b
C. 1. b   **2.** b   **3.** c   **4.** a

EXERCISE 1

likes, is, doesn't know, prefers worries
keeps, text, don't talk, connect, adds, doesn't use,
is texting, are making

EXERCISE 2

   3. 'm checking   **7.** use   **11.** know
   4. has   **8.** don't   **12.** worry
   5. 're singing   **9.** prefer
   6. Do   **10.** think

EXERCISE 3

   2. texting   **5.** 's failing   **9.** loves
   3. isn't doing   **6.** does   **10.** think
      (OR 's not doing)   **7.** say   **11.** 's becoming
   4. think   **8.** 's playing

EXERCISE 4

   2. wants   **4.** 's talking   **6.** is answering
   3. 's thinking   **5.** 's asking   **7.** 's

EXERCISE 5

I ~~hates~~ *hate* cell phones. My boss ~~is thinking~~ *thinks* he can call me anytime, even on weekends. I'x dislike email for the same reason. People in my company work all the time. There's no "off" time. Look at John over there. It's his lunchtime, but he *is* answering calls and ix checking email. This wasn't possible in my parents' day. I don't think it's right. Technology *is* great in some ways, but it's awful in other ways.

EXERCISE 6

A.

1. Bob	co-worker
2. Lydia	family
3. Natalya	family
4. Grandma Olga	family

B.

2. Lydia	studying late at school
3. Natalya	make final plans for trip
4. Grandma Olga	a smart phone

EXERCISE 7

B. a
C. b

EXERCISES 8–10

Answers will vary.

PART V   From Grammar to Writing (page 195)

3

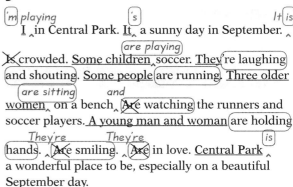

I *'m playing* in Central Park. It 's a sunny day in September. It *is* ix crowded. Some children *are playing* soccer. They're laughing and shouting. Some people are running. Three older women *are sitting* on a bench *and* Ax watching the runners and soccer players. A young man and woman are holding hands. *They're* Ax smiling. *They're* Ax in love. Central Park *is* a wonderful place to be, especially on a beautiful September day.

AFTER YOU READ

B. 1. bumpy   **3.** picked, up   **5.** canceled
   2. landed   **4.** freezing

C.   *a meal at a churrascuria*
   2. Karen and Julian enjoyed ~~dessert at a café~~.

                     at night
   3. Karen and Julian's plane arrived ~~in the afternoon~~.

                  helpful
   4. The people at the hotel were ~~unhelpful~~.

            canceled
   5. Mr. Grimes ~~attended~~ the spring conference.

EXERCISE 1

	BASE FORM
A. 2. walked	walk
3. invited	invite
4. baked	bake
5. (didn't look)	look
tasted	taste
6. cooked	cook
7. looked	look
(didn't taste)	taste
8. visited	visit
9. called	call
thanked	thank

B. last Friday, Yesterday afternoon, last night, yesterday morning, An hour ago

EXERCISE 2

2. landed   **4.** cooked   **6.** canceled   **8.** hugged
3. visited   **5.** walked   **7.** watched

EXERCISE 3

2. wanted, didn't want
3. rained, didn't rain
4. invited, didn't invite
5. helped, didn't help
6. watched, didn't watch
7. picked . . . up, didn't pick . . . up

EXERCISE 4

2. rained   **7.** climbed   **12.** didn't want
3. didn't stop   **8.** walked   **13.** wanted
4. carried   **9.** boarded   **14.** needed
5. shopped   **10.** watched   **15.** ordered
6. stopped   **11.** listened

EXERCISE 5

1. b. ago   **c.** last
2. a. last   **b.** last   **c.** ago   **d.** yesterday

EXERCISE 6

1. traveled
2. doesn't like, liked
3. opens, didn't open
4. don't travel, traveled
5. start, started
6. takes, didn't use, rented
7. bring, ate

EXERCISE 7

Dear Ilene,

   Paris is unbelievable at night! It's 10 P.M., and I'm writing to you from a café. We arrived here
          two days ago   *picked*
~~ago two days~~. Paul's friend Pierre ~~pick~~ us up.

   We toured the city during the day, and at night we
                        dined
~~did~~ walked along the Seine River. Today we ~~dining~~ in Montmartre, and we visited the Louvre Museum.
didn't like
I ~~not like~~ the food in Montmartre, but I ~~did~~ loved the area.

   We hope all is well with you. Don't work too hard.
Love,
Michelle and Paul

EXERCISE 8

A. 2. T   **3.** T   **4.** F   **5.** F
B. 1. 10 days   **3.** 1 day
   2. 2 nights   **4.** half an hour

EXERCISE 9

B.

	/t/	/d/	/ɪd/
1. I watched TV.	√		
2. I rented a movie.			√
3. I listened to music.		√	
4. I played a sport.		√	
5. I visited friends.			√
6. I worked.	√		

BEFORE YOU READ

b

AFTER YOU READ

B. 1. terrible   **3.** suddenly   **5.** shouted
   2. border   **4.** lucky   **6.** appeared

(continued on next page)

C.

__2__ A week later the horse came back with three other horses.

__1__ A horse appeared on a peasant's land. Two days later it ran away.

__3__ The next morning one of the horses ran into the peasant's son; he was hurt.

__4__ A month later soldiers rode into the village.

__6__ The other young men died. The peasant's son lived a long, happy life.

__5__ The soldiers took all the healthy young men to fight, but they didn't take the peasant's son.

EXERCISE 1

Past	Base Form
won	win
felt	feel
did	do
worried	worry
had	have
became	become
began	begin

EXERCISE 2

2. had	**8.** was	**14.** didn't let
3. went	**9.** didn't see	**15.** became
4. grew	**10.** came	**16.** led
5. split	**11.** gave	**17.** won
6. taught	**12.** ran	**18.** became
7. began	**13.** made fun	**19.** was

EXERCISE 3

2. began	**7.** said	**12.** did
3. didn't say	**8.** was	**13.** saw
4. wrote	**9.** got	**14.** became
5. made	**10.** went	**15.** won
6. knew	**11.** didn't have	**16.** was

EXERCISE 4

2. began	**7.** taught	**12.** didn't want
3. read	**8.** began	**13.** sold
4. became	**9.** had	**14.** gave
5. wasn't	**10.** was	**15.** wrote
6. went	**11.** didn't have	

EXERCISE 5

   My grandfather _was_ born in Peru. He had an older brother and sister. Their dad (my great-grandfather) ~~were~~ _was_ a dreamer. The family ~~have not~~ _didn't have_ much money. When my grandfather was 13, his mother ~~did~~ died

and his dad remarried. My grandfather ~~no like~~ _didn't like_ his stepmother so he ~~move~~ _moved_ in with his sister and her husband. All three ~~leave~~ _left_ for America. They ~~did begin~~ _began_ a small business. They worked hard, and the business ~~grow~~ _grew_. Today my sister and I direct the company.

EXERCISE 6

A. b

B.
2. didn't look	**7.** terrible
3. book bag	**8.** Forget about it.
4. book bag	**9.** forget, wrote
5. pencil case	**10.** son
6. lost, pencil case	

EXERCISE 7

C.

	/æ/	/ɛ/
2.		√
3.		√
4.	√	
5.	√	
6.		√

UNIT 20 (pages 219–229)

AFTER YOU READ

B.
1. play	**3.** mystery	**5.** be out
2. author	**4.** poem	

C. **1.** b **2.** b **3.** b **4.** b **5.** a **6.** a

EXERCISE 1

A.
1. watch	**3.** go	**5.** enjoy
2. see	**4.** understand	**6.** read

B. **1.** I read Hamlet.

  2. William Shakespeare.

  3. No, I got it at the library.

  4. Yes. I saw it three times.

EXERCISE 2

2. Did, enjoy	**5.** Did, like
3. Did, have	**6.** Did, expect
4. Did, understand	**7.** Did, see

EXERCISE 3

2. No, they didn't.

3. No, you didn't.

4. Yes, we did.

5. Yes, it did.
6. No, I didn't.
7. Yes, she did.

EXERCISE 4

2. Did you always want
3. Were you
4. Did you like
5. When did you start
6. How long did you work
7. Why did you start
8. Who helped you
9. How did you feel

EXERCISE 5

Q: When ˄John Steinbeck ~~was~~ born.　*was*

A: He ˄ born in 1902.　*was*

Q: Where ~~he was~~ born?　*was he*

A: He was born in Salinas, California.

Q: Where did he ~~studied~~ writing?　*study*

A: He studied writing at Stanford University.

Q: ~~He~~ graduate from Stanford?　*Did he*

A: No, he didn't.

Q: ~~Does~~ he marry?　*Did*

A: Yes, he did. He married in 1930.

Q: When ˄he ~~published~~ *Tortilla Flat*?　*did publish*

A: In 1936.

Q: What year did *The Grapes of Wrath* come out?

A: In 1938. It was his best book.

Q: What ~~were~~ it about?　*was*

A: It was about a family who lost their farm and became fruit pickers in California.

Q: Did he ~~won~~ many prizes?　*win*

A: Yes, he did. He won a Pulitzer Prize and a Nobel Prize in Literature.

Q: When did he ~~died~~?　*die*

A: He died in New York in 1968.

EXERCISE 6

D. 1. His initials are J.S.
2. He's good at storytelling, and some say he's a genius.
3. Does the J stand for Jack or John?
4. What year was he born?
5. We saw the movie *The Grapes of Wrath* yesterday.
6. At what age did he write his first book?

7. The language is not so difficult to understand.
8. Steinbeck wrote, "A journey is like marriage."

EXERCISE 7

A. 1. b　**2.** a　**3.** a
B.
Romeo and Juliet fell in love. They couldn't marry because of their families. In the last scene, they died (in each other's arms).

EXERCISES 8–9

Answers will vary.

PART VI From Grammar to Writing (pages 231–232)

1 and 3

The sentences are missing punctuation marks. The corrected sentences below are:
1. You're kidding!
2. She's 21 years old.
3. He said, "I love you."
4. He worked for many years before he became rich. Then he invested his money and became even richer.

4

Whose Baby Is It?

Solomon was a king. He lived about 3,000 years ago. Everyone came to Solomon because he was very wise.

One day two women approached King Solomon. One carried a baby. The woman said, "We live nearby and had our babies three days apart. Her baby died in the night, and she changed it for mine. This baby is really mine."

The other woman said, "No! That woman is lying. That's my baby."

The two women started arguing. They continued until King Solomon shouted, "Stop!"

He then turned to his guard and said, "Take your sword and chop the baby in two. Give one part to this woman and the other to that one." The guard pulled out his sword. As he was about to harm the baby, the first woman screamed, "No! Don't do it. Give her the baby. Just don't kill the baby."

King Solomon then said, "Now I know the real mother: Give the baby to the woman who has just spoken."

UNIT 21 (pages 234–246)

AFTER YOU READ

B. 1. b　**2.** a　**3.** b　**4.** a　**5.** a　**6.** a
C. 1. b　**2.** a　**3.** b　**4.** b　**5.** a　**6.** a　**7.** a

EXERCISE 1

Sentences with *Be* in the Past
2. When was that?
3. How long was he president?
4. Was he a good leader?
5. Kemal Ataturk was the father of modern Turkey.
6. He was also a great soldier and leader.
7. He was one of Korea's greatest leaders.

Sentences with Other Verbs in the Past
2. And before he became president, he led the army during the American Revolution.
3. He gave Turkey many things including a modern alphabet.
4. George Washington didn't do anything about the English alphabet.
5. King Sejong gave Korea an alphabet.
6. In South America, Simón Bolívar led many countries to independence.
7. He didn't change our alphabet, but spelling is not so hard in Spanish.

EXERCISE 2
2. were
3. was
4. practiced
5. moved
6. turned
7. went
8. wrote
9. became
10. had
11. started
12. gave
13. joined
14. promised

EXERCISE 3
2. married
3. had
4. lived
5. wore
6. worked
7. was
8. made
9. didn't like
10. didn't like
11. followed
12. invested
13. went
14. lost
15. didn't forgive
16. started
17. was
18. used
19. turned
20. did
21. didn't want
22. didn't want
23. died
24. left

EXERCISE 4
A. 2. When was Naismith born?
  3. What did he always love?
  4. How many degrees did he earn?
  5. When did he work as a gym instructor?
  6. How were his students?
  7. Why did he want them to play an indoor sport?
  8. Did he invent basketball?
B. 2. Was he a good student? Yes, he was.
  3. Did he finish college? Yes, he did.
  4. Did he become a lawyer? No, he didn't.
  5. Did he invent the game of volleyball? No, he didn't.

EXERCISE 5
1. Q: Who *was* Elizabeth Blackwell?
   A: She was the first woman physician in the United States.
2. Q: Where ~~she was~~ *was she* born?
   A: She was born in England.
3. Q: When was she born?
   A: She *was* born in 1821.
4. Q: When ~~she did~~ *did she* come to the United States?
   A: She ~~did come~~ *came* to the United States in 1835.
5. Q: Was it hard for her to become a doctor?
   A: Yes, it ~~were~~ *was*. Most medical schools didn't want women.
6. Q: How ~~was~~ *were* her grades in medical school?
   A: She was an outstanding student. Her grades were excellent.
7. Q: When *did* she graduate?
   A: In 1849.
8. Q: What did Dr. Blackwell fight for?
   A: She ~~did fight~~ *fought* for the admission of women to medical schools.
9. Q: Where did she ~~goes~~ *go* in 1869?
   A: She returned to London. She worked and wrote there for many years.
10. Q: When *did* she die?
    A: She died in 1910.

EXERCISE 7
A. a
B. 2. Q: was he born
      A: seventeenth
   3. Q: was Rembrandt born
      A: Holland
   4. Q: Rembrandt's full name
   5. Q: married
      A: John Lennon.
   6. Q: was the name, group
      A: The Beatles.
   7. Q: did the Beatles come from
      A: Liverpool, England.
   8. Q: did the Beatles make
      A: In 1966.

EXERCISE 10

C.
Information Gap questions for Student A
2. Where was he born?
3. What did he teach himself to play?
4. Where did he begin his career?
5. Who discovered him?
6. Where was he from 1958 to 1960?
7. What did he appear in after that?
8. When did he die?

Information Gap questions for Student B
2. When was he born?
3. What happened to him at the age of seven?
4. Where did he go to school?
5. What did he learn at school?
6. Where did he move?
7. How many years was he in the music business?
8. When did he die?

UNIT 22 (pages 248–256)

AFTER YOU READ

B. 1. a   **2.** b   **3.** a   **4.** a   **5.** b   **6.** b
C. 1. c   **2.** b   **3.** c   **4.** a   **5.** c

EXERCISE 1

2. I   **3.** I   **4.** G   **5.** G   **6.** I   **7.** I   **8.** G

EXERCISE 2

2. to move   **4.** to send   **6.** to complete
3. to work   **5.** to leave

EXERCISE 3

2. applying   **4.** working   **6.** going
3. doing   **5.** leaving

EXERCISE 4

2. to act / acting
3. to become
4. to have
5. to change
6. spending
7. to give up
8. trying out
9. to show

EXERCISE 5

2. to get   **4.** telling   **6.** to study
3. to meet   **5.** looking

EXERCISE 6

35 Main Street, Apt. 6
New Hope, New Jersey
07675

May 27, 2012
Head Librarian
Kennedy Library
7 West Street
New Hope, New Jersey 07675

To Whom It May Concern:

    I want ^*to* apply for a part-time job at Kennedy Library. I am in my senior year of high school. I expect ^*to* attend State College next year, and I plan to ~~majoring~~ *major* in library science. I enjoy ~~to read~~ *reading* and ~~to work~~ *working* with the public. I'm good at computers, and I like ^*to* keep things in order. I've enclosed a résumé. I hope ~~hearing~~ *to hear* from you soon.

EXERCISE 7

B. 1. out of juice
    2. out of order
    3. out of town
    4. out of eggs
    5. out of everything

EXERCISE 8

A. b
B. 1. True
    2. True
    3. True
    4. False. Cindy enjoys planning parties.
    5. False. Cindy likes to work with people.
    6. False. Ken wants to have dinner with Cindy on Saturday.

EXERCISES 9–12

Answers will vary.

UNIT 23 (pages 258–266)

AFTER YOU READ

B. 1. came up with   **3.** rejected
    2. comes after   **4.** accepted   **5.** invented
C. 1. F   **2.** T   **3.** F   **4.** T   **5.** F   **6.** T   **7.** T

EXERCISE 1

Present progressive: 'm looking, 'm trying, Are (you) kidding, 'm not kidding
Simple present: 's, need, 's, lives,
Simple past: divided, read, saw

EXERCISE 2

3. got	**8.** takes	**13.** makes
4. 's	**9.** feeds	**14.** did
5. travel	**10.** do	**15.** get
6. do	**11.** mean	**16.** bought
7. do	**12.** moves	

EXERCISE 3

3. come	**8.** use	**12.** are entering
4. are	**9.** didn't exist	**13.** open
5. 're using	**10.** wrote	**14.** didn't open
6. 're not	**11.** described	**15.** wrote
7. have	(OR describes)	

EXERCISE 4

Jay Leno is a comedian. He also ~~love~~ *loves* to collect cars. One of his cars ~~needs not~~ *doesn't need* gas. It's a Baker electric car. Baker ~~invent~~ *invented* an electric car in 1909. In the early 1900s, electric cars ~~was~~ *were* popular in the United States. Then Henry Ford ~~did produce~~ *produced* inexpensive cars that used gas. People stopped buying electric cars. But nowadays people ~~is~~ *are* trying to keep the air clean. So electric cars are ~~become~~ *becoming* popular once again.

EXERCISE 5

A. a
B. 2. b   **3.** b   **4.** a   **5.** b

PART VII   From Grammar to Writing
(page 268)

1

1. in the evening, At present

3

A Country Doctor

Michelle Hirch-Phothong is a country doctor. Her day begins at 6:30 <u>in the morning</u>. <u>At seven o'clock</u> she is at the hospital. She visits her patients and discusses their problems with the nurses and other doctors. Michelle enjoys talking to her patients. She listens carefully and never rushes.

<u>In the afternoon</u> Michelle works at a clinic. The clinic is busy, and patients are often worried about their health. Michelle and the other doctors try to help them.

<u>At six o'clock in the evening</u> Michelle leaves the clinic. She goes home and relaxes. <u>Every evening at seven o'clock</u> Michelle goes to Bangkok in the Boondocks. That's my restaurant, and Michelle is my wife. Michelle and I enjoy a delicious Thai dinner alone.

<u>Sometimes</u>, however, people come to the restaurant and tell Michelle their medical problems. I say, "Tell them to go to the clinic." But Michelle never sends them home without listening to their problems and offering advice. Michelle is a wonderful doctor.

UNIT 24   (pages 270–281)

AFTER YOU READ

B. 1. b   **2.** a   **3.** a   **4.** b   **5.** a   **6.** b
C. For the Fitness Center: b, c, f
   Against the Fitness Center: a, d, e

EXERCISE 1

A. 2. <u>'re going to build</u>, <u>'s going to have</u>
   3. <u>'s going to talk</u>
   4. <u>'re going to build</u>, <u>are going to provide</u>
   5. <u>is going to destroy</u>
B. 3. The mayor is giving a speech on Wednesday here at our school.

EXERCISE 2

3. is going to increase		**10.** 'm going to write
4. Is		**11.** are
5. going to lay off		**12.** going to say
6. are going to retire		**13.** 'm going to tell
7. is not going to hire		**14.** is
8. is probably going to increase		**15.** going to do
9. are probably not going to get		

EXERCISE 3

2. A: Where is it going to be?
   B: It's going to be on Oak Street.
3. A: When are the builders going to start?
   B: They're going to start next March.
4. A: How much is it going to cost?
   B: It's going to cost $45 million dollars.
5. A: How long is it going to take?
   B: It's probably going to take three years.

EXERCISE 4

2. is not going to look
3. is going to have
4. are going to be
5. are probably not going to be
6. 's going to be
7. 's going to look

EXERCISE 5

Conversation A

3. 's going to be   4. 's going to be

Conversation B

1. wants
2. 's going to make
3. do
4. know
5. announced
6. think
7. 're going to lose
8. did
9. say
10. is going to turn
11. is
12. going to do
13. 's going to offer
14. 's going to build
15. 's going to put

EXERCISE 6

2. **A:** What is he doing Monday afternoon?
   B: He's meeting with the California Energy Council.
3. **A:** Who is he meeting at 7:00 P.M. on Monday?
   B: He's meeting with the police commissioner.
4. **A:** What time is he flying home from Los Angeles?
   B: He's flying home at 11:30 P.M.
5. **A:** Where is he speaking in Washington, D.C.?
   B: He's speaking at State University.
6. **A:** When is he speaking to the senior citizens?
   B: At 3:00 P.M.
7. **A:** Where is he going for a dinner for the police chief?
   B: He's going to the Grand Hotel. (The dinner is going to be at the Grand Hotel.)

EXERCISE 7

Dear Residents:

Last week the mayor talked about building a sports stadium in our neighborhood. I think it's a terrible idea. It's going ˄*to* cost taxpayers millions of dollars. It ˄*'s* going to mean traffic jams. Parking is ~~being~~ *going to be* difficult, and it's going to ~~bringing~~ *bring* noise to the area.

Next Monday at 7:00 P.M. the mayor is ~~goes~~ *going* to answer questions at the public library. Please come out and speak out against the new stadium.

Sincerely,

Dale Ortiz
President, Residents' Association

EXERCISE 8

B.

going to	"gonna"
1. √	
2.	√
3.	√
4. √	
5.	√
6. √	
7.	√

EXERCISE 9

A. a

B. 1. **a.** There aren't enough apartments in the area.
   b. There's going to be a pool for everyone. (There are going to be shops on the street level.)
2. **a.** There's going to be more noise and traffic.
   b. It's going to spoil the view for people in nearby homes.
3. He's for the new building.

UNIT 25 (pages 283–292)

AFTER YOU READ

B. 1. vegetarian   3. disappear   5. spend time
   2. common   4. meal
C. 1. a   2. a   3. a, b   4. b, c

EXERCISE 1

2. d   3. c   4. e   5. a

EXERCISE 2

1. will be
2. will find, will save, won't miss
3. won't take, Will, give, 'll give
4. will send, will probably take
5. will, take place, will be, will, go, 'll probably go

EXERCISE 3

3. won't be   7. will   11. probably won't die
4. will like   8. check   12. will live
5. will help   9. Will   13. will
6. will have   10. disappear   14. happen

EXERCISE 4

2. Will the cost of health care stay the same?
   No, it won't. It will go down (decrease).
3. Will taxes stay the same?
   No, they won't. They will go down (decrease).

(continued on next page)

4. Will the percent of people under 25 decrease?
No, it won't. It will increase.

5. Will the percent of people over 65 decrease?
No, it won't. It will stay the same.

EXERCISE 5

3. was	**6.** 'll learn	**9.** Did
4. 'll be	**7.** 'll	**10.** like
5. 'll take	**8.** be	**11.** knows

EXERCISE 6

A: What did he say?

B: He said there _^ *will* be an increase in the population.

Many young people will ~~moves~~ *move* to the area. Taxes

will ~~increases~~ *increase*. The value of homes will also ~~to~~

increase.

A: How about crime? Will it ~~increases~~ *increase*?

B: No, it ~~doesn't~~ *won't*.

A: Well, it sounds like a great place to live.

EXERCISE 8

A. b

B. 1. a. She'll travel to the moon.

   b. She'll buy a house with room for her friends
and relatives.

   2. He'll give it away.

   3. They won't be upset for long.

UNIT 26 (pages 294–302)

AFTER YOU READ

B. 1. entire   **3.** flooding   **5.** highways   **7.** mild

   2. commute   **4.** predicted   **6.** storm

C. Sunday: cold and windy
Monday: heavy rain
Tuesday: rainy
Wednesday: rainy
Thursday: sunny, 20% chance of rain

EXERCISE 1

2. b   **3.** e   **4.** a   **5.** c

EXERCISE 2

2. might (may) take   **5.** may (might) be

3. may (might) cancel   **6.** may (might) leave

4. might (may) not have

EXERCISE 3

2. will probably rain,   **4.** Will, cancel
may not rain   **5.** might cancel

3. probably won't reach

EXERCISE 4

They may be
2. ~~Maybe they are~~ in the top drawer.

They may.
3. ~~Maybe~~.

We might
4. ~~Maybe we'll~~ meet at the mall.

She may.
5. ~~Maybe~~.

EXERCISE 5

1. A: Where's Bill?

   I think
   B: ~~I'm sure~~ he might be on vacation in Florida.

   need
   A: He may ~~needs~~ his winter jacket. It's 40
degrees there today.

   may
2. A: We ~~maybe~~ go to the park. Do you want to
join us?

   B: No thanks. It's very windy. Why don't you do
something indoors?

   Will
3. A: ~~May~~ you take the highway?

   B: Yes, I may. It's usually faster than the city
streets.

4. A: Are you going to finish your paper on climate
change today?

   might not
   B: I want to, but I ~~mightn't~~ have enough time.

5. A: What's the weather report?

   B: It's sunny now, but it may ~~be~~ rain this
afternoon.

EXERCISE 6

B. 1. 60   **2.** 30   **3.** 19   **4.** 15   **5.** 80

C. 1. 150   **2.** 60   **3.** 14   **4.** 13

EXERCISE 7

A. a

B. 2. It might rain.

   3. A sun hat because it might be sunny and a rain
hat because it might rain.

   4. He likes to read at night.

   5. They may go to a fancy restaurant.

PART VIII From Grammar to Writing
(pages 304–305)

1

1. When I was six years old, I loved to play with dolls. OR I loved to play with dolls when I was six years old.
2. When I graduate next year, I will work for a bank. OR I will work for a bank when I graduate next year.

3

Example paragraph:

When I was a child, I loved to play "make-believe" games. Sometimes I was a cowboy, and sometimes I was a prince. When I became a teenager, I got a job at a video store. I saw many movies. I also made a couple of videos and I acted in all the school plays. Now I'm studying film and acting at school. When I finish college next year, I will move to Hollywood. I hope to become a movie star.

UNIT 27 (pages 308–319)

AFTER YOU READ

B. 1. delicious   **4.** service
2. menu   **5.** atmosphere
3. main course   **6.** reservation
C. 1. AH   **2.** AH   **3.** AH   **4.** T   **5.** T

EXERCISE 1

A. 2. information—non-count noun
3. menu—singular count noun
4. customers—plural count noun
5. bread—non-count noun
6. napkin—singular count noun
7. server—singular count noun
8. miles—plural count noun
9. coffee—non-count noun
10. rolls—plural count noun
11. food—non-count noun
12. people—plural count noun
B. 1. a   **2.** b   **3.** a   **4.** b

EXERCISE 2

2. the   **4.** a   **6.** the   **8.** a   **10.** The
3. a   **5.** the   **7.** the   **9.** a   **11.** The

EXERCISE 3

Kel Warner is ˰*a* student. He's an English major. He has ˰*a* great part-time job. He writes for ˰*the* school paper. He's ˰*the/a* food critic. Kel goes to all ˰*the* restaurants in his town and writes about them. He can take ˰*a* friend to restaurants and ˰*the* school newspaper pays ˰*the* bill. Kel really has ˰*a* wonderful job.

EXERCISE 4

2. Some   **4.** any   **6.** any   **8.** some
3. some   **5.** some   **7.** any

EXERCISE 5

2. many   **4.** much   **6.** Many, Many
3. much   **5.** much, many

EXERCISE 6

2. many restaurants   **5.** many choices
3. much time   **6.** much information
4. many people

EXERCISE 7

2. a little   **4.** a few   **6.** many
3. a little   **5.** much   **7.** much

EXERCISE 8

My friend Mario is ˰*the* chef at a small French restaurant. He does most of the cooking. He doesn't have ~~the~~ *an* easy job. He works nights and weekends in ~~an~~ *a* hot kitchen. He manages ˰*a* lot of people. ~~Any~~ *Many* days the restaurant is very busy from 6:00 P.M. to 8:00 P.M. ˰ ~~Few~~ *A few* times a year the restaurant has a special deal. Mario has ~~much~~ *many* friends. They often eat at the restaurant. Mario's dishes are always delicious. He uses ~~many~~ *a lot of* wine in his sauces. Mario would like to go to a French cooking school, but he doesn't have ~~some~~ *any* (OR *the* OR *much*) time.

EXERCISE 9

C. 1. a little butter   **4.** a little salt,
2. a few eggs, a little cheese   a little pepper
3. a few minutes   **5.** a delicious dish

EXERCISE 10

A. soda, chips, salsa, tuna, ice
B. 1. He bought tuna for cats.
    2. Miguel usually eats the tuna for cats.

UNIT 28 (pages 321–332)

AFTER YOU READ

B. 1. taste   **4.** neighborhood
    2. in season   **5.** pretty good
    3. prepare   **6.** ingredients

                        wants
C. 1. Wasana ~~doesn't want~~ Carlos to try her dessert.
                           Tailand
    2. Wasana's dessert is popular in ~~Turkey~~.
          doesn't like
    3. Carlos ~~likes~~ the look of Wasana's dessert. OR
        Carlos likes the taste of Wasana's dessert.
                               rice
    4. Wasana's dessert has two kinds of ~~fruit~~.
                  cookies
    5. Carlos brought ~~fruit~~ from his country.

EXERCISE 1

A.

	Singular Count Noun	Plural Count Noun	Non-count Noun
milk		√	
eggs		√	
raisins		√	
sugar			√
juice			√
lemon	√		

B. 2. usually   **5.** often
    3. Once in a while   **6.** frequently
    4. Every weekend

EXERCISE 2

  1. many   **4.** How many, many
  2. How often, often   **5.** How much, much
  3. how much, much   **6.** How often, often

EXERCISE 3

  2. The coffee is always hot.
  3. The chocolate is almost always dark.
  4. It's never white chocolate.
  5. Hugo never drinks coffee in the evening.
  6. He usually drinks hot chocolate.
  7. Sometimes he drinks ginger tea.

EXERCISE 4

  2. enough drinks   **5.** enough cupcakes
  3. enough ice   **6.** enough chairs
  4. enough room   **7.** enough plates

EXERCISE 5

  2. container   **6.** cups
  3. pint   **7.** cups
  4. jar   **8.** tablespoons
  5. can

EXERCISE 6

  2. A: How often do you bake?
                always
     B: ~~Always~~ I ^ bake on the weekend.
                    enough cake
  3. A: Do we have ~~cake enough~~ for everyone?
     B: Yes, we do.
            much
  4. A: How ~~many~~ flour do you need?
     B: Two cups.
                eggs
  5. A: How many ~~egg~~ are there in the cake? And
        how much sugar~~s~~?
                        cups
     B: Four eggs and three ~~cup~~ of sugar.

EXERCISE 7

B. 1. Now   **4.** How, pounds
    2. How, brown   **5.** out
    3. about   **6.** How, ounces

EXERCISE 8

A. 1. T   **2.** T   **3.** F   **4.** T
B. cocoa powder, baking soda, salt, butter, eggs, sour
    cream, milk, red food color, vanilla extract, sugar

EXERCISE 10

Chocolate Chip Cookies

7 ounces of chocolate chips
2 1/2 cups flour
3 teaspoons baking powder
1 cup chopped walnuts
1 cup butter
3/4 cup sugar
3/4 cup brown sugar
2 eggs, slightly beaten
1 teaspoon vanilla extract

Apple Pie

The Crust
2 cups flour
1 teaspoon salt
2/3 cup shortening
5 tablespoons cold water

The Filling
1/3 cup sugar
1/4 cup flour
1/2 teaspoon ground cinnamon
1/2 teaspoon ground nutmeg
a pinch of salt
8 medium-size apples
2 tablespoons butter

UNIT 29 (pages 334–342)

AFTER YOU READ

B. 1. climate
2. pollution
3. crime
4. housing
5. free time
6. unemployment
C. 1. MB, NYC
2. MB, NYC
3. K
4. K
5. NYC
6. MB
7. K
8. NYC

EXERCISE 1

2. too crowded
3. too long
4. too many cars
5. too little information
6. too much crime
7. too few jobs

EXERCISE 2

2. too many storms
3. too much crime
4. too much pollution
5. too much noise
6. too many rats

EXERCISE 3

2. too long
3. too crowded
4. too small
5. too small
6. too long

EXERCISE 4

2. There wasn't enough rain
3. There aren't enough jobs
4. There isn't enough affordable housing
5. There aren't enough schools
6. There aren't enough parks

EXERCISE 5

2. too few
3. too few
4. too, too little
5. too many, too
6. too, too few
7. too
8. too, too many

EXERCISE 6

1. A: I'd like to move to the suburbs. The city is ^too^ noisy for me.
 B: Not me. I think the suburbs are ^too^ quiet.
2. A: What's wrong with that company?
 B: There are too many managers and too ~~little~~ *few* workers.
3. A: Did you buy that apartment?
 B: No. It was too ^*much*^ money for too ~~few~~ *little* space.
4. A: Don't go by bus. It will take too ~~many~~ *much* time. Take the train. It's a lot faster.
 B: Yes, but it's ~~too much~~ *much too* expensive. The bus is half the price.

EXERCISE 7

C. 1. I thought Ted taught about the environment.
 2. There are three trees in front of their house.
 3. It is true that the technician went through their house in only thirty minutes.

EXERCISE 8

A. c
B.

	What They Liked	What They Didn't Like
First apartment	beautiful street	too small, too few closets, wasn't big enough
Second apartment	the right size, great view	too noisy, too many people
Third apartment	big enough, not too noisy	the kitchen had too few cabinets

PART IX From Grammar to Writing
(pages 344–345)

1

1. at the top left of the page
2. below your address
3. below the date; skip two lines

(continued on next page)

4. *Dear* <u>Name:</u> OR *Dear Sir / Madam:* OR *To Whom It May Concern:*

5. explain what you want

6. thank you

7. *Sincerely yours,* OR *Yours truly,*

8. Your signature, and your name typed below your signature

UNIT 30 (pages 348–358)

AFTER YOU READ

B. 1. customs
   2. business receptions
   3. confusion
   4. consider
   5. insult

C. 1. F **2.** T **3.** F **4.** F **5.** F **6.** F **7.** T

EXERCISE 1

2. Q: <u>Should</u> I <u>translate</u> my card into Japanese?

3. Q: What <u>should</u> I <u>do</u> when I get my colleague's card?

4. A: You<u>'d better not start</u> your business before you exchange cards.

EXERCISE 2

2. shouldn't touch
3. shouldn't be
4. should, do, should wait
5. shouldn't say

EXERCISE 3

2. should arrive, shouldn't be
3. should, pay, should keep
4. should call
5. shouldn't surprise

EXERCISE 4

2. ought to send
3. ought to congratulate
4. ought to invite
5. ought to become
6. ought to ask

EXERCISE 5

2. 'd better not
3. 'd better
4. 'd better not
5. 'd better

EXERCISE 6

2. You'd better not eat everything on your plate in Cambodia.

3. In China, you'd better keep eating while your plate is full to show you like your food.

4. You'd better not touch a person's head or show the soles of your feet in Thailand.

5. You'd better not keep your hands in your pockets in Turkey. It's a sign of disrespect.

EXERCISE 7

A. 1. A: What ⌃*should* I wear?

   B: You ⌃*should* not wear jeans or shorts. Wear a skirt and blouse.

2. A: I think I insulted him.

   B: You ⌃*should* apologize.

3. A: They were really helpful. ⌃*Should* I send them a thank you note?

   B: That's a good idea.

4. A: ⌃*Should* I take my shoes off?

   B: Yes, please leave them by the door.

5. A: When ⌃*should* we leave for the business reception?

   B: At 6:15. The invitation is for 6:30, but we don't want to be the first ones there.

B. 2. A: You ⌃*'d better not* ~~don't~~ fly today. There's a bad hurricane and all flights are late.

   B: Good idea. I'll change my flight for tomorrow.

3. A: Can I call John Baker now?

   B: I don't think so. He's on U.S. time. You ⌃*'d better* call him at noon. You won't wake him then.

4. A: Is it OK to pay that bill on Friday?

   B: I don't think so. You ⌃*'d better* pay it today.

5. A: I told John about my birthday. He ⌃*'d better not* ~~doesn't~~ forget about it.

   B: John forgets everyone's birthday except his own.

EXERCISE 9

A. 1. To Japan
   2. By plane
   3. customs in Japan or ways to behave

B. 1. I meet someone
   Answer: You don't have to.
   2. my shoes, when I enter a home
   Answer: Yes, you should.
   3. a few phrases in Japanese
   Answer: Yes, you should.

UNIT 31 (pages 360–368)

AFTER YOU READ

B. 1. b   **2.** c   **3.** a   **4.** e   **5.** d

C.

	Gina	Jade
1.	√	
2.		√
3.	√	
4.		√
5.		√

EXERCISE 1

2. D   **3.** O   **4.** R   **5.** D   **6.** R   **7.** O   **8.** R

EXERCISE 2

2. Of course   **4.** Would you like
3. I'd like to do   **5.** I'd love to

EXERCISE 3

2. b   **3.** a   **4.** b   **5.** b   **6.** b   **7.** a   **8.** b

EXERCISE 4

2. Would (Could / Can) you please put the lemonade on the table over there?
3. And Roberto, could (would / can) you please put the juice over here next to the buns?
4. Can (Would / Could) you please bring it out?
5. What would you like—chicken or hamburgers?
6. Would you like chicken too?
7. No. I'd like a burger.
8. I'd like the recipe.

EXERCISE 5

1. A. Could you please move my car at 11:00?
    Sorry
   B: ~~No, I wouldn't~~. I'll be at work at that time.
    We'd   *you*
2. A: ~~We~~ like to rent this apartment. Could ˄
    please ~~you~~ give us an application?
   B: Of course.
                to
3. A: Would you like ˄come for dinner?
             Could/Can
   B: Yes, thank you. ~~Would~~ my friend come, too?
4. A: Would you help me with these boxes?
    Sure / Of course.
   B: ~~I would~~.

EXERCISE 7

A. c
B. 1. a   **2.** b   **3.** c   **4.** b

UNIT 32 (pages 370–380)

AFTER YOU READ

B. 1. pass   **5.** hard copy
   2. midterm, final   **6.** due
   3. average   **7.** outline
   4. percent

C.

	Students have to . . .	Students don't have to . . .
1.		√
2.	√	
3.		√
4.	√	
5.		√
6.	√	

EXERCISE 1

New York City (has) a special high school for music, art, dance, and drama. It's called LaGuardia High School. To be accepted, students <u>have to pass</u> an audition. In addition they <u>must</u> (have) good grades. The school usually (has) about 9,000 applicants a year. It accepts about 650 students. All prospective students, even the children of the rich and famous, <u>must audition</u>. They <u>must choose</u> to audition for acting, dance, music, or art.

Here are some of the requirements for students interested in art:
1. Each student <u>must submit</u> a portfolio of original artwork. The artwork <u>does not have to be</u> a special size, but all art <u>has to be</u> original. Students <u>mustn't bring</u> in photocopies.
2. Each student <u>must complete</u> three drawing exercises. Students <u>have to bring</u> a pencil and a transcript of their last report card. Students <u>don't have to bring</u> drawing materials. The school (has) all the necessary drawing supplies for the students.

EXERCISE 2

A. 1. have to take   **3.** have to bring
   2. have to perform   **4.** don't have to bring

B. 1. have to sing   **3.** have to use
   2. play   **4.** don't have to bring

EXERCISE 3

2. have to   **5.** have   **8.** have to
3. have to   **6.** have to   **9.** have
4. have to   **7.** have to   **10.** had to

EXERCISE 4

2. don't have to wear
3. have to pass
4. have to hand in
5. has to attend
6. doesn't have to buy
7. have to listen, don't have to say
8. doesn't have to pay

EXERCISE 5

2. You have to show (identification / I.D.) to get in. OR You must show (identification / I.D.) to get in.
3. You must not enter.
4. You must not get the hairdryer wet.
5. You mustn't drink (this bottle).
6. You mustn't text (when you drive / when you are driving).

EXERCISE 6

2. To learn a new vocabulary word, you must *hear* ~~hears~~ it seven times.
3. For me to remember a word, I *have* ~~has~~ to write it down.
4. Avi has a great memory. He just *has* ~~have~~ to hear a word once and he remembers it.
5. Our papers are due next week. I have *to* ˄start working on mine today.
6. We *don't have to* ~~mustn't~~ do any homework today. Tomorrow is a holiday.
7. You mustn't ⋊ bring any notes with you to the test.
8. You must ⋊ bring a photo ID to the testing center.

EXERCISE 8

A. an MBA (Masters of Business Administration)
B. 1. You have to take the GMAT.
  2. You don't have to go to business school right after college. You can get some work experience first.

1

  1. O 2. F 3. F 4. F 5. O

3

(I believe that Hollywood actors often set a bad example for young people). Young people look up to them, but these actors show bad values. For example, many stars spend huge amounts of money on homes, cars, and clothes. When young people try to copy their lifestyle, they often buy things they can't afford. Also, most Hollywood actors do not have long-term relationships. They change boyfriends and girlfriends frequently. Finally, many Hollywood actors have cosmetic surgery and go on strict diets, all in order to be more attractive.

(In my opinion, some Hollywood stars set a bad example because of their materialism, but others set a good example through their charity). For example, Angelina Jolie and George Clooney are big stars who help others. They give away a lot of their money to help the poor and the sick in different parts of the world. They also encourage others to give to good causes.

UNIT 33 (pages 386–397)

AFTER YOU READ

B. 1. coast   5. diverse
  2. port   6. personality
  3. mild   7. sea level
  4. ski   8. are located

C.

	Portland, Maine	Portland, Oregon
1.		√
2.	√	
3.		√
4.		√

EXERCISE 1

A. higher, older, younger, milder, better, bigger, more fun, larger, less expensive
B. 2. high   5. mild   8. fun
  3. old   6. good   9. large
  4. young   7. big   10. expensive

EXERCISE 2

A. 1. more expensive than
  2. hotter, hotter than
  3. higher, higher than

4. longer, longer than
5. better, than, cleaner
6. colder than
7. more popular, than
8. more humid than, more humid, than
9. farther, than, nearer
10. more polluted, than, cleaner
11. heavier
B. 2. less humid, than   **4.** more crowded, than
3. less polluted, than   **5.** more famous

EXERCISE 3

2. The average two-bedroom apartment in Middletown is more expensive than the average two-bedroom apartment in Lakeville.
3. A cup of coffee is less expensive in Lakeville than (it is) in Middletown.
4. It is probably harder to find work in Lakeville than (it is) in Middletown.
5. Healthcare is probably worse in Lakeville than (it is) in Middletown.
6. Summers are much warmer in Middletown than (they are) in Lakeville.

EXERCISE 4

2. bigger   **6.** more exciting
3. more polluted   **7.** quieter
4. worse   **8.** more expensive
5. busier   **9.** less expensive

EXERCISE 5

2. Florida is ~~more~~ hotter than Maine.
                  farther
3. Oregon is ~~far~~ north than California.
                    faster
4. A motorcycle is ~~more fast~~ than a bicycle.
                         heavier
5. Traffic at 8:00 A.M. is ~~more heavy~~ than traffic

   at 10:00 A.M.
                              milder
6. The climate in Portland, Oregon is ~~mild~~ than

   the climate in Anchorage, Alaska.
                                      sister's
7. Jake's apartment is sunnier than his ~~sister~~.

EXERCISE 7

A. He's making it a green city.
B. 1. livelier   **5.** harder
2. more comfortable   **6.** cleaner and safer
3. easier   **7.** dirtier and more
4. cleaner   dangerous

AFTER YOU READ

B. 1. b   **2.** a   **3.** b   **4.** a   **5.** a   **6.** a   **7.** b
C. 2, 4, 6

EXERCISE 1

clearly, long, fast

EXERCISE 2

2. well   **7.** dangerously
3. fluently   **8.** badly
4. clearly   **9.** slowly
5. fast   **10.** hard
6. carefully

EXERCISE 3

2. good   **5.** slowly
3. beautiful   **6.** slow
4. well   **7.** Nervous

EXERCISE 4

2. A: Was the food OK?
                                     good
   B: Everyone loved it. It really tasted ~~well~~.

3. A: Is Harry a good driver?
                                  slowly
   B: I don't think so. He drives too ~~slow~~.

4. A: How did they do?
                        hard
   B: They worked ~~hardly~~ and did well.

5. A: Did you hear him?
                              softly
   B: No, I didn't. He spoke too ~~soft~~.

6. A: How did she sound?
                      nervous
   B: A little ~~nervously~~.

EXERCISE 5

A. beginning (introduction), ending (conclusion), jokes
B. 2. Speak confidently.
3. Dress appropriately.
4. Speak freely and don't read your speech. Don't show a powerpoint slide with a lot of writing on it.
5. Summarize your talk and thank your audience sincerely.

AFTER YOU READ

B. 1. b   **2.** a   **3.** b   **4.** b   **5.** a
C. 1. F   **2.** F   **3.** T   **4.** T   **5.** F   **6.** T   **7.** T

EXERCISE 1

A. 2. The food wasn't spicy enough for him.

3. His dress shoes were too tight.

4. Her prom dress was very beautiful.

5. That tuxedo was too expensive.

6. The car wasn't big enough for all of us.
B. 1. Serena wore the same dress as Jasmin.
  2. He has the same voice as his father.
  3. He's different from his brother.
  4. Adam Rusk has the same initials as Ali Rogers.

EXERCISE 2

  2. too salty
  3. too sweet
  4. enough ice
  5. enough seats

EXERCISE 3

  2. It isn't warm enough to wear that dress.
  3. This steak is much too tough to eat.
  4. I'm too busy to call him right now.
  5. They weren't strong enough to move the sofa.
  6. That restaurant is much too expensive.
  7. That class was too important to miss.
  8. We don't have enough time to eat before the movie.
  9. His address wasn't clear enough to read.

EXERCISE 4

A. 1. too fast   **2.** too slowly   **3.** too carelessly
B. 2. Russ Tran has the same color eyes as Robert Trent.
  3. Russ Tran has the same initials as Robert Trent.
  4. Jean Philippe has the same weight as Robert Trent.

EXERCISE 5

1. very	**5.** very	**9.** too
2. very, too	**6.** too, very	**10.** too
3. too	**7.** very, too	**11.** very, too
4. too, very	**8.** very, too	

EXERCISE 6

  2. as serious an artist as she is
  3. as well as she does
  4. the same grades as she did
  5. the same art camp as she did

EXERCISE 7

  2. His girlfriend isn't as nice ~~than~~ *as* his old one.

  3. She's very different ~~than~~ *from* her sister.

  4. We're ~~very~~ *too* young to vote. You have to be 18

  years old. We're 17.

  5. She has the same dress ~~than~~ *as* I do.

  6. I'm as ~~taller~~ *tall* as my father.

  7. Dan's weight is the same as his ~~brother~~ *brother's*.

  8. Is your new book bag ~~enough big~~ *big enough* for all your

  books?

EXERCISE 8

B. 2. ox   **4.** honey   **6.** gold
  3. cucumber   **5.** feather

EXERCISE 9

A. b
B. 1. a   **2.** b   **3.** b

UNIT 36 (pages 421–431)

BEFORE YOU READ

  1. F   **2.** F   **3.** T   **4.** F

AFTER YOU READ

B. 1. inches   **5.** species
  2. centimeters   **6.** extinct
  3. pounds   **7.** feathers
  4. kilogram   **8.** explorer
C. 1. Emperor Penguins
  2. Little Blue Penguins
  3. the Antarctic
  4. Greenland and Iceland
  5. Galapagos Penguins

EXERCISE 1

A. 2. the cleanest
  3. The . . . heaviest
  4. The best
  5. the most famous

B. 2. cleanest
    3. heaviest
    4. best
    5. famous
C. on earth, in the cleanest kitchens, in a novel

EXERCISE 2

     1. the loudest
_a_ **2.** the largest
_d_ **3.** the tallest
_c_ **4.** the smallest
_f_ **5.** the fastest
_e_ **6.** the most colorful

EXERCISE 3

2. the deadliest   **7.** the most frightening
3. the highest   **8.** The heaviest
4. largest   **9.** the longest
5. scariest   **10.** deadliest
6. the oldest

EXERCISE 4

2. one of the most beautiful birds
3. one of the smartest animals
4. One of the best nature shows
5. one of the funniest animals
6. one of the best collections

EXERCISE 5

1. shorter, larger, taller   **5.** larger
2. the richest   **6.** more active, colder
3. The smallest   **7.** the most dangerous
4. The largest

EXERCISE 6

2. It is one of the most popular ~~zoo~~ *zoos* in the world.
3. The zoo has ^*the* biggest collection of different

    species in the world.

4. The zoo is very crowded Sunday afternoon.
    That is the ~~most bad~~ *worst* time to visit.
5. The pandas are the most popular ~~resident~~ *residents* of the

    Berlin Zoological Garden.
6. The Birdhouse is one ^*of* the most modern

    bird houses in Europe. There are more than

    500 species of birds, many of them quite rare.
7. The ~~most good~~ *best* time to visit the zoo is in the

    spring or the fall.

EXERCISE 8

A. 1. a   **2.** b   **3.** a   **4.** a
B. 1. Answer one: elephant
    Answer two: cheetah
    Answer three: monkey
    Answer four: mosquito
  2. thirty-six thousand dollars

PART XI   From Grammar to Writing
(pages 433–434)

1

  1. funny little brown monkey
  2. beautiful red silk dress

3

  1. big brown Asian
  2. new black Italian leather
  3. beautiful Mexican silver

Single-User License Agreement

System Requirements

WINDOWS®	MACINTOSH®	BOTH
• Windows XP/Vista/7 • Intel Pentium processor 1GHz or higher • Internet Explorer® 7.0 or higher OR Firefox® 2.0 or higher	• Mac OS X (10.4 & 10.5) • PowerPC & Intel processor 1GHz or higher • Safari® 2.0 or higher OR Firefox® 2.0 or higher	• 256 MB RAM minimum (512+ MB recommended) • Monitor resolution of 1024 x 768 or higher • Sound card and speakers or headphones • 500 MB hard disk space • 10X CD-ROM drive or higher • Adobe Flash 8 plug-in or higher • Internet Connection: DSL, Cable/Broadband, T1, or other high-speed connection • Microsoft® PowerPoint Viewer

Installation Instructions

WINDOWS®	MACINTOSH®
• Insert the CD-ROM into the CD-ROM drive of your computer. On most computers, the program will begin automatically. If the program does not begin automatically: • Open "My Computer." • Right-click on the CD-ROM icon. • Click on Open. • Double-click on the "Start" file. Leave the CD-ROM in the computer while using the program.	• Insert the CD-ROM into the CD-ROM drive of your computer. • Double-click on the CD-ROM icon on your desktop. • Double click on the "Start" file. Leave the CD-ROM in the computer while using the program.

Note: The original CD-ROM must be in the CD-ROM drive when you use the program.

TECHNICAL SUPPORT

For Technical Product Support, please visit our support website at www.PearsonLongmanSupport.com. You can search our **Knowledgebase** for frequently asked questions, instantly **Chat** with an available support representative, or **Submit a Ticket/Request** for assistance.